Dr. Daniel Amen is not only a great friend, but he is also one of the kindest people I know, and this kindness comes out in his tireless search for answers to help people manage their mental health. His latest book is a testament to this and, combined with his extensive research studying more than 200,000 brain scans of people from over 155 countries, is guaranteed to give insight to all who read it!

DR. CAROLINE LEAF, clinical neuroscientist, mental health researcher, and author of *Cleaning Up Your Mental Mess*

Dr. Amen eloquently reveals the simple and yet profound notion that happiness can be cultivated. We've long had the tools to achieve important goals like losing weight and gaining strength, but the science underlying how we can bring about brain changes to create and enhance happiness has remained obscure until now. *You, Happier* is your guide to make happiness manifest in your life. And why not?

DAVID PERLMUTTER, MD, author of the #1 *New York Times* bestseller *Grain Brain* and *Brain Wash*

During these challenging times, *You, Happier* is the book we've all been waiting for. And it delivers on its promise! Putting Dr. Amen's brain-based happiness secrets into daily practice will give you a major mood boost.

AWARD-WINNING ACTRESS JENNIE GARTH

I have known and worked with Dr. Amen for the past 30 years. The gems he's mined during this time after completing over 200,000 scans have resulted in seven sound neuroscience principles that will help you have a happier today and a more joyful tomorrow! Buy this book for you and your families and friends . . . help people find happiness and joy!

EARL R. HENSLIN, PsyD, board certified expert in traumatic stress; diplomate, the American Academy of Experts in Traumatic Stress; functional and integrative neuroscience coach

The seven secrets of happiness that Dr. Amen reveals in *You, Happier* should be taught in schools everywhere. If you want to feel more joy, positivity, and contentment, make it part of your own personal "core curriculum."

LEWIS HOWES, *New York Times* bestselling author and host of *The School of Greatness* podcast

Ever wonder why one-size-fits-all happiness advice doesn't actually work for everyone? In this encouraging, hope-filled book, Dr. Amen reveals the revolutionary concept that happiness depends on your brain type. Imagine that—a happiness recipe targeted to *your* brain!

JIM KWIK, celebrity brain coach, *New York Times* bestselling author of *Limitless: Upgrade Your Brain, Learn Anything Faster, and Unlock Your Exceptional Life*

I'm a big fan of books that help you understand what's going on in your brain and follow that up with actionable steps to make the changes you desire. *You, Happier* does just that. By understanding your brain type and the brains of those around you, you can turn on your happiness switch, experience more joy, and connect with loved ones (and the world) on a much deeper level. You'll discover that the power to do so is yours, and it only takes a few minutes per day.

CHALENE JOHNSON, *New York Times* bestselling author, health and lifestyle expert

Dr. Daniel Amen does it again—another amazing book with all the science-backed evidence he is known for. If doctors wrote as many prescriptions for happiness the way they hand out medications for physical or mental health issues, this book would be the nation's number one script! So if you're feeling down, anxious, or stressed, read *You, Happier*!

DR. UMA NAIDOO, Harvard nutritional psychiatrist, chef, nutrition specialist, and author of the national bestseller *This Is Your Brain on Food*

A SAMPLE OF OTHER BOOKS BY DANIEL AMEN

Your Brain Is Always Listening, Tyndale, 2021

The End of Mental Illness, Tyndale, 2020

Conquer Worry and Anxiety, Tyndale, 2020

Feel Better Fast and Make It Last, Tyndale, 2018

Memory Rescue, Tyndale, 2017

Stones of Remembrance, Tyndale, 2017

Captain Snout and the Superpower Questions, Zonderkidz, 2017

The Brain Warrior's Way, with Tana Amen, New American Library, 2016

Time for Bed, Sleepyhead, Zonderkidz, 2016

Change Your Brain, Change Your Life (revised), Harmony Books, 2015, *New York Times* Bestseller

Healing ADD (revised), Berkley, 2013, *New York Times* Bestseller

The Daniel Plan, with Rick Warren, DMin, and Mark Hyman, MD, Zondervan, 2013, #1 *New York Times* Bestseller

Unleash the Power of the Female Brain, Harmony Books, 2013, *New York Times* Bestseller

Use Your Brain to Change Your Age, Crown Archetype, 2012, *New York Times* Bestseller

Unchain Your Brain, with David E. Smith, MD, MindWorks, 2010

Change Your Brain, Change Your Body, Harmony Books, 2010, *New York Times* Bestseller

Magnificent Mind at Any Age, Harmony Books, 2008, *New York Times* Bestseller

The Brain in Love, Three Rivers Press, 2007

Making a Good Brain Great, Harmony Books, 2005, Amazon Book of the Year

ADD in Intimate Relationships, MindWorks, 2005

New Skills for Frazzled Parents, MindWorks, 2000

YOU, HAPPIER

THE 7 NEUROSCIENCE SECRETS OF FEELING GOOD
BASED ON YOUR BRAIN TYPE

#1 *NEW YORK TIMES* BESTSELLING AUTHOR

DANIEL G. AMEN, MD

TYNDALE
REFRESH™

Think Well. Live Well. Be Well.

MEDICAL DISCLAIMER

The information presented in this book is the result of years of practice experience and clinical research by the author. The information in this book, by necessity, is of a general nature and not a substitute for an evaluation or treatment by a competent medical specialist. If you believe you are in need of medical intervention, please see a medical practitioner as soon as possible. The case studies in this book are true. The names and circumstances of many of those profiled have been changed to protect the anonymity of patients.

Visit Tyndale online at tyndale.com.

Visit Daniel G. Amen, MD, at danielamenmd.com.

Tyndale and Tyndale's quill logo are registered trademarks of Tyndale House Ministries. *Tyndale Refresh* and the Tyndale Refresh logo are trademarks of Tyndale House Ministries. Tyndale Refresh is a nonfiction imprint of Tyndale House Ministries, Carol Stream, Illinois.

You, Happier: The 7 Neuroscience Secrets of Feeling Good Based on Your Brain Type

Designed by Julie Chen

Published in association with the literary agency of WordServe Literary Group, www.wordserveliterary.com.

For information about special discounts for bulk purchases, please contact Tyndale House Publishers at csresponse@tyndale.com, or call 1-855-277-9400.

Library of Congress Cataloging-in-Publication Data

A catalog record for this book is available from the Library of Congress.

ISBN 978-1-4964-5452-2 (HC)
ISBN 978-1-4964-6558-0 (ITPE)

Printed in the United States of America

28	27	26	25	24	23	22
7	6	5	4	3	2	1

Contents

PART 4: THE SOCIAL CONNECTIONS OF HAPPINESS

PART 5: THE SPIRITUALITY OF HAPPINESS

Introduction

I am writing this book at a time when the world is in turmoil and Americans are the unhappiest they've been in 50 years.[1] There is a lot to be unhappy about: As of July 2021, more than 30 million people in the United States have contracted the COVID-19 virus, and more than 600,000 Americans have died in the global pandemic that brought social isolation, grief, and fear to almost every household in the country. Add that to subsequent high unemployment rates, an economy in tatters, and the ongoing political divide, and you can see why we have been brought to our emotional knees. As a nation, we are feeling so stressed and unhappy that it has sparked a dramatic rise in the number of new prescriptions for antidepressants, anti-anxiety medications, and sleep aids.[2] In early 2020, rates of depression—the opposite of being happy—tripled from 8.5 percent, which was already at record highs, to a horrifying 27.8 percent just a few months later.[3] The statistics may seem grim, but you deserve to be happy, and you can cultivate happiness even when it seems like the world is crumbling around you.

I've seen it happen. In 2021, I knew people were hurting emotionally in the wake of the pandemic, so I launched an online 30-Day Happiness Challenge that attracted an astounding 32,000 participants. (You can do the challenge at 30DayHappinessChallenge.com.) On each day of the challenge, I shared science-backed tips and strategies—some of the same ones you will find in this book—that ramp up happiness and positivity. I wanted to see how much the participants could improve over the course of the challenge, so I asked them to take the Oxford Happiness Questionnaire, a well-respected assessment that provides a score on a scale of 1 to 6.[4] (See page 35 for more information on this questionnaire, which you can take as part of my 30-Day Happiness Challenge.) People took the quiz twice, once at the beginning of the program and once at the end. The average happiness score for participants on Day 1 was 3.58, which correlates to being "not particularly happy." Among people who completed the course, the average score on Day 30 had jumped to 4.36, a 22 percent improvement, which correlates with being "rather happy; pretty happy"! Even more impressive, their self-reported happiness levels increased by 32 percent. And they did it in just about 10 to

15 minutes a day. This shows that not only can you develop happiness, but also that you can do it quickly. Take it from one of the participants who wrote in a post, "Thirty days ago I was so miserable, so hopeless, and so depressed! This has literally transformed my life and made my life not only bearable but JOYFUL."

I want the same for you. In the following pages, you will discover how to do it.

CHAPTER 1

THE SEVEN SECRETS TO HAPPINESS NO ONE IS TALKING ABOUT

Success is not the key to happiness. Happiness is the key to success.
ALBERT SCHWEITZER, MISSIONARY SURGEON
TO AFRICA AND NOBEL PRIZE WINNER

Contrary to what most people believe, happiness is not reserved for the rich, famous, fortunate, or beautiful. I've treated many of these people, and they are some of the unhappiest people I know. You don't have to win the genetic lottery to be blessed with a happy disposition, and you aren't doomed to always feel down when life doesn't go your way. You can learn how to consistently generate positive feelings no matter your age, income, or situation by using practical neuroscience and knowing the seven secrets to happiness no one is talking about.

Why should we focus on being happy? As a psychiatrist, I've written about anxiety, depression, bipolar disorder, attention deficit hyperactivity disorder (ADHD), aging, violence, obesity, memory loss, love, parenting, and other important topics. Yet underlying the reasons most people come to see us at Amen Clinics is the fact that they are unhappy. Helping people be happier day to day is at the core of getting and staying mentally and physically healthy. Extensive research has shown that happiness is associated with a lower heart rate, lower blood pressure, and overall heart health. Happier people get fewer infections, have lower cortisol levels (the hormone of stress), and fewer aches and pains. Happy people tend to live longer, have better relationships, and be more successful in their careers. Plus happiness is contagious because happier people tend to make others happier.[1]

One of my favorite short videos that I encourage all of my patients to watch is by Dennis Prager. In "Why Be Happy," he suggests that happiness is a moral obligation. He says:

Whether or not you're happy, and most importantly, whether or not you act happy is about altruism, not selfishness—because it is about how we affect others' lives. . . . Ask anybody who was raised by an unhappy parent whether or not happiness is a moral issue, and I assure you the answer will be "yes." It is no fun being raised by an unhappy parent or being married to an unhappy person or being the parent of an unhappy child or working with an unhappy coworker.[2]

THE LIES OF HAPPINESS

Before discussing how to use neuroscience to be happier and unveiling the seven secrets no one is talking about, it's important to recognize the lies of happiness. For financial gain, marketers have been brainwashing populations for decades into believing happiness is based on things that actually damage our brains, ruin our minds, increase depression, and make us unhappy.

Lie #1: Having more and more of something (love, sex, fame, drugs, etc.) will make you happy. Unfortunately, if you are not careful, the more pleasure you get, the more you will need in the future to continue making you happy, something called hedonic adaptation. Your brain will adapt to high-pleasure experiences, so you'll need more each time to get the same effect, much like cocaine. Seeking more and more of a pleasure high often leads to depression because it wears out the pleasure centers in your brain, which we will discuss. I have seen this phenomenon repeatedly in Olympic and professional athletes, movie stars, and recording artists who never learned to manage their minds.

Lie #2: A "Don't Worry, Be Happy" mindset, promoted by the popular 1988 Grammy Song of the Year of the same name by Bobby McFerrin, will make you happy. In fact, this mindset will make you unhappy and kill you early. According to one of the longest longevity studies ever published, the "don't worry, be happy people" die early from accidents and preventable illnesses.[3] You need some anxiety to be happy. Appropriate anxiety helps us make better decisions. It prevents us from running into the street as children, risking broken bodies, and running headlong into toxic relationships as adults, risking broken hearts.

Lie #3: Advertisers and fast-food restaurants know what will make you happy. Take McDonald's Happy Meals (and kids' meals on most restaurant menus), for example. They certainly will not make children happy. These meals should be called Unhappy Meals as the low-quality, nutrient-sparse, processed food-like substances increase inflammation and have been linked with depression, ADHD, obesity, cancer, and a lower IQ.[4]

Lie #4: Someplace else will make you happy. The notion that happiness lies elsewhere is wrong. A prime example is Disneyland, which claims to be "the happiest place on earth." I grew up in Southern California, and Disneyland opened in 1955 when I was just a year old. I've been many times. Depending on whom I'm with, it can be fun or it can be stressful and exhausting because of the large crowds, long lines, crying children, and expensive trinkets. I'm hoping it's not the happiest place on earth, as stress can shrink the major mood and memory centers in the brain.[5]

Lie #5: You need a smartphone, watch, tablet, or the latest technology to make you happy. Technology can be addicting; gadgets and apps grab our attention and distract us from more important things such as family, friends, fitness, or faith. Many people eat at the same table but engage with their phones rather than with each other. Current research has found that many teens spend more hours on social media (average 9 hours) than they do sleeping.[6] Children 8 to 12 are online 6 hours a day. Technology has hijacked developing brains, with potentially serious consequences for many.

Lie #6: Video games make you happy. Depression and obesity rise for people who spend more and more time on video games and technology. Ian Bogost, famed video game designer (*Cow Clicker* and *Cruel 2 B Kind*) and chair of media studies and professor of interactive computing at the Georgia Institute of Technology, deemed habit-forming technologies as "the cigarettes of this century," cautioning about their equally addictive and potentially destructive side effects.[7] The World Health Organization added gaming disorder to the ICD-11 (International Classification of Diseases) in 2018.[8]

Lie #7: Constantly being "in the know" by following your favorite news outlet will make you happy. News outlets repeatedly and purposely pour toxic thoughts into our brains, making us see terror or disaster around every corner—all in an effort to boost their ratings and profits. Seeing repeated scary images activates our brains' primitive fear circuits (in the amygdala) that are meant to ensure our survival but are now obsolete.

The news always highlights scandalous and terrifying stories to keep you hooked on their channels or websites. Unless you purposefully monitor your news intake, these companies succeed in raising your stress hormones, which you now know shrink the major mood and memory centers in your brain and may put excessive fat around your waist.

Do you pick up your phone or tablet when you first wake up to see the latest world news? You might not know that just a few minutes of negative news in the morning can lower your happiness later in the day by 27 percent,[9] but now you do. I was on the *Dr. Phil* show when writing this book and evaluated a woman who had a brief psychotic episode around the 2020 election, thinking one of the candidates had brainwashed her daughter and was out to get her. She had never been political but started watching the news 24-7, and it contributed to her briefly losing her mind.

Lie #8: Alcohol makes you happy. Not so fast. The American Cancer Society links any alcohol consumption to seven types of cancer. Cancer is not a happiness maker. Alcohol can help you feel better quickly, but it can also damage your brain, decrease the quality of your decisions, and harm your relationships. If you are vulnerable to addiction, alcohol can hijack your pleasure centers and ruin your life.

Lie #9: Marijuana makes you happy. Maybe in the short run, but over time, marijuana prematurely ages the brain and lowers overall blood flow, which is not associated with a happy brain.[10] Plus, teens who use marijuana have a 450 percent increased risk of psychosis[11] as well as a heightened risk of depression and suicide in young adulthood.[12]

Lie #10: Sweet treats and desserts—any sugar—make you happy. Yes, sweets can provide a brief moment of bliss but definitely not long-term happiness. Sugar is addictive, pro-inflammatory, and associated with depression, obesity, diabetes, and dementia. As an example of this lie, just look at Coca-Cola's soft drink, which has the slogan "Open happiness." The slogan should actually read, "Open depression, obesity, diabetes, addiction, dementia, and early death."[13] When you drink a Coke or other soft drinks, you are drinking sugar water that is pro-inflammatory (inflammation increases depression, cancer, diabetes, and dementia), salt that makes you thirsty, and caffeine that brings your energy up then drops you like a rock and can negatively impact sleep.

Lie #11: Money makes you happy. This is true but only up to about $75,000 a year in the US; then the relationship completely falls off. Anyone who says money is irrelevant should look at the homeless; anyone who says money buys happiness should look at the suicides of the beautiful, wealthy, and famous. Neither is true. Money can change your circumstances to a certain point, but money doesn't help much once you have your basic needs met. When wealthy people were asked what they needed to be a perfect 10 in happiness, most said 2 to 10 times more.[14] The need for more makes many people unhappy because it can never be fully satisfied. Interestingly, a recent study about some very poor nations found that those citizens experienced happiness by being connected to their community and family and spending time in nature. For them, money played a minimal role in their subjective sense of well-being.[15] We can learn from their example. At the same time, if you shift the focus of your money toward giving to causes and people that matter to you, money can contribute to happiness. Likewise, spending money to have experiences with others actually gives us greater happiness than buying stuff. So, instead of going on a shopping spree at the mall, use that money to enhance your happiness quotient by catching a game, going to a concert, or having a delicious meal with people you enjoy.[16]

THE SEVEN SECRETS TO HAPPINESS NO ONE IS TALKING ABOUT

For decades, social scientists have been searching for the roots of happiness. Based on their research, it is generally accepted that happiness is about 40 percent genetic (you inherit it from your ancestors), 10 percent your situation in life or what happens to you, and 50 percent habits and mindset. This means you have a higher degree of control over happiness than most people think.

Researchers typically report happiness being associated with novelty, fun experiences, positive relationships, laughter, gratitude, anticipation, helping others, staying away from comparisons, meditation, nature, living in the moment (rather than the past with regret or the future with fear), productive work, a sense of purpose, spiritual beliefs, and wanting what you have as opposed to wanting more. Yet most happiness research completely misses seven important aspects:

1. It is critical to target happiness strategies to your unique brain type—a one-size-fits-all approach will never work.

2. Brain health (the actual physical functioning of the organ) is the most important foundational requirement of happiness.

3. Your brain needs targeted nutrients every day to boost happiness.

4. The foods you choose to eat either elevate happiness or steal it.

5. Mastering your mind and gaining separation or psychological distance from the noise in your head is essential to protecting happiness.

6. Noticing what you like about others more than what you don't is a recipe for happy relationships and happiness overall.

7. Having clearly defined values, purpose, and goals are essential to a strong foundation for happiness.

Consistently making high-quality decisions will give you a high-quality life. In researching happiness, together with my clinical experience over the last 40 years, I've summarized seven questions to ask yourself on a regular basis. *You, Happier: The 7 Neuroscience Secrets of Feeling Good Based on Your Brain Type* will explore each of the seven secrets and seven questions to help you be happier and more successful in everything you do.

HAPPINESS TRANSFORMATION IN 30 DAYS

How can 30 days pass so quickly? I am so glad to be learning how to apply the seven secrets and develop good habits these past 30 days.

—WMC

Secret 1: Know your brain type.

Question 1: Am I focused on what makes me uniquely happy?

In the late eighties, when I started looking at the brain, I was searching for tools to help me be more effective with my patients. I loved being a psychiatrist but quickly realized psychiatrists were handicapped compared to other medical specialists. Making diagnoses solely based on symptom clusters—such as anxiety, depression, addiction, or a short attention span—was inadequate. Symptoms didn't tell us anything about the underlying biology of the problems. All other medical professionals look at the organs they treat, but as psychiatrists, we were taught to guess and assume the underlying biological mechanisms for issues such as depression, ADHD, bipolar disorder, and addiction without ever looking at the brain, even though our patients were every bit as sick as those with heart disease, diabetes, or cancer.

My colleagues and I started looking at the brain with a study called quantitative EEG (qEEG), which evaluates electrical activity. Once we knew an individual's brain pattern, we could then teach patients to change it using medications, nutraceuticals (nutritional supplements with a pharmaceutical effect), and techniques such as neurofeedback (using the mind to control your physiology). This is where I first got the inspiration for my book *Change Your Brain, Change Your Life.* You are not stuck with the brain you have; you can make it better, and we could prove it.

In 1991, we added brain SPECT imaging to our toolbox. SPECT (single photon emission computed tomography) scans evaluate blood flow and activity patterns in the brain. Structural CT or MRI scans, which you've probably heard of, only assess brain anatomy. SPECT looks at how the brain functions and basically tells us three things about brain activity: if it is healthy, underactive, or overactive. Initially, my team started by naively looking for unique electrical or blood flow signature patterns for each of the major psychiatric issues—such as depression, anxiety disorders, addictions, bipolar disorder, obsessive-compulsive disorder (OCD), autism, and ADD/ADHD (attention deficit disorder/attention deficit hyperactivity disorder)—but we soon discovered there was not one brain pattern associated with any of these illnesses. They all had multiple types that required their own treatments, which made sense because there will never be just one pattern for depression given that not all depressed people are the same. Some are withdrawn, others are angry, and still others are anxious or obsessive. Taking a one-size-fits-all approach to people with any mental health issue based solely on their symptoms invites failure and frustration.

The SPECT scans helped us understand the type of depression, anxiety, ADHD, obesity, or addiction a person had so we could better target treatment to their individual brain. This one idea led to a dramatic breakthrough in our effectiveness with patients and opened up a new world of understanding and hope for more than 100,000 people who have come to see us and the millions of people who have read my books or seen my public television programs. In previously published books, I have written about seven types of anxiety and depression, seven types of ADD/ADHD, six types of addicts, and five types of overeaters. Understanding your type of brain is critical to getting the right help.

When I first started performing SPECT scans, I would often read them blindly without any information on the patient. I came to realize that the scans all by themselves could tell us a lot about a person. Of course, whenever we evaluate a new patient, we gather detailed information about their lives. Still, it was fun to say, "I wonder if you tend to act this way . . ." solely based on their scans.

I once saw the head of the local Alzheimer's association, Jim, who wanted to learn more about our process in helping people with memory problems. He asked to be scanned as part of his due diligence. When I asked Jim about his history, he refused to give me any information, saying he only wanted me to tell him about himself from looking at the scans. I told him that was not how we practiced. We always try to put the scans in the context of a person's life. Again, he refused. The front part of his brain worked way too hard (compared to our healthy group), which correlated with a brain type we call Persistent.

In front of his wife, I said, "Okay, you tend to be persistent and goal-oriented and to follow through with whatever you start."

Jim nodded I was correct.

"At the same time," I continued, "you can be worried, rigid, inflexible, and if things don't go your way, you can be easily upset. You also tend to hold grudges, take the opposite position in arguments whether you believe them or not, and can be argumentative and oppositional."

While I was reporting my observations, his wife was nodding her head: yes . . . yes . . . yes . . . and yes. Jim's scan gave me so many clues about his brain type and personality.

As we clinicians were working on understanding brain type and psychiatric issues, we also began to realize we were seeing features of personality in the scans.

- If your brain showed full, even, symmetrical activity overall, we called it **Balanced**.
- If the front part of your brain was sleepy or lower in activity compared to others, you were more likely to be creative, impulsive, and **Spontaneous**.
- If the front part of your brain was much more active than average, like Jim's, you tended to worry and be more **Persistent**.
- If your emotional or limbic brain was more active than average, you tended to be more vulnerable to sadness and be more **Sensitive**.
- If your amygdala and basal ganglia were more active than average, you tended to be more anxious and **Cautious**.

The scans began to tell an important story about who people are, how they think, how they act, how they interact with other human brains, and what makes them happy. For example, when my wife, Tana, was a child, her mother, Mary, took her to see R-rated horror movies, such as *The Hills Have Eyes* and *The Silent Scream*. Mary has the Spontaneous brain type and loves excitement and stimulation. She loves horror movies. They turn on her sleepy brain. Tana has a combination of a Spontaneous-Persistent-Cautious Brain Type and found the movies disturbing and had trouble letting go of the horrific images. Knowing your specific brain type and the brain types of your loved ones can help you feel better and get along better with those around you.

Consider 11-year-old Anna and 16-year-old Amber, two sisters who share the same room. Anna has the Persistent brain type (the front part of her brain is very active), loves a neat and orderly space, and becomes unhappy when items are out of place. Amber has the Spontaneous brain type (with low activity in the front part of her brain), is always looking for the next social engagement, and doesn't notice anything out of place. She has to work very hard to keep her room clean. This led to conflict and unhappiness for both of them. Balancing their brains helped them get along better without having to criticize and judge each other.

Secret 2: Optimize the physical functioning of your brain.

Question 2: Is this good for my brain or bad for it?

Your brain is involved in everything you do and everything you are. After looking at more than 200,000 brains scans on patients from over 155 countries, it is very clear to me that when your brain works right, you work right; and when it doesn't, you are much more likely to have trouble in your life. Your brain is the organ of happiness. With a healthy brain, you are happier (because you've made better decisions), healthier (also better decisions), wealthier (better decisions), and more successful in relationships, work, and everything else you do. The quality of your decisions (a brain function) is the common denominator of happiness and success in every area of life.

What most happiness researchers and writers are not talking about is that when the brain is troubled, for whatever reason, people tend to make poorer decisions, which leads to them being sadder, sicker, poorer, and less successful, which leads to depression and unhappiness. If the brain is not healthy, you can have all the features of a happy life mentioned above and still want to end your life. Having all the things that "should" make you happy only accentuates your unhappiness. If you want to be happy, it is critical to assess and optimize the physical functioning of your brain like my patient Stephen did.

Stephen Hilton, 46, suffered with depression for most of his life. He remembers often feeling sad for no reason when he was a child. He also struggled with weight issues and began to use food to help him cope with sadness. At school, Stephen often felt disconnected, and just the thought of going made him feel anxious. He tended to skip school and dropped out early to pursue music. At 16, he found methamphetamines and said it was like "the light in his head came on." This is a common statement among my patients with ADHD, although this was not the case here.

By the age of 18, he stopped using methamphetamines and switched to alcohol to cope with his depression and anxiety. Stephen immediately became a heavy user, and throughout his young adulthood, he continued to heavily consume alcohol on a near daily basis. During these years, his depression persisted despite using alcohol. And although he was able to function and grow in his music career—working on many blockbuster movies, such as *Die Another Day*, *Ocean's Eleven*, and *The World Is Not Enough*—he would often feel very low, hopeless, and "shut down." Eventually, Stephen entered a drug and alcohol rehabilitation program and was sober for 10 years. However, after moving from England to Los Angeles, he lost contact with his sponsor and stopped attending AA (Alcoholics Anonymous) meetings. He soon began abusing prescription medications and entered another rehab program. He had been sober for six years before coming to Amen Clinics.

I met Stephen after evaluating his wife, actress and comedian Laura Clery, who came to see us for trouble focusing, anxiety, and dark thoughts. Laura filmed her evaluation with me and posted the videos online, where they received more than 10 million views. As part of the clinical evaluation of Stephen, we took a detailed history to understand the story of his life, ran a complete set of laboratory tests, and did a SPECT scan. The following image represents a healthy SPECT scan, showing full, even, symmetrical activity.

HEALTHY SURFACE SPECT SCAN

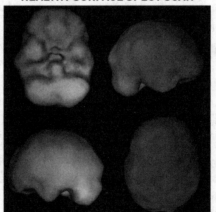

Top left view: looking up from bottom of brain
Top right image: looking at right side of the brain
Bottom left image: looking at left side of brain
Bottom right image: looking down from top of brain
Healthy = full, even symmetrical activity

STEPHEN'S SURFACE SPECT SCAN

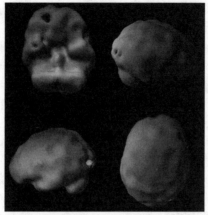

Top left view: holes indicate low blood flow in prefrontal cortex and right temporal lobe
Top right and bottom left views: decreases in left and right occipital lobes

Stephen's SPECT scan showed clear evidence of a prior head injury with low blood flow in the right prefrontal cortex, right temporal lobe, and the left and right occipital lobes. In his history, he told us that when he was very young, he had fallen down a flight of stairs and been knocked unconscious.

Could the early fall have caused a lifetime of sadness? Absolutely. Undiagnosed brain injuries are a major contributing factor to depression, anxiety, ADHD, addictions, homelessness, and suicide. Despite seeing psychiatrists, psychologists, and other therapists, Stephen's brain history had never been addressed because no one had ever looked at his brain. After just two months of repairing his brain by using bright light therapy and targeted nutraceuticals geared to his brain type and by learning not to believe every bad thought he had, Stephen felt happier, more hopeful, and more in control of his emotions.

While I was writing this book, we at Amen Clinics administered the Oxford Happiness Questionnaires to 344 of our patients who also had SPECT scans. From the scan data, it became clear that with a healthier brain comes a happier life. You'll learn more about this fascinating study in chapter 2.

Secret 3: Nourish your unique brain.

Question 3: Am I nourishing my unique brain?

Prior to going to medical school, I was interested in natural ways to heal. My grandfather, Dan, after whom I was named and who was my best friend growing up, had a heart attack when I was a teenager. As part of his recovery, my mother took him to natural health practitioners who changed his diet and started him on natural supplements. Health was a common discussion with my mother. Yet in medical school and five years of my psychiatric residency and fellowship, there was very little education on the impact of diet on mental health and virtually nothing on natural supplements, which unfortunately is still the case today. To my surprise there was already an extensive literature in 1991 about nutraceuticals and health, including mental health, which has since grown exponentially. For example, a search of PubMed.gov from the National Library of Medicine will return over 2,400 scientific abstracts on omega-3s and mood,[17] over 3,900 on vitamin D and mood,[18] and over 3,500 on St. John's Wort, a commonly used nutraceutical for mood issues.[19]

New research suggests we can produce up to 700 new brain cells a day if we put them in a nourishing environment (meaning good nutrition, omega-3 fatty acids, oxygen, blood flow, and stimulation).[20] If we nourish our brain and body, the hippocampi (which resemble seahorses) can grow stronger. We have two hippocampi, one in our left temporal lobe and another in our right temporal lobe. They are critical for learning, memory, and mood (happiness). If you hurt your biology, they shrink.

With a few basic nutrients and targeted supplements, you can improve the health of your brain, support the brain chemicals involved in your happiness, and balance the specific needs for your brain type.

Secret 4: Choose foods you love that love you back.

Question 4: Do I choose foods today I love that love me back?

Scientists in the fields of psychiatry and psychology are increasingly finding that food is tightly linked to mood and mental health issues, such as depression and anxiety. In a 2017 study in *BMC Medicine*, researchers found that when people with moderate to severe depression received nutritional counseling and ate a more healthful diet for 12 weeks, their symptoms improved significantly.[21] In fact, depressive symptoms got so much better that over 32 percent of the participants achieved what psychiatrists call "remission criteria." This means they no longer qualified as having a mood disorder. Based on these results, the research team suggested that dietary changes could be an effective treatment strategy for depression. It is becoming abundantly clear that if you want to feel good, you need to eat well.

Think back to the "Lies of Happiness." Coca-Cola's "Open happiness" campaign and McDonald's "Happy Meals" are made with low-quality ingredients that taste good going down but that downgrade your happiness over time.

As a general rule, fast food is sad food. Just look at the findings of this study on food and depression from two small islands in the Torres Strait located between Australia and New Guinea.[22] One of the islands is dotted with fast-food joints, while the other more remote island doesn't have a single fast-food outlet. On the fast-food island, residents reported lower fish consumption, while those living on the other island said they had higher fish consumption. When the researchers screened the residents for depression, 16 people from the fast-food island reported moderate-to-severe depressive symptoms, compared to only three people from the other island. This represents a 500 percent increase in the incidence of depression based on food consumption.

What you eat and drink has a direct effect on your brain and its ability to balance chemicals, promote health, and operate optimally—all factors in your happiness.

Secret 5: Master your mind and gain psychological distance from the noise in your head.

Question 5: Is it true? What went well today?

Your mind can be a troublemaker. Mine often is. Thoughts and feelings come from many sources, such as:

- How your brain is working at any given moment (which is influenced by your diet, gut health, immunity, inflammation, exposure to toxins, and sleep)

- Experiences from your ancestors that have been written in your genetic code

- Genetic tendencies. For example, my oldest daughter was shy when she was very young and would often hide behind my leg whenever a new person came by, while her younger sister said, "Hi, my name is Kaitlyn," to everyone she met, and Chloe, our youngest, came out of the womb extremely verbal (12-word sentences at the age of 2), claiming, "I'm the leader; I am the boss" as a toddler.

- Personal experiences (conscious and unconscious) and memories

- Your interpretation of the words and body gestures of your parents, siblings, friends, enemies, and acquaintances

- The news, music, and social media you're exposed to, and much more

You are not your mind. Your ability to separate from, manage, and not be a victim of your mind is essential to feeling happy. Yet it was not until I was 28 years old, starting my psychiatric residency, that I learned I was not my mind and I did not have to believe every stupid thought that came into my awareness. I learned that my thoughts create my feelings; my feelings create my behaviors; and eventually my behaviors create my outcomes in relationships, work, finances, and how healthy I am physically and emotionally. If I could separate myself from my thoughts and look at them dispassionately, then I could feel and act in a more consistently happy way over time.

One helpful psychological distancing technique, found in chapter 12, is to give your mind a name. This allows for separation, and you choose whether to listen to it. As you'll learn, I named my mind Hermie after the pet raccoon I had when I was 16 years old. I loved her, but she was a troublemaker, like my mind, and got me into hot water with my parents, siblings, and girlfriend. (I'll tell you more about Hermie later.) I often imagine Hermie holding up signs in my head with random negative thoughts, such as:

- You're a failure.
- You're a fool.
- You'll get sued.
- You're not enough.
- Others are better than you.

Knowing that I am not my mind, I can choose to ignore Hermie—metaphorically putting her in her cage. Always ask yourself whether your thoughts help you or hurt you. When Hermie is causing trouble, I often imagine petting her, playing with her, or putting the little troublemaker on her back and tickling her. I don't have to take Hermie, or my mind, seriously. I can gain psychological distance, and so can you. Hermie will show up throughout the book to illustrate how psychologically distancing yourself can contribute to your happiness.

Secret 6: Notice what you like about others more than what you don't.

Question 6: Am I reinforcing the behaviors I like or dislike in others today?

One day my patient Jessie, 16, stormed into my office, sat on a couch, and told me that she hated her mother, was running away from home, and I couldn't stop her. She was clearly unhappy. In the few years I had been seeing Jessie, I had gotten to know her family well. It was clear to me that her mother had untreated ADD and tended to pick on Jessie as a way to stimulate her own brain. Conflict-seeking behavior is very common among people with untreated ADD. I tried to convince her mother to get help, but she wouldn't have it . . . and now she was driving her daughter away.

In the middle of the rant, Jessie turned her anger on me. "Tell me, Dr. Amen. Why does a grown man collect penguins?" she asked.

In my office at the time were hundreds of penguins . . . pretty much any type of penguin that you could imagine: penguin pens, dolls, and puppets; a penguin vacuum; and even a penguin weather vane. I laughed and said, "I've seen you for two years, and you're just now noticing the penguins? Let me tell you the story.

"A long time ago, when my son was seven, he was difficult for me. As a way to work on our relationship, I took him to a sea animal park. We had fun at the whale show and the sea lion show, and at the end of the day my son wanted to see the penguin show. The penguin's name was Fat Freddy. He was an amazing chubby little penguin. He dove off a high diving board, bowled with his nose, counted with his flippers, and jumped through a hoop of fire. Then, toward the end of the show, the trainer asked Freddy to go get something, and Freddy went and brought the item right back.

Wow, I thought to myself. *I ask this kid to get something for me, and he wants to have a discussion for twenty minutes, and then he doesn't want to do it.* I knew my son was smarter than the penguin.

"So, after the show, I went up to the trainer and asked her how she got Freddy to do all of those really cool things. The trainer looked at my son and then at me and said, 'Unlike parents, whenever Freddy does anything I want him to do, I notice him. I give him a hug, and I give him a fish.'

"Even though my son didn't like whole raw fish like my sushi-loving daughter Chloe did, a light turned on in my head. Whenever my son did things that I liked, I paid no attention to him at all because, like my own father, I was a busy guy. But when he didn't do what I wanted him to do, I gave him a ton of attention because I didn't want to raise bad children. I was inadvertently teaching him to act badly in order to get my attention. So now I collect penguins as a way to remind myself to notice the good things about the people in my life a lot more than the bad things."[23]

As I finished telling the story, I told Jessie that I had this really crazy idea. "What if we trained your mother to be less angry and less likely to pick on you?" I began.

"I'm listening," she said.

"I know this will be hard, but whenever your mother starts in on you, I want you not to overreact. Don't challenge her or get emotional."

At this point, Jessie's eyes got big. "I don't think I can do that," she said, her voice trailing off.

"Hold on," I said. "Here's what I'm asking you to do. Whenever she is nice to you, listens to you, or is more appropriate with you, I want you to tell her how much you love and appreciate her."

Jessie was starting to understand. Like the trainer who shaped Freddy's behavior, she could influence her mother's behavior by noticing what she liked a lot more than what she didn't like. I was teaching Jessie personal power.

Clearly, Jessie knew how to push her mother's buttons. With a look or a word, she could send her mother into orbit. But if she had that power, she also had the power to calm things down and make life better.

That night, I got a text from Jessie saying that she decided not to run away from home. A week later, she said our plan was working. Two weeks after that, when I saw her again, she said things were much better at home, and she brought me a penguin to add to my collection.

I know you've heard the phrase "It takes two to make a relationship better." It's just not my experience as a psychiatrist. When I teach my patients how powerful they are, they realize they can clearly make things better with their loved ones or they can make things worse.

Secret 7: Live each day based on your clearly defined values, purpose, and goals.

Question 7: Does it fit? Does my behavior today fit the goals I have for my life?

Over the years, I've seen many patients who feel disconnected and insignificant. They lack a sense of meaning and purpose. They lack a relationship with God or something bigger than themselves. Regardless of religion, denomination, or even personal belief in God, without a spiritual connection, many people experience an underlying sense of despair or meaninglessness. At their core, they are unhappy. It doesn't have to be that way.

We are all spiritual beings created with divine purpose, whether or not we believe in God. Each person has a role to play in the lives of those around them and a mission to fulfill. Having a deep sense of meaning and purpose gives you a reason to get up and take great care of your brain. Purpose gives you a sense of what matters most in the grand scheme of life and eternity, and it is essential for happiness. Without knowing your purpose, it's hard to have values and goals that matter. When you make decisions based on your purpose, it shifts your focus away from self and onto others. I like to ask people the following question to help them discover why their life matters: Why is the world a better place because you breathe? If you don't know the answer to this question, think it over. Ask those closest to you for their insights. What skills do you have that could be helpful to someone today? What can you do to make the world a better place?

Knowing your purpose guides your goals and decisions in what I call the Four Circles—the four areas of your life that make up the essence of who you are. Let me explain.

In evaluating and treating patients, I never think of them as their symptoms but rather as whole people in four big circles: biological, psychological, social, and spiritual (underlying meaning and purpose). This book will be divided into sections that honor these circles, as they all contribute to happiness or unhappiness.

If you were one of my patients, I'd ask you to do my Four Circles of Happiness exercise to identify what makes you happy in each of the Four Circles.

HAPPINESS TRANSFORMATION IN 30 DAYS

I am so happy that I did the challenge. I loved all the interventions. My husband also took this challenge. We asked each other the seven questions each night, and I believe doing this challenge has brought us closer together. I feel so much more motivated to live my life differently so I can be happier.

—MT

- **Biological Circle:** how your physical body and brain function
- **Psychological Circle:** developmental issues and how you think
- **Social Circle:** social support, your current life situation, and societal influences
- **Spiritual Circle:** your connection to God, the planet, past and future generations, and your deepest sense of meaning and purpose

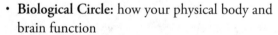

Look for the Micro-Moments of Happiness

Keep in mind that the big "H" doesn't require major life-changing events, accomplishments, or milestones. Start finding joy in the smallest things you can: hearing a bird sing outside your window, feeling the warmth of the sun on your face when you step outside, petting your dog or cat, taking that first sip of your favorite brain healthy smoothie, or cracking open a new book (like this one!). I call these micro-moments of happiness. Most of us gloss over these little things, searching instead for the big experiences. I want you to savor these precious times because, when your brain pays attention to them, they add up to more overall contentment and satisfaction with your life. The more micro-moments you cherish, the greater your sense of joy. Throughout this book, I will introduce you to some of my own micro-moments of happiness and will offer suggestions to look for your own based on your brain type. (Just look for the smiley face icons.) Let's get happier, one micro-moment at a time!

Let me show you what this looks like when I do this exercise:

DR. AMEN'S FOUR CIRCLES OF HAPPINESS

Biological

A great night's sleep

Waking up feeling rested

Feeling mentally sharp

Great health numbers, such as: BMI, blood pressure, vitamin D, omega-3 index, C-reactive protein, HbA1C, fasting blood sugar, ferritin, etc.

Exercises I love, especially table tennis, lifting weights to feel strong, and walks on the beach with Aslan, my white shepherd

Warm weather

Foods I love that love me back: my brain-healthy shake in the morning, perfectly cooked eggs, Copper River salmon

Physical affection with Tana

Being in nature: the beach, woods, and mountains, especially Muir Woods, a redwood forest north of San Francisco

Being pain-free

☺ **Biological Micro-Moments:** the first sip of a brain-healthy cappuccino or hot chocolate, the first bite of an orange from my father's ranch, guacamole made from his avocados, Aslan getting excited when I put on my sneakers, holding Tana's hand when we walk, having eye contact with her, seeing the fireplace come on or watching it, hearing a song I love

Psychological

Healthy routines

Starting my days with "Today is going to be a great day"

Ending each day with the treasure hunt of "What went well today?"

Happy memories, such as giving the graduation commencement speech at my university 40 years (almost to the day) after graduating with an undergraduate degree

Correcting negative thought patterns

Writing and creating new ideas

Feeling productive

New learning

Listening to great audiobooks

Movies, especially comedies

Fun TV series

Working toward achieving our goals

☺ **Psychological Micro-Moments:** making a great play in a Sudoku puzzle, laughing at a joke or funny scene in a movie or TV show, listening to a cool plot twist in an audiobook, putting words together to make someone laugh

Social

Being connected to Tana

Being connected to my kids and grandkids on a regular basis

Spending time with my mother

Being connected to siblings, friends, and coworkers

Smooth-functioning executive team at work with people I care about

Great conversations

Speaking and teaching

Financial security; being a value spender

Watching sports (Lakers, Dodgers, tennis, especially Rafael Nadal)

Recognition for doing a good job

Being with our dog and cat

☺ **Social Micro-Moments:** hearing my mother's voice on the phone when she first recognizes it's me, thinking of the grandkids, getting a fun text from a friend or patient, petting/cuddling the dog and cat

Spiritual

Being close to God

Attending religious services with people I care about

Caring for the planet (recycling)

Being connected to the past (especially my grandfather and father who are both dead but live in me)

Being connected to the future (my grandchildren and the future of
   Amen Clinics and BrainMD)
Doing work that matters
Living a life that matters and changing how mental health care is
   practiced worldwide
Feeling purposeful
Making a difference in the lives of others
Not being afraid to die

☺ **Spiritual Micro-Moments:** saying a prayer each night, randomly remembering a Bible verse that applies to a situation I am in, being grateful for another
day, remembering my grandfather and father

Now it's your turn. I urge you to do your own Four Circles of Happiness
on a sheet of paper or on your smart device right now. Inside each of the
circles, write the following titles:

FOUR CIRCLES OF HAPPINESS

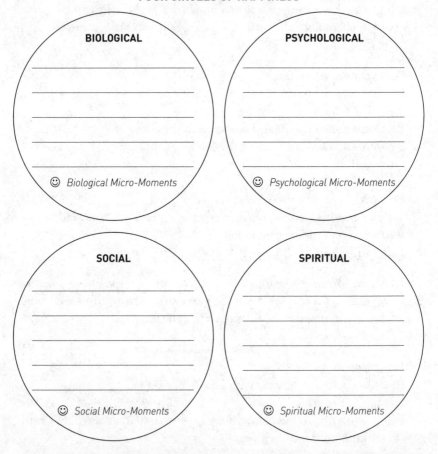

BIOLOGICAL

☺ *Biological Micro-Moments*

PSYCHOLOGICAL

☺ *Psychological Micro-Moments*

SOCIAL

☺ *Social Micro-Moments*

SPIRITUAL

☺ *Spiritual Micro-Moments*

Within each circle, write down what makes you happy while keeping these questions in mind:

- What brings a smile to your face?
- What makes you feel good about life?
- What do you value most?

Don't forget to add a section for micro-moments in each circle. When you have finished, look at how many things you have listed in each circle. Does one circle have a much shorter list? Are you out of balance in any of these areas? If so, you may be neglecting one of your circles. Be sure to look at your Four Circles of Happiness every day as a way to remind yourself about the things that bring you joy. Focusing on doing what you love to do is a surefire way to make you happier.

Now that you know the seven secrets of happiness no one is talking about, let's get serious about helping you and your loved ones become and stay happier.

PART 1

THE NEUROSCIENCE OF BRAIN TYPES AND HAPPINESS

CHAPTER 2

FINDING HAPPINESS IN THE BRAIN

Being able to instantly respond to sarcasm is a sign of a healthy brain.
ANONYMOUS

Your brain is the organ of happiness. Your brain is the organ of liking, wanting, and learning—all essential ingredients that go into happiness. Your brain is also the organ of sadness, anxiety, panic, anger, and storing past emotional trauma—the enemies of happiness. Deciding to assess and optimize the three pounds of tissue between your ears is the first foundational decision to a happier life. Yet most people never think about their brains, which is a huge mistake, because success and happiness start in the physical functioning of the brain.

Evidence that most people never think about their brains is everywhere. Adults still let kids play football despite all the evidence of brain damage, hit soccer balls with their heads, and do dangerous gymnastics routines. Head trauma, as we saw with Stephen in the first chapter, is a major cause of unhappiness. I live in Newport Beach, California, where there are more plastic surgeons than most places in the world, and I often think that as a society we care more about our faces, breasts, bellies, and butts than we do our brains. The thinking among many people is that if you look perfect, you will be happy. Of course, that is a lie. Looking perfect will *not* make you happy—just remember the stunning actress Marilyn Monroe and supermodel Margaux Hemingway, who took their own lives.

Why do most people never think about the health of their own brains? Because you can't see the brain. You can see the wrinkles in your skin or the fat around your belly, and you can do something when you're unhappy with how you look. Yet, since most people never see their brains, they just don't care until it is showing signs of real trouble. Physicians screen hearts, bones, cervices, and prostate glands, but it is rare for them to assess brain health unless you have a significant problem, such as migraines, dizziness, seizures, or memory issues.

When I first started looking at the brain in 1991 using SPECT imaging, I didn't care about my own brain, even though I was the top neuroscience student at my medical school and, at the time, was a double board-certified psychiatrist (general psychiatry, and child and adolescent psychiatry). I don't remember one lecture on brain health during my five-year psychiatric training program. As embarrassing as it sounds now, I hadn't thought about the physical health of my brain, even though the brain is the main target organ in psychiatry. That all changed in an instant.

Shortly after I started ordering SPECT scans, I scanned my 60-year-old mother as part of a healthy database project. I discovered that she had a stunningly beautiful brain, which looked much younger than her 60 years.[1] Her scan reflected her life. At the time, she had seven children, dozens of grandchildren, and was an active, positive presence in everyone's life. She also played golf and was the Newport Beach Golf Club Women's Champion in 1976. After seeing her brain, I worked up the courage to scan my own brain. It was not healthy, looking significantly older than my 37 years. As I wondered why, I remembered I had played football in high school (bad for the brain), had meningitis twice as a young Army soldier (also bad for the brain), and had bad brain habits. Although I was never one to drink alcohol (I hate being out of control), smoke, or use drugs, at the time I was under chronic stress at home and work, often didn't sleep more than four hours a night, was about 30 pounds overweight, and ate mostly fast food on the run.

Seeing my SPECT scan compared to my mother's scan, I developed brain envy. I wanted a healthy brain like hers, so I began working to improve it. My brain became healthier quickly and stayed that way. Decades later, my scan was fuller, fatter, and healthier, which became the foundational principle behind our work at Amen Clinics: "You are not stuck with the brain you have. You can make it better, and we can prove it." We saw this not only in me but also in the tens of thousands of patients we treated. With a better brain comes a better, happier, and more successful life.

MY MOTHER'S BEAUTIFUL SPECT SCAN AT AGE 60

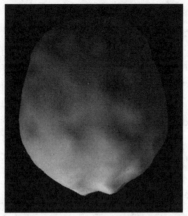

Full, even, symmetrical, healthy appearance

DANIEL, AGE 37

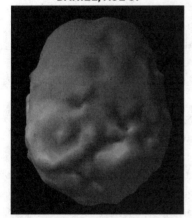

Bumpy, toxic appearance

DANIEL, AGE 62

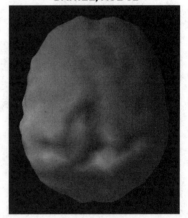

Much healthier

TAKE A TOUR OF THE HUMAN BRAIN

Your brain is an integrated community of parts that work together to create and sustain who you are.[2] Specific parts of the brain are designed to do certain things, but its functions are rarely simple. With that in mind, I like to teach some generalizations to help you learn about your brain. The human brain is like a modern ancient city—think Athens, Rome, or Paris. Like these famous cities, your brain has different neighborhoods connected by billions of neural pathways. Let's take a brief tour.

Your brain houses a primitive section, responsible for the activities essential for survival. Neuroscientists call this the "reptilian brain," and it includes the brain stem and cerebellum, which control breathing, heart rate, body temperature, balance, and coordination. The brain stem and cerebellum play a critical role in happiness, as they are also involved in processing speed and producing some of the chemicals, such as dopamine and serotonin, that are involved in mood, motivation, and learning, which we will discuss in detail.

The human brain also has the limbic neighborhood, or emotional brain, that is situated around the brain stem and cerebellum. This brain region colors our emotions as positive or negative and is involved with our basic needs for survival, including bonding, nesting, and emotions. The limbic brain records memories of what sustains or threatens our survival and is responsible for our urges and cravings (our wants and desires) and how pleasurable something is (our likes). The limbic brain exerts a strong, often unconscious, influence on our behavior.

Limbic brain structures include:

- **Hippocampus:** mood and the formation of new memories
- **Amygdala:** emotions, including fear, as well as signaling the presence of food, sexual partners, rivals, or children in distress
- **Hypothalamus:** helps control body temperature, appetite, sexual behavior, and emotions
- **Basal ganglia:** motivation, pleasure, smoothing motor movements
- **Anterior cingulate gyrus:** shifting attention and error detection

Finally, the brain has one other area known as the cerebral cortex, which is built around the reptilian and limbic neighborhoods. This part of the brain is involved in creating and understanding language, abstract thought, imagination, and culture. It has endless learning possibilities and creates the story of why we are happy or sad, which may or may not have anything to do with the truth. The cerebral cortex is the largest structure in the human brain. The wrinkly walnut-shaped mass sits atop and covers the rest of the brain and has four main lobes on each side of the brain:

- **Frontal lobes:** The frontal lobes consist of the motor cortex, which is in charge of directing movement; the premotor cortex, which helps to plan movement; and the prefrontal cortex, which is considered the executive part of the brain. This region is the most evolved part of the human brain and is involved with focus, forethought, judgment, organization, planning, impulse control, empathy, and learning from mistakes. It makes up about 30 percent of the human brain, compared to just 11 percent for chimpanzees, 7 percent for dogs, 3 percent for cats (perhaps why they need 9 lives), and one percent for mice (which is why they are eaten by cats). On the underside of the prefrontal cortex is an area called the orbitofrontal cortex, located just above the orbits of your eye sockets, that is intimately involved in happiness.

- **Temporal lobes:** The temporal lobes, situated underneath the temples and behind the eyes, are involved in language, processing what you hear, learning and memory, and emotion. The temporal lobes have been called the "What Pathway" because they name "what" things are. On the inside of the temporal lobes are two critical structures of the limbic system (emotional brain): the hippocampus (memory and mood) and the amygdala (emotional reactions and fear).

- **Parietal lobes:** The parietal lobes, to the top side and back of the brain, are the centers for sensory processing (touch), perception, and sense of direction. Called the "Where Pathway" because they help us locate where things are in space, they're also involved in manipulating numbers, dressing, and grooming.

- **Occipital lobes:** The occipital lobes, at the back of the cortex, are concerned primarily with vision and visual processing.

The cortex is divided into two hemispheres, left and right. While the two sides significantly overlap in function, the left side in right-handed people (may or may not be opposite in left handers) is generally the seat of language and tends to be the analytical, logical, detail-oriented, and more positive part of the brain. The right hemisphere tends to see the big picture and is involved more with hunches and intuition. It also tends to see and admit problems and has been associated with being the anxious side of the brain. One psychiatric treatment called transcranial magnetic stimulation uses a fast electromagnetic frequency to stimulate the left prefrontal cortex to help depression and a low frequency to the right prefrontal cortex to calm anxiety.

Information from the world enters your brain through your senses and goes to the limbic brain, where it is tagged as meaningful, safe, or dangerous; then it travels to the back part of the brain (temporal, parietal, and occipital lobes), where it is initially processed and compared with past experience; then it travels to the front part of the brain for you to evaluate and decide if you will act on it. Information in the brain travels up to 270 miles per hour, and the transmission of information from the outside world to your conscious awareness happens almost instantaneously.

OUTSIDE VIEW OF THE BRAIN

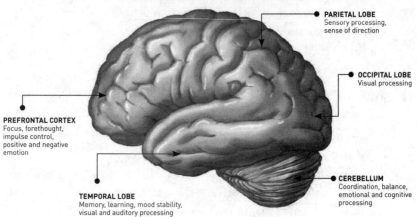

PARIETAL LOBE
Sensory processing,
sense of direction

OCCIPITAL LOBE
Visual processing

PREFRONTAL CORTEX
Focus, forethought,
impulse control,
positive and negative
emotion

CEREBELLUM
Coordination, balance,
emotional and cognitive
processing

TEMPORAL LOBE
Memory, learning, mood stability,
visual and auditory processing

INSIDE VIEW OF THE BRAIN

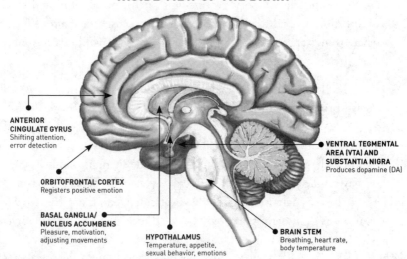

**ANTERIOR
CINGULATE GYRUS**
Shifting attention,
error detection

**VENTRAL TEGMENTAL
AREA (VTA) AND
SUBSTANTIA NIGRA**
Produces dopamine (DA)

ORBITOFRONTAL CORTEX
Registers positive emotion

**BASAL GANGLIA/
NUCLEUS ACCUMBENS**
Pleasure, motivation,
adjusting movements

HYPOTHALAMUS
Temperature, appetite,
sexual behavior, emotions

BRAIN STEM
Breathing, heart rate,
body temperature

YOUR BRAIN ON HAPPINESS

Now that you have an overview of the neighborhoods of the brain, let's turn
our attention specifically to research on happiness, which seems to stem from
an interaction of three important brain areas:

- **Orbitofrontal cortex**, located in the front, underside part of the
  cerebral cortex
- **Basal ganglia**, especially in the front half of the nucleus accumbens,
  which responds to rewards and the anticipation of rewards, in the
  limbic area

- **Brain stem**, which is where the neurotransmitters dopamine, serotonin, and phenylethylamines are produced; part of the reptilian brain

Orbitofrontal cortex: why you should never allow children to hit a soccer ball with their head

The orbitofrontal cortex sits right behind your forehead and directly above your eyes, surrounded by hard, ridged bones that can damage it. This brain region has been shown to be intimately involved in happiness, which is why you should never allow children (or adults) to hit a soccer ball with their head. In over 90 percent of people with traumatic brain injuries, the prefrontal cortex and orbitofrontal cortex have been hurt. Brain imaging studies have shown that the orbitofrontal cortex is an important region for coding pleasure. The medial (middle) aspect is associated with subjective pleasure (liking), such as to foods (like chocolate), sexual orgasms, drugs, and music. This region also helps you learn and remember what makes you happy. Unpleasant sensations are coded in the more lateral (outside) parts of the orbitofrontal cortex.

Basal ganglia

The basal ganglia are large structures deep in the brain involved in pleasure, motivation, habit formation, and motor movements. They contain the nucleus accumbens, part of the reward system that motivates you to go toward pleasure (wanting) and away from pain, and are exquisitely responsive to the neurotransmitter dopamine, which is involved with cravings and addictions. When the nucleus accumbens is underactive, people tend to feel flat and depressed, and they are more vulnerable to addictions and craving substances that activate it, such as drugs, alcohol, sex, or high-calorie sugary foods. The substantia nigra (part of the basal ganglia) and ventral tegmental area (located in the brain stem) produce dopamine. When either of these areas is underactive or starts to die, dopamine is reduced and people develop Parkinson's disease, apathy, and often depression.

Brain stem

This area of the brain is critical to supporting life and, as mentioned, has groups of cells in a region called the ventral tegmental area that produces dopamine, which is involved with motion, motivation, and pleasure. The raphe nuclei (another cluster of cells) produces the well-known neurotransmitter serotonin, which is involved with mood and cognitive flexibility.

In addition to the interplay of these three brain regions, happiness also relies on quieting the misery-producing areas of the brain. In particular, this means calming activity in the amygdala, an area that registers fear, and the insular cortex, a region located between the frontal and temporal lobes that is more active when people feel angst or unhappiness.

WANTING VERSUS LIKING

Now the limbic system, or emotional brain, also plays another role in happiness. It distinguishes wants and likes. Imagine people in a casino at the slot machines putting in coins and pulling the levers repeatedly for hours. Most look tired and bored and barely smile when they win. This is an example of compulsive persistence with little joy. Their brains *want* to do what they are doing, but there is little evidence they actually *like* it. Wanting and liking are both important to happiness, but they are separate in the brain. This is why we can want something we do not like, such as craving (wanting) drugs that put a mother at risk for losing her children or gambling that causes a man to lose his home and family.

Using a personal example, I love holidays at my mother's home. She's an incredible cook and even now, at the age of 89, puts so much effort into making these times special for her family. I want her sausage pizza, buttered rice, Syrian bread dripping with honey, and other unhealthy foods. However, I don't like how they make me feel (overly full, self-loathing, and unhappy) or what they do to my body since I work hard to be at a healthy weight and to have the energy needed to do the work I love for as long as possible. Over time, I found that if I eat something healthy an hour before I go to my mother's home, it helps stabilize my blood sugar levels, and I can have a small piece of whatever I want without the overwhelming urge to eat more or to jeopardize my happiness or health. I've learned to balance the wanting and liking systems in my brain.

- **Wanting** is "anticipatory desire," which is looking forward to getting a reward in the future, such as craving a brownie, a cigarette, or a trip to a casino. Wanting relies on dopamine, the chemical of possibility, as we will see. The "wanting" system in the brain is large, robust, and powerful, which is why you need a healthy prefrontal cortex to control it.

- **Liking**, "consummatory pleasure," involves a much smaller brain system and is more fragile and uses serotonin and endorphins to signal pleasure from what you are doing in the moment. Addictive substances create pleasure in the moment *and* appropriate the wanting circuitry, which means, if you are not careful, they can literally hijack your brain and life.

The major difference between wanting and liking has to do with how our brain operates: consciously or unconsciously. Nobel prize–winning psychologist Daniel Kahneman has divided the information processing into two systems: System 1, unconscious or automatic, and System 2, conscious.[3] Liking is conscious, meaning you are aware of it. Wanting is often unconscious, meaning your desires occur automatically and often without you noticing them. System 1 is where most of the work of our mind gets done: automatic skills, intuition, and dreaming are examples of unconscious processing. As much as 95 percent of cognitive activities happen in the unconscious mind.

You have to like something first before the wanting system kicks in. Psychologists call this the arousal template, which is the complete array of thoughts, images, behaviors, and sensory input that first triggered happiness or pleasure. This is why soothing a child with sugar or electronic devices is a bad strategy. It can set them up for later food or gadget addictions. The stronger the liking, the more power it might have over you later in life, which is why many people never get over their first loves. The first time the explosion of new love chemicals— oxytocin and dopamine—hit the nucleus accumbens, it leaves a lasting imprint on the pleasure centers in the brain. Anything that reminds you of your first love can retrigger an explosion of those same chemicals.

FINDING HAPPINESS IN THE BRAIN

As I was writing this book and learning more about brain systems and happiness, I decided to see if I could indeed find happiness in the brain imaging work we do at Amen Clinics. We had 344 patients, ages 9–89, take the respected Oxford Happiness Questionnaire, which was developed by Drs. Michael Argyle and Peter Hills of Oxford Brookes University. The questionnaire, which you can take as part of my challenge at

HAPPINESS TRANSFORMATION IN 30 DAYS

Oh my goodness! I just took the quiz and then compared it to my Day 1 happiness score. I jumped from 2.69 to 4.79! Mind blown. This course was amazing. The timing was absolutely perfect for me, as I had a lot of alone time to ponder each day's message and thought prompts. You really made me think about things in a new light.

—HJ

30DayHappinessChallenge.com, asks respondents how much they agree or disagree with 29 questions on a 6-point scale:

1 = strongly disagree
2 = moderately disagree
3 = slightly disagree
4 = slightly agree
5 = moderately agree
6 = strongly agree

Some of the statements are phrased positively and some negatively. Examples of positive ones include:

- I feel that life is very rewarding.
- I laugh a lot.
- I often experience joy and elation.

Examples of negative statements include:

- I am not particularly optimistic about the future.
- I don't think I look attractive.
- I don't have a particular sense of meaning or purpose in my life.

When finished, questionnaire takers calculate their scores.[4]

1–2: Not happy, you may be seeing yourself and your situation worse than it really is
2–3: Somewhat unhappy
3–4: Neutral, not really happy or unhappy
4–5: Rather happy
5–6: Very happy
6: Too happy

People with particularly low scores may be viewing their lives as worse than they actually are; those with a perfect score are actually too happy and less likely to thrive in daily life. Their health may also suffer. Being too happy may lower healthy anxiety and decision-making ability.

Our research team compared the bottom 50, with scores ranging from 1.03 to 2.72, to the top 50, with scores ranging from 4.38 to 5.76. Then our statistician, Dr. David Keator from the University of California, Irvine, did an additional set of analyses correlating the happiness scores for all participants. The results were fascinating.

The brain SPECT scans of the high happiness group showed increased activity and blood flow overall, meaning the healthier your brain, the happier you are likely to be. We also saw increased activity and blood flow in the orbital prefrontal cortex and in the basal ganglia and nucleus accumbens in the limbic part of the brain.

INCREASES IN HIGH HAPPINESS GROUP

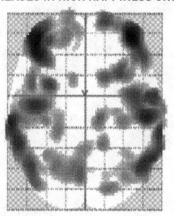

Overall increased blood flow in the high happiness group, especially in prefrontal cortex

In the low happiness group, the SPECT scans showed increased activity in the anterior cingulate gyrus, which I think of as the brain's gear shifter, meaning these people are more likely to get stuck on negative thoughts.

LOW HAPPINESS GROUP WITH INCREASED ANTERIOR CINGULATE ACTIVITY

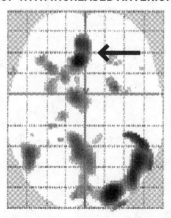

Arrow points to increased anterior cingulate activity in low happiness group

HAPPINESS TRANSFORMATION IN 30 DAYS

I've had my share of life-shattering events beyond the pandemic, but I'm so glad I stayed with the Happiness Challenge. It was an epiphany to realize a happy life doesn't just land on your doorstep, nor is it the responsibility of others to give it to you. You must work at it every day. I now feel armed, and with these tools, I can hold myself accountable for my own happiness.

—KP

According to Dr. Keator, the most interesting result from our study was found in the reward or happiness circuits, composed of the ventral tegmental area, nucleus accumbens, and orbitofrontal cortex. These circuits have been associated with smiling, laughter, pleasurable feelings, and happiness.[5] The higher activity in these areas correlated with higher total happiness scores.

Now that we have found happiness in the brain, let's dive into the neuroscience of brain types, which are associated with what makes you uniquely happy.

KNOW YOUR BRAIN TYPE

QUESTION 1

*Am I focused on
what makes me uniquely happy?*

CHAPTER 3

AN INTRODUCTION TO BRAIN TYPING

*I think I, like a lot of people, have that type of brain where
I find it interesting or fulfilling to worry about something.*

MARIA BAMFORD

Why do you do what you do?

Why do others do what they do?

What makes you happy?

What makes your loved ones happy?

To answer these central questions, it is critical to know about your brain, especially your brain type, and the brain types of others.

Throughout history, we've categorized people and their personalities in many ways. Hippocrates, the fifth-century Greek physician, explained four fundamental temperaments he believed were caused by an excess or lack of bodily fluids (blood, yellow or black bile, and phlegm). The four temperaments are:

- Sanguine (outgoing, social, risk-taking)
- Phlegmatic (relaxed, peaceful, easy-going)
- Choleric (take-charge, decisive, goal-oriented)
- Melancholic (thoughtful, reserved, introverted, sad, and anxious)

In one of my first college psychology classes, Temperament and Personality, I wrote a paper comparing the Peanuts characters to Hippocrates's temperament types. (Quick confession: I've been a huge fan of the Charles Schulz *Peanuts* comic strip since I was a child. When I was a young soldier in the Army and stationed in Germany, I even had Snoopy sheets on my bed. Shhh, don't tell anyone.) Obviously, Snoopy was sanguine; Schroeder, phlegmatic;

Lucy, choleric; and Charlie Brown, melancholic. Ever since that paper, I was hooked on looking into the science of how we classify personality.

These days, many personality tests are available, but some of the most well-known assessments include:

Myers-Briggs: This test classifies people into 16 personality types, based on four sets of behaviors—Extroversion vs. Introversion, Sensing vs. Intuition, Thinking vs. Feeling, and Judging vs. Perceiving.

DiSC: Often used in business, this test is based on four traits: Dominance, influence, Steadiness, and Conscientiousness.

Big Five: This test examines five basic dimensions of personality, which are Extroversion, Agreeableness, Openness, Conscientiousness, and Neuroticism.

Schools, businesses, and therapists use these tests and others to better understand students, employees, and patients. Personality assessments give people a sense of uniqueness and belonging. Yet, despite their widespread use, there is surprisingly little neuroscience underlying their practical application. Of these tests, most neuroscientists consider the Big Five model as an accepted framework.

A NEW MODEL BASED ON 200,000 BRAIN SPECT SCANS AND 3 MILLION QUESTIONNAIRES

As our brain imaging work became more widely known to help people with mental health issues, many people wanted to get scanned but did not have the resources or were not near one of the Amen Clinics. Wanting to help as many people as possible, we developed a series of questionnaires to help them predict what their brain might look like if we could scan them. The questionnaires were based on tens of thousands of scans. Obviously, they were not as accurate as getting scanned, but they were the next best thing. In the last three decades, we have had thousands of mental health professionals use our questionnaires in their practices, and they've told us that knowing a person's brain type completely changed the way they think about and help their patients.

In 2014, our team published our online Brain Health Assessment, which takes about six minutes to complete and helps people know which of the 16 brain types they may have, along with their Brain Health Score.[1] We drew on our four decades of experience helping patients and then validated the questions in the Brain Health Assessment by comparing brain region activity to the answers to 300 questions and choosing the most predictive 38 questions. As of this writing, more than 2.5 million people from around the world have taken our assessment.

We discovered five primary brain types:[2]

1. Balanced
2. Spontaneous
3. Persistent
4. Sensitive
5. Cautious

Brain Types 6–16 are a combination of Types 2–5.

6. Spontaneous-Persistent
7. Spontaneous-Persistent-Sensitive
8. Spontaneous-Persistent-Sensitive-Cautious
9. Persistent-Sensitive-Cautious
10. Persistent-Sensitive
11. Persistent-Cautious
12. Spontaneous-Persistent-Cautious
13. Spontaneous-Cautious
14. Spontaneous-Sensitive
15. Spontaneous-Sensitive-Cautious
16. Sensitive-Cautious

Knowing your brain type helps you know more about how you interact with the world, but it also helps you know how to optimize your specific brain to smooth out some of the rough edges in your life and understand what is more likely to make you or your loved ones happy. Here is an example:

Kimberly and Kate

Kimberly struggled with an addiction to alcohol for years, and eventually her husband left her and gave her an ultimatum: Enter an addiction treatment program or their marriage was over. Kimberly desperately wanted her spouse back, so she joined a program to help her stay clean. During the marital crisis, her mother, Kate, came to live with Kimberly, but they fought constantly, which was incredibly stressful for them both.

Kimberly was Brain Type 13 (Spontaneous-Cautious) and struggled with low activity in her prefrontal cortex—giving her a short attention span, disorganization, and poor impulse control—combined with increased activity in her basal ganglia and amygdala (emotional brain), causing her to struggle with anxiety and predicting the worst. Her alcohol addiction was her attempt to medicate her anxious feelings, and her poor impulse control made it harder for her to consistently stick with her program.

Kate was Brain Type 3 (Persistent) and was great at taking charge and getting things completed, but she became furious when things were out of place (Kimberly was a slob). Negative thoughts looped in her head, and she had a tendency to go over and over the hurts of the past, which only stressed Kimberly more.

When I was asked to help, I realized that for Kimberly to maintain her sobriety so she could reunite with husband, we would have to balance not only her brain but also Kate's brain, using supplements and lifestyle interventions targeted to each individual brain type. Within a few weeks, the harmony in the home increased, and several months later Kimberly's husband took her back.

CHEMICALS OF HAPPINESS

In addition to the brain systems that play crucial roles in happiness, there are important neurochemicals that influence your level of joy because they are involved in mood, motivation, and learning, and that's the short list. Neurotransmitters are the molecules used by the nervous system to transmit messages between neurons or from neurons to target cells in muscles, glands, or other nerves. Since these chemical messengers communicate information between the brain and our bodies, they are incredibly important to good health. Neurotransmitters are the chemical messengers that stimulate or inhibit nearby cells.

In terms of happiness, I want to focus on seven neurotransmitters. Some of these neurochemicals play a more critical role in certain brain types as you will see in the next few chapters. For now, let me briefly introduce these important molecules to you:

- **Dopamine: The Molecule of More**—This unique transmitter helps with focus and staying on task while supporting the brain's ability to remember things. This brain chemical helps you remember significant moments, whether good or bad, and is involved with anticipation, pleasure, and love. I liken dopamine to a "chemical of more" because you always want more of it since this is the principal neurotransmitter that makes you feel good.

- **Serotonin: The Molecule of Respect**—This brain chemical is involved with mood, sleep, and flexibility, and it helps you to be open and adaptable to change. Serotonin increases when you feel respect from your peers and decreases when your feelings get hurt.

- **Oxytocin: The Molecule of Trust**—Whereas dopamine is the "chemical of more," oxytocin can be called the "chemical of love" for the way it enhances bonding and trusting relationships. This powerful neurotransmitter has a reputation for playing Cupid because it's released when you snuggle up, have sex, or socially bond with friends. But some researchers believe oxytocin also leads to feelings of jealousy and suspicion, especially toward those outside our social circles.

- **Endorphins: The Molecule of Pain Relief**—Almost everyone has heard about these neurotransmitters. These "feel good" brain chemicals released by your body during a workout or physical exertion cause your immune cells to flood the cardiovascular system, which protects your body against illness and lifts your mood.

- **GABA: The Molecule of Calmness**—GABA, which stands for gamma aminobutyric acid, is the brain's chief inhibitory neurotransmitter in the brain. GABA's primary role is to reduce brain cell excitability and slow down the firing of neurons. It helps balance more stimulating neurotransmitters, such as dopamine and adrenaline. Too much stimulation can cause anxiety, insomnia, and seizures, while too little nerve cell firing can cause lethargy, confusion, and sedation. It is all about balance.

- **Endocannabinoids: The Molecule of Peace**—These molecules play a role in regulating mood, sleep, and appetite. Excessive endocannabinoid activity contributes to overeating and obesity, while low activity is a risk factor for developing depression, anxiety, posttraumatic stress disorder, inflammation, and immune system problems. Marijuana and hemp contain more than 100 naturally occurring cannabinoids that, when absorbed, interact with the endocannabinoid system's receptors to produce a response. The best known are tetrahydrocannabinol (THC) and cannabidiol (CBD). While they have a similar chemical makeup, THC and CBD interact with cannabinoid receptors completely differently. THC is the cannabinoid people associate with marijuana. It directly stimulates endocannabinoid receptors to cause the intoxicating effects. CBD does not cause a high because it works indirectly.

- **Cortisol: The Molecule of Danger**—This hormone gets a bad rap. It's critical for your survival and has important benefits, but it's also a hormone that you want less of—not more of—because, when cortisol production gets out of control, it drains your happiness. Why is that? Cortisol is the body's "stress hormone," and chronically high levels are linked to depression, anxiety, grief, memory loss, and weight gain as well as conditions like type 2 diabetes and hypertension. The body also releases cortisol whenever you feel like you're in danger or involved in a fight-or-flight response. When stress seems never-ending and remains high for too long—like during the pandemic—then cortisol will make you feel awful. This explains why researchers have found that the happiest people tend to have lower cortisol levels.[3]

Balance is key for all of the brain chemicals (neurotransmitters) we will discuss.

KNOW YOUR BRAIN TYPE AND THE BRAIN TYPES OF YOUR INNER CIRCLE

Knowing your brain type can help in so many areas of your life. To help you get the most out of this book, I encourage you to take our free brain type quiz at brainhealthassessment.com. It will only take five to seven minutes. Also, share it with your family and friends. In addition to knowing your brain type, you will also get scores on important areas of brain health. No matter what your type is, this assessment tool, along with this book, will help you understand your strengths and vulnerabilities and show you how to optimize your overall brain health and happiness. When your brain works right, regardless of your brain type, you tend to work right, and that leads to a happier life.

Even if you know your brain type, read each chapter about the five general types to help you better understand your own brain in case you have a combination type, as well as the people in your life. They influence your happiness too. For each of the five primary brain types, you will discover the characteristic traits, what our brain SPECT imaging shows about each type, which specific brain systems and neurochemicals are most influential, and what you can do to optimize your brain so you can be happier. You will also discover what it means to have a combination brain type.

CHAPTER 4

THE BALANCED BRAIN TYPE

Happy Brain Systems and Balanced Neurochemicals

To expect a personality to survive the disintegration of the brain is like expecting a cricket club to survive when all of its members are dead.

BERTRAND RUSSELL

The first brain type—Balanced—is an excellent place to start and a good place to be, if that's what your Brain Health Assessment determined. If I had to make an estimate, I'd say that a third of the general population belongs in the Balanced camp, which is good for our society. We need Balanced brains since they are the foundation of a productive, happy community. People with the Balanced Brain Type tend to go through life in an organized fashion and generally do well in school and on the job. They are the neighbors we want next door.

COMMON TRAITS IN BRAIN TYPE 1: BALANCED

People with this type tend to score high on the following traits:

- Focus
- Good impulse control
- Conscientiousness
- Flexibility
- Positivity
- Resilience
- Emotional stability

They tend to score low on:

- Short attention span
- Impulsivity

- Undependability
- Worry
- Negativity
- Anxiety

If you have the Balanced Brain Type, then you are a focused, flexible, and emotionally stable individual. You show up on time for meetings, whether they occur in a conference room or online through Zoom. You do what you say and say what you do. You don't like to take big risks and prefer to follow the rules. You're not the type to color outside the lines.

Your coping skills are formidable, and if there's anything you learned from the pandemic, it's that you know how to go with the flow. When the pandemic hit, you were able to adapt to the many changes in your everyday life without feeling overly stressed, anxious, or blue.

Balanced types don't struggle with acting impulsively. They think about the consequences of their actions and are equipped with an inner five-second delay that keeps them from blurting out inappropriate comments. In addition, they're not the sort to mope around the house all day long. Optimists at heart, they see the glass as half full. Their balanced attitudes generally come from having a healthy brain where the frontal lobes (such as the prefrontal cortex) and the limbic or emotional brain work in a healthy, balanced way.

Another plus is that Balanced types carry the right amount of anxiety. You read that correctly. A lot of my patients are surprised when I tell them that having some anxiety is a good thing. So many people are under the false impression that eliminating anxiety is a great goal to shoot for. It isn't. Having a healthy dose of anxiousness keeps people from getting into trouble. They don't rob convenience stores because they would be anxious about getting caught and being locked up for years behind bars. They don't drive 100 miles per hour down the freeway because they'd be worried about crashing into another car and killing themselves or innocent victims. Because they are conscientious, they go through life consistently and predictably, which helps them live longer and healthier.

Balanced types tend to be generally happy, but who doesn't want to be happier? We all want happiness in our lives. But we've all learned that life can rear back and throw a massive curveball at any time, causing even the most well-adjusted people to lose their balance. A sudden illness, a death in the family, a job loss, or loneliness—any of these can mess with brain function. As you will see, it's the daily decisions you make that either keep you feeling stable and positive or rob you of your happy nature.

Keep in mind that you need every edge you can get in today's competitive and challenging environment. If you want to enhance creativity, sharpen your memory, achieve greater success at work, become a stronger public speaker, develop a deeper relationship with your significant other, or get better at soothing yourself in stressful situations, it all starts with your brain.

Following the brain-optimization strategies and focusing on the seven secrets outlined in this book can help you go beyond the average to reach peak performance. Doing your best and experiencing success will make you happier.

I also have to mention that some of the people who scored Balanced on the Brain Health Assessment questionnaire may have "gamed the system" by not being totally honest in their answers. Or perhaps they just aren't in touch with their own strengths and weaknesses. To be sure, you may ask your spouse, sibling, or a good friend to take the Brain Health Assessment with you. As you go through the questions a second time, ask them if they agree with your answers. If you take this extra step, then *You, Happier* will help you all the more. Keep reading even if your brain does not fall into this category.

WHAT SPECT SCANS SHOW ABOUT THE BALANCED BRAIN

Our brain imaging work shows that people who have the Balanced Brain Type tend to have healthy brains overall with full, even, symmetrical activity and high levels of activity in the cerebellum, which is one of the brain's major processing centers (part of the reptilian brain).

BALANCED BRAIN TYPE

HEALTHY SURFACE BRAIN SPECT SCAN

HEALTHY ACTIVE BRAIN SPECT SCAN

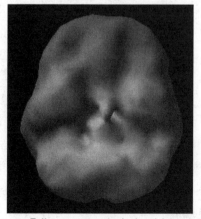

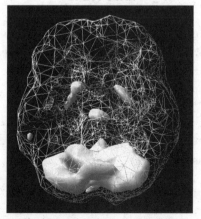

Full, even, symmetrical activity

Healthy activity in the cerebellum

In people with the Balanced Brain Type, the brain areas that cause misery—including the amygdala and insular cortex, which you read about in chapter 1—tend to be calmer.

BRAIN TYPE 1:
BALANCED CHEMICALS OF HAPPINESS

In people with Brain Type 1, the chemicals of happiness tend to be balanced—not too high, not too low. There isn't one neurochemical that dominates the others, and they play nicely with each other.

Optimizing the Balanced Brain Type

You optimize your brain by using the seven brain-based secrets to happiness and constantly asking yourself the seven simple questions. Eating a balanced diet, exercising regularly, engaging in meditation or prayer, getting massages, and generally taking care of your brain and body are essential so that you can continue producing balanced amounts of dopamine, serotonin, oxytocin, endorphins, GABA, endocannabinoids, and cortisol.

On the nutritional supplement side, you can support Brain Type 1 health by taking a broad-spectrum multivitamin with a strong mineral complex. Key as well are the omega-3 fatty acids found in highly potent and ultrapurified fish oils. Because the health of your gut is essential to the health of your brain, I recommend top-notch probiotics as nutritional supplements. And don't forget vitamin D, which plays many roles in regulating brain health, including keeping cognitive function in older adults (more details in chapters 10 and 11).

Happiness prescription for Brain Type 1: Balanced

Support your brain type. To maintain a Balanced brain, learn to love your brain, engage in brain healthy behaviors, and avoid things that hurt your brain. This will help you remain emotionally stable and cope well with life's ups and downs.

Understand your career path. Balanced people are a human resources department's dream: steady, conscientious employees who are good executive material and task-oriented.

Appreciate your learning style. You're the type who follows instructions, likes to take notes in church, and makes an effort to be organized and prepared for meetings.

Know what you want in a relationship. Because you're even-keeled, not too up and not too down, you tend to be a drama-free person. You can adapt to friends and family with other brain types to make a relationship blossom.

When You're in a Relationship with the Balanced Brain Type

Having someone with Brain Type 1 in your life—whether it's a spouse, sibling, or supervisor—can be a source of comfort. You can count on them to do what they say, follow through on things, and roll with life's ups and downs. If problems arise, you can generally expect people with this type to address them in a reasonable, solutions-based way because they have strong interpersonal skills. Typical relationship advice works for this type because they are adept at RELATING.

Responsibility: the ability to respond to any situation
Empathy: the ability to feel what others are feeling
Listening: being a good listener and having effective communication skills
Assertiveness: expressing thoughts in a firm yet reasonable way
Time: giving the actual physical time necessary to build a relationship
Inquiry: questioning and correcting negative thoughts and thinking patterns
Noticing: seeking out what you like more than what you don't like
Grace: finding healthy ways to move forward and forgive after being hurt

You'll learn more about RELATING in chapter 14 and how it can make your relationships happier.

What their romantic partners say:
"She's usually in a good mood."
"He's really considerate."

What their coworkers say:
"He's a great team player."
"I can always count on her to hit her deadlines."

What their friends say:

"He's always willing to be the designated driver."

"I love that she's so reliable."

Watch for times when you get off track. You realize that too many fast-food and takeout meals, which were necessary for many during the pandemic, leave your brain and body without the essential nutrients to function in a high-performance way.

Know what makes you uniquely happy. You focus on the things that give you joy.

What makes people with the Balanced Brain Type happy?

- Healthy relationships
- Meaningful work
- Financial security
- Following the rules
- Being on time
- Participating in traditional holidays such as Thanksgiving, Christmas, and Hanukkah
- Having fun

What makes people with the Balanced Brain Type unhappy?

- Chaos
- Excessive risk-taking
- Running late
- Going out on a ledge
- Missing assignments
- Being around people who are undependable, negative, or don't play by the rules

☺ **Look for the micro-moments of happiness.**

- When your spouse rubs your shoulders
- Your first bite of a delicious salmon dinner
- Feeling the cool sheets when you get in bed at night
- Your morning ritual to prepare for the day
- Having FaceTime or Zoom to stay connected with family and friends who live far away

CHAPTER 5

THE SPONTANEOUS BRAIN TYPE

The Prefrontal Cortex and Dopamine

---

*With the prefrontal cortex down-regulated, most impulse
control mechanisms go offline too. For people who aren't used
to this combination, the results can be expensive.*

STEVEN KOTLER, *STEALING FIRE: HOW SILICON VALLEY, THE NAVY SEALS,
AND MAVERICK SCIENTISTS ARE REVOLUTIONIZING THE WAY WE LIVE AND WORK*

One of the greatest things about my job is that I get to meet interesting people like Laura Clery, the actress and comedian I mentioned in chapter 1. Actually, she left Hollywood behind and turned to making improv videos and comedy sketches that she shares with millions of people on her Instagram and YouTube channels. She has 3 million Instagram followers and more than 800,000 subscribers on YouTube, where she posts outrageous skits in her alter egos: Pamela Pupkin and Helen Horbath. In the world of social media, she's known as a "mega-influencer."

Like many of our patients, Laura wanted to get her brain scanned at Amen Clinics because she had a number of concerns. She went through periods of not wanting to get out of bed and was having problems with her memory. Mind you, she's far from old—a young mother in her thirties with two children under the age of four.

Laura grew up in Chicago as the class clown, the funny blonde always cracking jokes about herself and the world around her. When she moved to New York City in her late teens to pursue an acting career, she developed a drug problem and smoked a "ton of weed"—a disclosure that she had no problem sharing with me or with the millions on her social media feeds. To her credit, she has been clean for nearly ten years, but she was concerned that her past drug use might have damaged her brain.

Her team filmed the entire evaluation process at our Costa Mesa clinic, including taking computer-based psychological and cognitive tests, filling out patient history forms, preparing for her SPECT scan, lying down on the flat bed, and remaining still for about 15 minutes while technology took over. Lying still proved challenging for the always-on-the-move influencer, and she had to redo her SPECT scan.

Two days later, Laura arrived at our clinic to go over the results. Her first words to me: "Have you looked at my brain?"

"I have," I replied with a grin and led her into my office. I sat down opposite her and opened up a folder containing printouts of her SPECT scans.

Laura, dressed casually in jeans and a blue-and-white-striped long-sleeved shirt, clasped her hands. I've seen nerves like hers thousands of times over the years.

"One of the things I was concerned about is my memory is not great," she began. "My husband will say, 'Do you remember this movie?' And I'm like, 'I don't know what you're talking about.' Oftentimes, I don't remember things he does, so that's concerning."

I nodded in understanding. "I've read what you filled out, and I've looked at your scans," I said, holding them in my hands. "Your history is very consistent with a female with attention deficit disorder or ADD."

"Oh, wow," she replied, clearly surprised.

"Is that anything you've ever thought about?" I asked.

"ADD? Ah, I never really went to a doctor for that, even though I really struggled to focus growing up. I struggled to take tests, and I never felt very smart, but I felt very funny, so I focused on that. But I've never gotten diagnosed with ADD."

Based on her evaluation, testing, and brain scans, I was confident that Laura had ADD, also referred to as attention deficit hyperactivity disorder (ADHD). Her scans revealed a brain pattern commonly seen in people with ADD: lower activity in the prefrontal cortex (or the PFC, as I like to call it), especially when she tried to concentrate. In people who don't have ADD, concentration increases activity in this brain region. In people with ADD, however, it's the opposite, meaning that the harder they try to concentrate, the worse it gets. Laura has Brain Type 2, but not all individuals with the Spontaneous Brain Type have ADD.

COMMON TRAITS IN BRAIN TYPE 2: SPONTANEOUS

People with this type tend to score high on the following traits:

- Spontaneity
- Risk-taking
- Creativity, out-of-the-box thinking
- Curiosity
- Wide range of interests
- Short attention span
- Impulsiveness; careless mistakes
- Restlessness
- Disorganization
- Love of surprises
- Tendency toward ADD

They tend to score low on:

- Hatred of surprises
- Risk aversion
- Routine
- Affinity for sameness
- Convention
- Practicality
- Attention to detail
- Impulse control
- Feeling settled

Spontaneous Brain Types can be the life of the party. They're the ones who love trying new things, get a thrill from skydiving or bungee jumping, and are willing to walk away from a secure job to throw the dice on starting their own business. In a way, the traits seen in the Spontaneous Brain Type represent some of the characteristics we admire most as Americans—risk-taking, creativity, and adventurousness. Just think about the protagonists in Hollywood movies—they're often the ones who throw caution to the wind to attempt the impossible.

Although America seems to have a love affair with this type, there are some challenges people with the Spontaneous Brain Type face. Restless and easily distracted, they need to be highly interested, excited, or stimulated in what they're doing if they're going to focus on a task set in front of them.

Think firefighters and race car drivers. Organization can be a struggle for them too, and I can almost guarantee you that they won't show up on time for anything. Smokers and heavy coffee drinkers tend to fit this type, as they use these substances to turn their brains on.

Their risk-taking behavior can get them into trouble. A small example happened when I treated a man who liked to hide behind a corner in his house and then jump out and scare his wife when she walked by. He liked the charge he got out of her screams that woke up half the neighborhood. Unfortunately for his wife, she developed an irregular heart rhythm and brought him to Amen Clinics to save her life.

Many people with the Spontaneous Brain Type, however, know when to cool it, and they may feel happier than most people. A study found that respondents who identified as a "spontaneous personality" were 40 percent more likely to consider themselves happy. They were also 38 percent more likely to report being content and satisfied.[1]

WHAT SPECT SCANS SHOW ABOUT THE SPONTANEOUS BRAIN

The SPECT scans of Spontaneous individuals typically show lower activity in the PFC.

SPONTANEOUS BRAIN TYPE

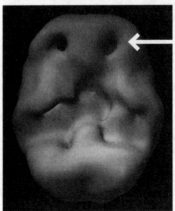

Low PFC activity at front of brain

THE PREFRONTAL CORTEX: OUTSIDE VIEW OF THE BRAIN

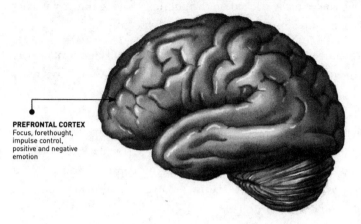

PREFRONTAL CORTEX
Focus, forethought,
impulse control,
positive and negative
emotion

The PFC is situated in the front third of the brain behind the forehead and is the most evolved part of the brain. It is responsible for higher-level cognitive processes that are necessary for you to act with long-term goals in mind. The PFC acts like the CEO of the brain—supervising, directing, observing, and guiding your behavior. Think of the PFC as your brain's boss, pushing you to achieve your goals, be efficient, and collaborate well with others. The PFC's primary functions include:

- **Focus:** The PFC (especially the dorsolateral PFC) plays an important role in focus and attention, which are necessary for learning, short-term memory, and follow-through. The PFC is what helps you stay focused on a task at hand, such as compiling a report for work or writing an essay for an English class at school, so you can complete the project. At the same time, it transmits signals to calm activity in other parts of the brain in an effort to filter out distracting input like your coworkers chatting or your phone buzzing to signal a new text has arrived. When there is underactivity in the PFC, a common trait in people who have the Spontaneous Brain Type, you are more easily distracted and may struggle with follow-through.

- **Forethought:** I like to think of the PFC as the brain's brake, if you will. The PFC helps you think about the consequences of what you say or do before you actually say or do it. For example, let's say you run into a friend after not seeing them for months and they've gained some weight. If you have good PFC function, you can focus on telling them how happy you are to see them again. If you have poor function in this brain region, you are more likely to blurt out something hurtful, such as, "Wow, you've really packed on the pounds!" Saying things you later regret is common among those with Brain Type 2.

- **Impulse control:** A healthy PFC provides good impulse control to keep you from engaging in behaviors that don't serve you. With low activity in this brain region, you're more vulnerable to a lack of control. For example, you may say yes to drinking too much alcohol even though you will be driving, you may give in to your urges to have an affair with the neighbor, or you might gamble away your paycheck on a whim. This type of impulsivity can have damaging consequences on your relationships, health, financial status, and overall well-being. And that can make you decidedly unhappy.

- **Judgment:** The PFC is the little voice in your head that helps you make good decisions. When it is functioning well, it enables you to opt for the banana rather than the banana split. Poor function means you may not make the best decisions, and consistently making bad choices is a recipe for unhappiness.

- **Organization:** Staying organized is a sign of a finely tuned PFC. With lower activity in this region, which is common in the Spontaneous Brain Type, you may have trouble keeping track of everything. Your desk may be a mess with sticky notes posted all over the place. A lack of organization contributes to problems with follow-through, causes you to take longer to accomplish tasks, and makes you more prone to being late.

- **Planning:** A well-functioning PFC enables you to plan ahead, problem-solve, and anticipate potential issues before they happen. Think about a chess game, for example, where the best players plan several moves in advance. In the game of life, it's this brain region that helps you plan the best moves. When the PFC isn't operating at peak capacity, however, it hinders your ability to navigate curveballs, and you may find yourself a step behind.

- **Learning from experience:** This powerful brain region is also critical in helping you learn from your mistakes. Having a strong PFC doesn't mean that you'll never slip up; rather, it keeps you from repeating your mistakes. When there is low activity in this area of the brain or it is "sleepy," as I like to say, it means you are more likely to make the same bonehead mistakes over and over. This can lead to friction in relationships, trouble at work, and problems in school. When you struggle with any of these areas of your life, it's harder to feel happy.

- **Ability to feel and express emotions:** You can thank this powerhouse brain system for allowing you to feel happiness, joy, and love. The PFC is also what gives you the ability to feel sadness and other emotions. When the PFC is damaged or has too little activity, it is harder to express thoughts and feelings, and the risk of depression increases.

- **Empathy:** Being able to understand other people's feelings or to step into their shoes and see things from their viewpoint is associated with healthy activity in the PFC. Underactivity here, which is seen in people with Brain Type 2, makes it harder to grasp what others may be thinking or feeling. This doesn't mean that the Spontaneous Brain Type is uncaring but, simply, that their brains tend to work differently.

BRAIN TYPE 2: SPONTANEOUS NEUROCHEMICALS OF HAPPINESS

Brain Type 2 can be associated with lower levels of dopamine, which may cause people to be more restless and willing to take needless risks. In chapter 3, I gave you a brief look at the "molecule of more," which is involved with focus and motivation. Now, let's take a deeper dive into this fascinating brain chemical.

Synthesized in the ventral tegmental area in the brain stem and substantia nigra, dopamine is the neurotransmitter of wanting, especially wanting more. It is involved with anticipation, possibility, love, and seeking success to maximize future resources. Dopamine is released when you expect a reward (food, sex, money, shopping) or when you get an unexpected happy surprise. It is involved with motivation (going toward a reward), memory, mood, and attention. Dopamine is a salesman that drives you to pursue a better life. But like many salesmen, it can also lie to you and promise you pleasure when, in fact, pain will result (such as engaging in drug abuse or affairs). Dopamine also helps to regulate motor movements, which is why you jump when you get excited, such as I did when the Los Angeles Lakers won the 2020 NBA Championship and the LA Dodgers won the World Series just a few weeks later.

Too much dopamine has been associated with agitation, obsession, compulsions, psychosis, and violence. I once evaluated and testified in the capital murder trial of Louis Peoples, who killed four people when he was heavily using methamphetamines, which made him paranoid and violent. Of the more than 100 murderers we have scanned at Amen Clinics, nearly half of them committed their crimes when they were on methamphetamines, which raises the brain's dopamine levels.

Too little dopamine can cause depression, low motivation, apathy, fatigue, boredom, Parkinson's disease, impulsivity, sugar cravings, and thrill-seeking and conflict-seeking behavior. Low dopamine is also thought to be the primary issue in ADD (often associated with short attention span, distractibility, disorganization, procrastination, and impulse control issues). Many people with ADD play the game of "Let's have a problem" in an unconscious attempt to stimulate dopamine. Many mothers of ADD children tell me if they have a bad morning at home with their child (crying, screaming, and threatening), the child will have a good day at school; but if they have a good morning at home (loving, sweet, kind), the child will often have a bad day at school.[2]

There are two main brain dopamine systems that relate to happiness:

1. The *dopamine reward center* in the front half of the nucleus accumbens of the basal ganglia (involved with seeking pleasure and addiction). Think of the dopamine reward system involved with wanting and desire.

2. The *dopamine control center* that enhances the activity of the PFC/orbitofrontal cortex and helps you think before you act and stop unhelpful behaviors. The dopamine control center is involved with forward thinking, judgment, planning, impulse control, and long-term happiness.

I think of these two systems as the gas (dopamine reward center) and the brakes (dopamine control center); both are essential to get anywhere special.

Dopamine is known as the molecule of more because once it stimulates the pleasure centers, tolerance often develops, and you may need more and more of something to get the same feeling. It is called "hedonic adaptation." From the book *The Molecule of More* by Daniel Lieberman and Michael Long,

If you live under a bridge, dopamine makes you want a *tent*. If you live in a *tent*, dopamine makes you want a *house*. If you live in the most expensive mansion in the world, dopamine makes you want a castle on the *moon*. Dopamine has no standard for good, and seeks no finish line. The dopamine circuits in the brain can be stimulated only by the possibility of whatever is shiny and new, never mind how perfect things are at the moment. The dopamine motto is "More."[3]

Dopamine is lowered by monotonous routine, reward frustration (not getting what you want), disappointment, familiarity, and diets high in processed foods. Dopamine-lowering drugs are used to treat severe depression and anxiety, bipolar disorder, and schizophrenia. Unfortunately, those life-saving drugs can also cause apathy, emotional blunting, and abnormal motor symptoms, such as tremors or restlessness.

Dopamine is stimulated by the thrill of chasing something (Mick Jagger of the Rolling Stones has been romantically linked to thousands of women over the years, which adds new meaning to the lyrics "I can't get no satisfaction"), anticipation, discovery, novelty, reward prediction error—when things are better than we expect, such as the surprising gold medal victory of the underdog 1980 US Olympic hockey team over the powerhouse Soviet team. Dopamine is also stimulated by random rewards (think slot machines in Las Vegas), high-intensity exercise, gambling, sex, caffeine, nicotine, and most drugs of abuse, particularly cocaine and methamphetamines. So you can see how people with the Spontaneous Brain Type can easily be drawn into risky behaviors or activities. Their brain is looking for a dopamine boost.

Fame also initially increases dopamine, as having mass numbers of people recognize you for your accomplishments meets so many basic human needs (achievement, being noticed, security, love, etc.). The more pleasure you get, the more you will want, and over time, it wears out your pleasure centers, leaving you feeling flat and depressed. Throughout my career, I've been blessed to treat many famous people, from Olympic athletes, professional golfers, football, hockey, baseball, and basketball players to Oscar-winning actors,

Hall-of-Fame musicians, politicians, Pulitzer prize–winning writers, models, and more. The dopamine highs of fame often lead to tolerance, where it takes more and more to get the same desired feeling, which is why many famous people often resort to drug abuse, affairs, fast cars, and gambling just to feel normal. Newly married celebrities are five times more likely to get divorced than ordinary people.[4]

My prayer for young people is often "Please, God, do not let them be famous before their brains are developed." The dopamine control center is not finished developing until about age 25. Early fame and drug abuse can cause lasting damage to the brain. At Amen Clinics we spend our time in therapy working to rebuild the pleasure centers and orbitofrontal cortex by avoiding anything that hurts the brain and doing things that help it.

10 natural ways to balance dopamine to benefit the Spontaneous Brain Type

1. **Eat foods rich in tyrosine, the amino acid building block for dopamine.** In order to make dopamine, your body needs tyrosine, which can be found in almonds, bananas, avocados, eggs, beans, fish, chicken, and dark chocolate. Note: Dark chocolate seems to balance all the chemicals of happiness.

2. **Eat a high-protein, lower-carbohydrate diet. Ketogenic diets have been shown to increase dopamine availability in the brain.**[5] Eating highly processed and sugary foods like cookies, snack cakes, muffins, and pies leads to cravings and overeating, which leave a strong imprint on the pleasure centers in the prefrontal cortex and lead to weight gain. Being overweight can impair dopamine pathways.

3. **Exercise regularly.** In general, physical exercise is one of the best things you can do for your brain. It increases the production of new brain cells and your levels of dopamine, while slowing down brain cell aging. Exercise has also been associated with improved mood and overall a better outlook on life. Exercise helps to balance all the chemicals of happiness. For people with Brain Type 2, be sure to choose an aerobic sport or heart-pumping activity you love.

4. **Learn to pray and meditate.** Hundreds of research studies have demonstrated the overall health benefits of prayer and meditation (or

focusing your mind). Many of those have shown that meditation increases dopamine, leading to improved focus and concentration, which can be beneficial for people with the Spontaneous Brain Type. Meditation also helps balance the other chemicals of happiness.

5. **Get a massage.** One way to keep dopamine levels high is to avoid stress, which is nearly impossible in this day and age. To counter the effects of stress, research has demonstrated that massage therapy increases dopamine levels by about 30 percent while decreasing the stress hormone cortisol.[6]

6. **Sleep.** To ensure that your brain increases dopamine naturally, make sure you get enough sleep. This includes setting aside time before bed away from screens. Sleep helps all the cells in the body repair and renew. It gives the brain a chance to wash away toxins that build up during the day and helps keep the nerve cell connections and pathways active and constantly self-renewing. Lack of sleep has been shown to reduce concentrations of neurotransmitters, including dopamine, and their receptors.

7. **Listen to music.** It is no surprise that listening to calming music can increase pleasurable feelings, improve mood, reduce stress, and help with focus and concentration. Research has demonstrated that much of this occurs because of an increase in dopamine levels.[7]

8. **Get more sunshine.** Sunlight exposure has been found to increase dopamine in the brain.[8]

9. **Supplements.** The herbals ashwagandha, rhodiola, and panax ginseng have been found to increase dopamine levels, promoting improved focus and increased energy while enhancing endurance and stamina. Other supplements that also increase dopamine include curcumins, l-theanine, and L-tyrosine, which promote alertness, attention, and focus. These nutraceuticals (supplements with a pharmaceutical

HAPPINESS TRANSFORMATION IN 30 DAYS

Thank you for the fabulous challenge; it is helping me in so many ways to be happier and calmer. I enjoy listening to music most days and sometimes don't even turn on the TV. The type of music I enjoy varies with my mood or needs.

—CE

effect) support healthy brain function for the Spontaneous Brain Type. Taking a comprehensive, powerful multivitamin with a strong mineral complex profile, omega-3 fatty acids found in highly potent and ultrapurified fish oils, and probiotics also support Brain Type 2.

10. **Set goals.** Always have new positive goals to strive for no matter your age or situation. Dopamine provides the energy for the journey, not just the destination.

If you have Brain Type 2 and ADHD and the above natural treatments are not as effective as needed, consider medications to treat ADHD. See my book *Healing ADD: The Breakthrough Program That Allows You to See and Heal the 7 Types of ADD* for more information. Untreated ADHD is associated with school failure, job failure, divorce, incarceration, substance abuse, and bankruptcy—all factors in unhappiness.

Happiness prescription for Brain Type 2: Spontaneous

Support your brain type. Follow the suggestions to boost dopamine and engage in brain healthy behaviors that protect and nourish the prefrontal cortex.

Understand your career path. Having Brain Type 2 is common among entrepreneurs, entertainers, politicians, salespeople, and realtors.

Appreciate your learning style. You're easily distracted and struggle with organization, so even though you may be highly intelligent, it can be hard for you to perform up to your potential. Take advantage of technology by creating alerts and notifications for meeting times, deadlines, and appointments. If possible, hire an assistant who can help keep you organized, or ask a friend to teach you organizational skills.

Know what you want in a relationship. Because you crave excitement in your life, you may have a tendency to create drama in your relationships. Understand that if you fall for someone who has the Persistent Brain Type and loves routine or the Cautious Brain Type and likes to follow the rules, it may create friction.

When You're in a Relationship with the Spontaneous Brain Type

Being in a relationship with someone who has the Spontaneous Brain Type can be exciting, fun, and unpredictable. They may inspire you to try new foods, take a last-minute weekend getaway, or get romantic on the beach. At work, they are often the ones who bring the most innovative ideas to meetings, close the most sales, and naturally schmooze their way into new accounts. On the downside, their tendency to be impulsive in what they say or do can lead to problems in relationships at home and at work. If your significant other, friend, or coworker falls in this category, you may occasionally be the target of hurtful comments, which can make you think they are being deliberately mean. You may also interpret their habitual tardiness, tendency to get distracted when you're talking to them, or cavalier attitude about following through on things as a lack of respect for you. In more extreme cases, if a Spontaneous spouse has an extramarital affair, you're likely to think it's because they don't love you anymore.

In reality, if their PFC is sleepy, it means their brain's brakes are not working optimally. Understanding this and encouraging them to follow the suggestions to boost activity in the PFC and enhance dopamine production can be helpful. Helping them with organization, giving them specific deadlines for chores and projects, and having conversations while walking (to boost focus) can be relationship savers.

What their romantic partners say:
"I love that she's always ready to jump in the car and go on an adventure."
"Sometimes she says things that are rude to me."

What their coworkers say:
"If we need to come up with something really innovative, he's the one to ask."
"If you're giving the project to him, you have to tell him it's due several days earlier than the real deadline."

What their friends say:

"If you want to have a great party, be sure to invite him."

"I don't feel like I can always count on him to be there for me."

Watch for times when you get off track. You may engage in risky behavior, such as drinking too much, taking drugs, or having extramarital affairs. Be aware that this brain type is vulnerable to ADD, depression, and addiction. If your spontaneous nature goes beyond being fun and adventurous and starts interfering with your daily life or causing problems at work, school, or in relationships, it's time to seek professional help.

Know what makes you uniquely happy. Be sure to focus on the things that give you joy.

What makes people with the Spontaneous Brain Type happy?

- Trying new things
- Surprises
- Getting off work
- Brainstorming
- Creative projects
- Deciding to fly to Europe the next day
- Moving to a new place
- Having multiple interests
- Trying an extreme sport
- Watching scary movies
- Staying up all night
- Playing devil's advocate to get a rise out of people

What makes people with the Spontaneous Brain Type unhappy?

- Boredom, sameness, and familiarity
- Having to sit in one place for too long
- Having a deadline
- Being told you can't do something
- Not getting answers to your questions
- Being stuck in traffic
- Having to wait in line

☺ **Look for the micro-moments of happiness.**

- Receiving a last-minute text invite to a party (even if it's on Zoom)
- Seeing that there's a new flavor at your favorite smoothie shop
- Waking up and having no plans
- Trying a new fitness class at the gym
- Hearing your favorite song play on the radio while driving to work

CHAPTER 6

THE PERSISTENT BRAIN TYPE

The Brain's Gear Shifters and Serotonin

---

*Notice that the stiffest tree is most easily cracked, while the
bamboo or willow survives by bending with the wind.*

BRUCE LEE

A few years back, during the morning break in an all-day seminar I was giving
in Seattle about the beautiful and mysterious brain for a group of medical
and mental health professionals, a doctor whom I'll call Greg approached me
and said, "Dr. Amen, I love you and love your work. You have transformed
my practice and my marriage."

"Really?" I asked.

"Yeah. My wife has the cingulate from hell."

I laughed out loud. For those who don't get the joke, what my colleague
was saying was that his wife's anterior cingulate gyrus, located deep in the
front part of the brain, was at the root of his marital difficulties. I think of the
anterior cingulate gyrus as the brain's gear shifter. It allows you to be flexible
and go with the flow. When it works too hard, people can get stuck on negative thoughts or behaviors. It was likely working too hard. Greg and I both
knew the anterior cingulate gyrus had connections to both the emotional
limbic system and the cognitive PFC. Those connections are responsible for
brain functions such as emotional processing and shifting attention. For Greg
and his wife, those wires of communication were getting crossed.

Greg continued, "If things don't go her way, she gets upset. She is argumentative and oppositional, rigid and inflexible. When I ask her to go to the
store with me, she gets angry. 'I can't go to the store,' she'll say. 'Don't you see
how busy I am?' No matter what I ask her to do, even fun things, she'll say
no before the words leave my mouth."

"So what happened?" I ventured. "You said your marriage was
transformed."

"I heard you say one time that when you're with someone who has a Persistent Brain Type—which she does—then you have to ask things in the opposite way. So I started saying, 'You probably don't want to go on a bike ride with me, so I'll be back in a—' She'd stop me right there and say, 'Of course I want to go.' I'm telling you, Dr. Amen, it works so well. As long as I say, 'You probably don't want to,' she wants to join me."

"Well, that's wonderful to hear." I meant it. I thanked him and was about to continue to the next person in line waiting to talk to me when he looked over his shoulder and whispered, "Dr. Amen, I'm having problems with the sex thing because it doesn't sound right to say, 'You probably don't want to have sex with me.' Do you have any ideas?"

I loved that question because it shows just how practical neuroscience can be. I answered, "People with the Persistent Brain Type can use sex as a weapon, which is just death to a relationship, but you just have to understand how to respond. Let me give you a couple of ideas. With Persistent people, you have to look for ways to increase serotonin production."

He nodded, signaling that he knew what the neurotransmitter serotonin was all about. Produced mainly in the brain stem and the gut, serotonin helps with mood regulation, memory, and healthy digestion. Serotonin also assists the body with sexual function, sleep, bone health, and blood clotting. This feel-good neurotransmitter is often low in people with the Persistent Brain Type.

"Here's what I want you to do," I began, drawing him closer. "Get a babysitter. Before dinner, take her for a long walk because exercise boosts serotonin. Then take her out to an Italian restaurant. Order pasta but not too much." Now, I'm not normally a fan of pasta because it spikes your blood sugar, but spikes in blood sugar increase serotonin production, which is why people like to eat carbohydrate-heavy meals like spaghetti or lasagna in the evening. Small amounts of carbs—preferably complex carbs—lower anxiety, improve mood, and help with sleep. I gave Greg another tip: "When you come home from the Italian restaurant, put on a bit of baby powder."

Greg gave me a funny look. "Baby powder?"

I explained that baby powder is one of the most powerful aphrodisiacs because the brain works through association. What do women associate with baby powder? Freshly diapered, cute little babies, and then they unconsciously want one. Then I gave Greg advice that's firmly rooted in neuroscience. I told him to give his wife one square of dark chocolate because chocolate has a chemical in it called phenylethylamine or PEA, which goes to work on the brain stem signaling to the body that something fun is about to happen. "But don't give her a whole box of chocolates because then she'll have all the fun she needs," I pointed out. "Oh, and there's one more thing: When you go to bed that night, rub her shoulders but don't ask for anything directly. Because as soon as you say, 'Would you like to?' she's going to say, 'No.'"

Greg shook my hand, and I wished him all the best. I never thought I'd hear from him again, but I received an email from him several weeks later thanking me profusely. That's a happy ending to a story about a young doctor who is married to someone who is Brain Type 3: Persistent.

COMMON TRAITS IN BRAIN TYPE 3: PERSISTENT

People with this brain type tend to score high on the following traits:

- Persistence
- Strong will
- Preference for routine
- Inflexibility or stubbornness
- Easily "stuck" on thoughts
- Resentment
- Tendency to see what is wrong
- Opposition/argumentativeness
- Obsessive-compulsive tendencies

They tend to score low on:

- Adaptability
- Timidity
- Spontaneity
- Flexibility
- Letting go of negativity easily
- Letting go of hurts easily
- Tendency to see what is right
- Being noncritical
- Cooperation

If you have the Persistent Brain Type, you like to get up in the morning and attack the day. You want to get things done, checking off items on your to-do list as you complete each task. You refuse to take no for an answer, and you go through life with a "my way or the highway" attitude. This is why others may see you as argumentative. You thrive when things go your way but get bent out of shape when something unexpected happens. You have trouble adjusting on the fly. You may be a worrier who has trouble letting go of past hurts.

I grew up as the third of seven children and quickly learned that my father's response to anything I asked was an automatic no. So frustrating! He was so set on his opinion and his ways that anything you said to him bounced off like he was wearing Teflon body armor. Before he passed away in 2020, my dad was as Persistent as they come, so I'm well aware of what it's like to live with this brain type. I had asked him twelve times to get scanned as part of a study I was doing on high achievers—he was a self-made man, who owned a chain of grocery stores and was the chairman of the board of a $4 billion company—before he finally agreed. It was no, no, no, no, no, no, no, no, no, no, no . . . okay. When I finally did scan him, his anterior cingulate gyrus was overactive, which gave me a bit of emotional relief. It showed me that his behavior was not always will-driven (he didn't intentionally mean to be difficult); his behavior was brain-driven (less in his control than most people imagine).

DAD'S ACTIVE SPECT SCAN (LEFT SIDE VIEW)

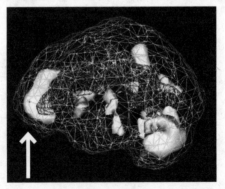

Increased anterior cingulate gyrus

WHAT SPECT SCANS SHOW ABOUT THE PERSISTENT BRAIN

Brain imaging work shows that people with the Persistent Brain Type, like my father, often have increased activity in the anterior cingulate gyrus. I know it is a mouthful, so let's just call it the ACG for the remainder of this chapter. In the Persistent Brain, this gear shifter works too hard, which is why these people tend to get stuck on thoughts or behaviors. An overactive ACG also makes them experts at picking up errors, which can cause problems in relationships. The primary functions of the ACG include:

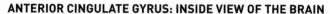

ANTERIOR CINGULATE GYRUS: INSIDE VIEW OF THE BRAIN

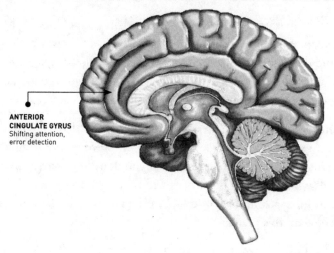

**ANTERIOR
CINGULATE GYRUS**
Shifting attention,
error detection

- **Ability to shift attention and go from idea to idea:** When activity levels in the ACG are balanced, it means you can shift easily from one thought to another or from one activity to another. When activity is higher in this brain region, common in people with the Persistent Brain Type, you are more likely to get caught in looping negative thoughts or have trouble breaking bad habits. It's as if you can't get out of your own way even when you want to change your thinking patterns and behaviors.

- **Cognitive flexibility, adaptability, and going with the flow:** Being able to cope with change, go with the flow, and successfully handle life's little (or big) emergencies is a function of the ACG. Whether you're moving into a new home, starting a new relationship, or taking on a new client, you need to be able to adapt, and flexible thinking helps you do it. Being able to handle transitions is a critical component of happiness that is often in short supply in Persistent people. Because of their rigid thinking, unexpected changes breed frustration and drain happiness for them.

- **Ability to see options:** When you're faced with a problem at work or in a relationship, it's the ACG that either helps you see a number of possible solutions or locks you into one course of action even if it isn't the best option. People in the Persistent camp have a tendency to zero in on a goal and then pursue it doggedly. This can be a beneficial trait that helps you achieve goals and stay focused on what you want out of life. On the flip side, this type can be resistant to adopt new ideas or new technology.

- **Ability to cooperate:** The ACG is involved in cooperation, which requires adaptability, a willingness to adopt other people's way of doing things, and the open-mindedness to change course based on new information. When the ACG works too hard, it can hinder your cooperative nature and give the impression that you aren't a "team player."

- **Error detection:** The ACG plays an important role in detecting errors. An overactive ACG sends error detection into overdrive, causing you to be overly critical and to focus on what you don't like. These are the individuals who can point out what's wrong while on vacation on the most beautiful beach in the world—"I can't enjoy myself; there are too many people on this beach!"

Problems When the ACG Works Too Hard

- Worrying
- Holding on to hurts from the past
- Getting stuck on thoughts (obsessions)
- Getting stuck on behaviors (compulsions)
- Oppositional behavior ("No. No way. Never! You can't make me do it.")
- Argumentativeness
- Uncooperativeness
- Tendency to say no automatically
- Addictive behaviors (alcohol or drug abuse; eating disorders)
- Chronic pain
- Cognitive inflexibility
- Obsessive-compulsive disorder (OCD)
- OCD spectrum disorders
- Eating disorders
- Road rage

For people who have the Persistent Brain Type, these challenges may be mild annoyances (for you or the people around you), or they can be debilitating and rob you of your happiness.

BRAIN TYPE 3: PERSISTENT NEUROCHEMICALS OF HAPPINESS

Persistent types are often associated with lower levels of the neurotransmitter serotonin, the "molecule of respect." Researchers were mapping serotonin receptors in the brain and found that the ACG contained many of them.[1] Synthesized in the GI tract and multiple groups of cells (raphe nuclei) in the brain stem, serotonin is a neurotransmitter that enhances and stabilizes mood, regulates stress, and helps us be more flexible, open, and adapt to changes in our environment. It also helps us shift our attention away from unhelpful worries and be more open to cooperating with others. There is evidence that serotonin increases when you feel respected by others, which promotes self-esteem, and decreases when you feel disrespected.

Serotonin is also involved with sleeping, eating, digestion, blocking pain, and blood platelet function to heal wounds. Low levels are involved in depression, anxiety, worry, poor memory, pain, aggression, suicidal behavior, poor self-esteem, being oppositional or argumentative, and being rigid or cognitively inflexible.

The low serotonin levels associated with Brain Type 3 lead to struggles with perseverative behaviors where their brain gets stuck in specific states, such as obsessions or compulsions. They also hate surprises. Living in Southern California, I've treated several children who have had massive tantrums in the Disneyland parking lot because their parents surprised them for their birthdays. Even though the kids loved Disneyland, they couldn't shift their mindsets into spending the day at the park on the spur of the moment.

Higher levels of serotonin are associated with better moods, improved feeling of social status or respect, and flexibility. Higher levels can also decrease motivation. Serotonin and dopamine counterbalance each other. As one goes up, the other tends to go down. Being balanced between the two is important. Tryptophan, the amino acid precursor for serotonin (meaning your body uses it to make serotonin), decreases tendency to argue, increases cooperation, and lifts mood.[2]

Certain medications increase serotonin, especially selective serotonin reuptake inhibitors (SSRIs), which are the most commonly prescribed antidepressant medications (such as Prozac, Paxil, Zoloft, Celexa, Lexapro, and Luvox). Psychedelic drugs, including LSD and magic mushrooms, stimulate serotonin receptors, which helps people feel more open to change,[3] but these can be addictive and have detrimental side effects.

To boost serotonin levels for the Persistent Brain Type—or at least level them out—I recommend the following.

1. **Increase the intake of tryptophan.** This amino acid found in foods such as turkey, chicken, fish, carrots, blueberries, pumpkin seeds, sweet potatoes, and garbanzo beans helps drive tryptophan into the brain, where serotonin is made. Although 90 percent of serotonin in the body is produced in the gut, which keeps your digestive tract healthy and happy, the brain needs to make its own, which is why dietary tryptophan is essential. Stay away from sweets: Sugar quickly raises serotonin but doesn't maintain the boost, which is why many people become addicted to it. Avoid sugary desserts because they can cause long-term health problems for Brain Type 3.

2. **Eat seafood and lots of it.** Not only does seafood provide ample tryptophan, but its long-chain omega-3s increase serotonin production in the brain.[4] Watch the wine intake, however. Persistent types often feel they need a nightly glass of wine—or two or three—to calm their worries. Those are steps in the wrong direction.

3. **Make an effort to compare yourself to others in a positive way.** Comparing yourself to others in a negative way is the most predictable way to lower your self-esteem. I recommend that my patients focus on what they have in life rather than what they don't have. For example, my wife, Tana, and I adopted our nieces because they grew up in a chaotic household with people who had addictions. We

lovingly told the girls that they had a choice to focus on what they did not have—a stable home environment in their early childhood—or what they did have—an aunt and uncle who promised to provide a loving, predictable, and healthy home life for them.

4. **Perform regular exercise.** Exercise helps to drive tryptophan into the brain, which can turbocharge serotonin levels. Multiple research studies have demonstrated that exercise can boost mood and cognitive flexibility.

5. **Take certain nutritional supplements.** The ones I recommend are saffron, l-tryptophan, 5-HTP, St. John's Wort, magnesium, vitamin D, vitamins B6 and B12, and curcumin. Be aware that caffeine and diet pills tend to worsen the negative traits in Persistent people because this brain type does not need more stimulation.

6. **Indulge in regular massages.** One study evaluated 84 pregnant women with depression. Those whose partner gave them 20 minutes of massage therapy twice a week reported feeling less anxious and depressed and had higher serotonin and dopamine levels and lower cortisol levels after 16 weeks.[5]

7. **Try out a bright light therapy lamp in the morning.** This increases serotonin levels and improves mood.[6] The mood-lowering effect of acute tryptophan depletion in healthy women was completely reversed by bright light (3,000 lux) therapy.[7]

8. **Engage in meditation and "quiet times."** Serotonin levels have been found to increase in response to nearly any form of spiritual reflection or meditation.

9. **Focus on what you like more than what you don't like.** Research demonstrates that where you bring your attention determines how you feel and the serotonin level your brain makes.[8] Using positron emission tomography (PET) scans, researchers obtained a measure of serotonin in the brains of healthy participants who focused on positive, negative, and neutral thoughts. Focusing on positive thoughts was correlated with increased levels of serotonin in the ACG. This means that serotonin can be bidirectional. When it is low, you feel sad, but you can feel better when you focus on what you love.

Happiness prescription for Brain Type 3: Persistent

Support your brain type. Follow the strategies to boost serotonin to help "grease" your brain's gear shifter and calm the ACG.

Understand your career path. The Persistent Brain Type is common among chief operating officers, accountants, event planners, and account managers.

Appreciate your learning style. You're a top student—or quick study—when you're given some leeway in how to learn the material. You don't like to be told, "You have to know this." You want to decide that for yourself.

Know what you want in a relationship. You can be stubborn and tend to remember every slight and every fight you have had with your spouse or partner. If your significant other also has the Persistent Brain Type, beware that you could end up butting heads.

When You're in a Relationship with the Persistent Brain Type

People with the Persistent Brain Type are strong-willed, opinionated, can-do types. Being around someone who knows who they are, what they believe, and works hard to gets things done can be intoxicating, especially when so many people seem aimless and uninspired. The trouble can start if you disagree with these types or want a change of pace. Whether the Persistent person is a partner, parent, or pal, you may hear "no" a lot, which can be frustrating. They may also frequently remind you of something you did wrong ages ago—when you said you didn't like her new hairdo, when you changed the filing system at work and he couldn't find his client's account information for a big meeting, or when you set her up on a blind date that didn't go so well.

Learning to give Persistent Brain Types options helps them avoid the automatic no. Exercising with them and cooking complex carbohydrates for them help boost serotonin production, which makes them a little less intense, so you can be happier together.

What their romantic partners say:
"I don't think I've ever heard him say he's sorry."
"She still brings up something I did three decades ago. I wish she would get over it."

What their coworkers say:
"She sticks to her goals no matter what."
"He has trouble shifting gears when things in the market change."

What their friends say:
"If I need someone to help me plan something, he's the guy."
"When our plans change, she gets upset."

Watch for times when you get off track. When your brain's ACG is overactive or overstimulated, you can get stuck on negative thoughts and go to a dark place. This mindset impacts your happiness and is associated with anxiety, depression, obsessive-compulsive disorder (OCD), and eating disorders.

Know what makes you uniquely happy. Make a list of the things that bring you joy and look at it every day to remind yourself of the activities you love.

What makes people with the Persistent Brain Type happy?

- Being in charge
- Having the respect of others
- Predictable days
- Seeing the big picture
- Sameness and familiarity
- Keeping traditions
- Maintaining a routine
- Making his or her own decisions

What makes people with the Persistent Brain Type unhappy?

- People who don't do what they said they were going to do
- Failure
- Getting told no
- Being kept waiting
- Not finding a parking place
- Being stymied by higher-ups
- Having the rules changed

☺ **Look for the micro-moments of happiness.**

- Checking something off your to-do list
- Making plans
- Waking up and knowing exactly what your day will look like
- Spending time reading a great book
- Watching the sunset after a successful day

CHAPTER 7

THE SENSITIVE BRAIN TYPE

The Limbic System and Oxytocin and Endorphins

I will protect my energy around draining people.
I will learn how to set healthy boundaries.
I will learn how to say "no" at the right times.
I will listen to my intuition about the
relationships that are nurturing for me.

JUDITH ORLOFF, MD, *THE EMPATH'S SURVIVAL GUIDE*

Do you feel that you can tune into the feelings of people around you, especially family members?

Do you feel empathetic about people's troubles and setbacks? Can you sense the emotions going on in other people?

Are you an emotional sponge, where you can absorb what others' feelings in your own body? Before the pandemic, were you uncomfortable around big crowds?

If you answer yes to any or all of these questions, there's a strong chance that you're Brain Type 4: Sensitive. You have a way of sensing and feeling emotions in ways that many people aren't capable of doing. Because of your brain type, someone else's pain and happiness become part of *your* pain and happiness, part of *your* experience.

COMMON TRAITS IN BRAIN TYPE 4: SENSITIVE

People with this type tend to score high on the following traits:

- Sensitivity
- Deep feelings
- Empathy
- Mood variability
- Pessimism

- Lots of ANTs (automatic negative thoughts)
- Depression

They tend to score low on:

- Superficiality
- Consistent happiness
- Positive thoughts

Another way to describe the Sensitive Brain Type is "empathetic." When you are an empath, you have an innate ability to understand others' experiences and feelings outside of your own. You tend to be sensitive and feel deeply.

Sensitive people typically shy away from crowds, and their idea of a lovely Saturday afternoon is more likely to involve a book of poetry, the solitude of a quiet walk through a deserted forest, or traipsing all alone through an uncrowded park or nature reserve. Anytime Sensitive Brain Types can get away from honking horns, the hustle and bustle of commercial zones, loud parties, or excessive stimulation, they are in their happy zone.

Sensitive people are happiest when they can chill out. They would love to go on a silent retreat at a monastery, spend a quiet night at home, or go out to dinner with just one friend or loved one instead of meeting a dozen friends at a crowded pizzeria. They aren't usually fans of small talk and prefer to dive deeper with people. They don't want to be "scheduled" all the time, preferring some wiggle room or unplanned gaps in their days. A long shower and plenty of time to get ready is heaven to Brain Type 4. So is having time to write in a personal journal or spend time with a book that recharges their spiritual batteries.

Insights from an Expert

While I'm not this brain type, I've long been fascinated with people who are, which is why I invited one of the pioneers in understanding sensitive people to be on *The Brain Warrior's Way Podcast* that I host with Tana. Our guest was Dr. Judith Orloff, author of *Thriving as an Empath: 365 Days of Self-Care for Sensitive People*.

Check Out
The Brain Warrior's Way Podcast

I love listening to audiobooks, which is why I also love listening to podcasts. If you're the same, you'll enjoy listening to the fascinating guests that Tana and I host on our podcast. I love having Tana, a neurosurgical ICU trauma nurse, lend her perspective to the discussions that unfold.

We started the podcast in 2016, and we've already reached over 10 million downloads on nearly 1,000 episodes on a variety of topics related to brain health. Each show lasts only 10–15 minutes so you can enjoy it in bite-size chunks. It's hard to pick a few that stand out, but some of the most popular have been with Jay Shetty, a former monk who has become a social media phenom, hosts the *On Purpose* podcast, and is the author of *Think Like a Monk*, and Dr. Caroline Leaf, a cognitive neuroscientist and author of *Cleaning Up Your Mental Mess*.

Whatever your interest, you'll find something to listen to as you drive to your destination or engage in exercise. Visit our website: brainwarriorswaypodcast.com.

Dr. Orloff was eager to talk about how to thrive as a "sensitive empath," saying they have beautiful, wonderful skills, but they also have to learn self-care to deal with the challenges of being highly sensitive.

"The secret is not to get less sensitive, to get a thicker skin, as my physician mother told me over and over, 'Dear, just get a thicker skin. You've got to toughen up,'" Dr. Orloff began. "That's not the answer. The answer is to expand your sensitivities, but learn how to center yourself. Learn how to set good boundaries. Learn how to practice fierce self-care. Learn how to have enough alone time. Learn the signs of when you go on sensory overload so you can nip it in the bud before it explodes and then you say something you regret because you're so overwhelmed."

I was curious how Dr. Orloff, an admitted sensitive person, discovered these traits about herself. She described how she was the only child of two physicians with 25 medical doctors in her family heritage. When she was little, she was a quiet girl who found that wading into crowds left her anxious and depressed. "I didn't know what happened in that crowded place that would cause such a change in my body," she said.

Her mother's admonition to "toughen up" wasn't helpful. "I had no self-care techniques at all growing up. I was totally alone," she told us. This led to a fascinating exchange between Tana and Dr. Orloff:

> **Tana:** *So being an empath is different than just having empathy for people? What I'm hearing you say is I can have empathy. If I see a child hurt, I can have empathy, but I don't feel that pain the way they feel it. It's different to have empathy versus being an empath, right?*
>
> **Dr. Orloff:** *Exactly. There's a spectrum of empathy and in the middle of the spectrum are regular beautiful people who have empathy and feel the joy and pain of others. But if you go higher on the empathic spectrum, you get the highly sensitive person who's sensitive to noise, smells, sounds, excessive talking, light.*
>
> *Then if you go even higher, you have all those sensory characteristics plus the emotional sponge and the physical sponge characteristic where you literally become one with [that person], which is a positive thing in a spiritual sense, that onement, but it's not a helpful thing in terms of taking on other people's emotions.*
>
> **Tana:** *Do you feel more for some people than other people? Do you feel more things when you're around one person or is it the same no matter who you're around?*
>
> **Dr. Orloff:** *No, it varies according to the person. It depends. I can feel all the positive things. Empaths have incredible gifts. Part of the self-care is taking care of your gifts: intuition, depth, the capacity for love, creativity, love of nature, knowing that there's a oneness in the world, that we're all brothers and sisters in one family, that anything else is an illusion; we know that without a doubt. . . . That's very clear and that clarity is extremely helpful.*

I thought back to the imaging studies on people with sensory disorders and highly sensitive people I'd conducted as part of our work at the Amen Clinics. What I often saw was that their parietal lobes—the top back part of their brains that are responsible for sensing the world—were working way too hard compared to other people's.

> **Dr. Amen:** *How would someone know if they or one of their children or their spouse was an empath?*

Dr. Orloff: *Well . . . there's some very basic questions you can ask yourself, such as:*

- *"Have you been labeled as 'overly sensitive' all your life as a putdown?"*
- *"Do you need a lot of alone time to decompress and replenish yourself?"*
- *"Do you prefer alone time to being with people when you replenish yourself?"*

Some extroverts love going out and being with people and that's how they get their energy back, but when I'm on sensory overload, I go to solitude. I go alone. That aloneness is my nurturing place. It's my . . . spirit. It's manna from heaven, being alone, because that decreases stimulation.

. . . Or other questions: "Am I sensitive to noise, smells, or excessive talking?" Empaths have a very strong sense of smell. We could go into an elevator and there could be perfume there and I could feel like I'm being nuked by it and you might feel like, "Oh, what a pretty smell." If you take your sensory capacity and magnify it by about a million, then you can understand an empath.

The reason this is beautiful is that my capacity for love is very deep. My capacity for spiritual connection and connection to nature and all the things that matter to me is very, very deep. Connection is what's important to me. As an empath, that connection is available.[1]

Many studies have found that feeling connected to nature is positively correlated with feeling happy and having a sense of well-being. So Sensitive Brain Types need to get outside as much as possible to boost daily happiness.[2]

Inner workings of Brain Type 4

Sensitive people are among the 20 percent of the population whose brains process things more deeply than others, and to understand, we can look to the brain's neurotransmitters. Consider this:

1. **Your brain responds to dopamine differently.** You've learned that dopamine is the "molecule of more," the brain's reward chemical. You like dopamine because its presence propels you to "want" to get certain things done, but recognition or external rewards don't drive Sensitive Brain Types. That's why you feel reserved in certain situations, holding back as you observe others and processing that information until you feel comfortable taking action. Your body also reacts differently to overstimulation from a loud concert—the heavy

bass, blaring music, and strobe lights. Your brain doesn't produce as much dopamine as the brains of, shall we say, party animals.

2. **Your brain is more active in processing information than others.** When you're observant, your brain is working. While other brain types might "take five" and daydream, you're constantly processing the world around you. Your brain is fine-tuned to observe and interpret the behavior around you. This explains why you're hypersensitive to violent movies, profanity-laced language, and onscreen sex scenes. Others can shrug off the mayhem, raw language, or naked bodies, but you can't "compartmentalize" those images like others can.

3. **You experience emotions more deeply and vividly than others.** If you're a nurse, patients say you have a wonderful bedside manner. If you're a therapist, clients praise you for your listening skills. If you're a pastor, people appreciate your wisdom and humbleness.

   You experience your emotions more deeply than most others because you can tap into an area of the brain called the ventromedial prefrontal cortex (vmPFC). You're likely blessed with a gene that increases the vividness of your feelings. So while you may appreciate the love from a toddler falling into your lap more than others, you're also more likely to stew over losing a sale or not getting the promotion.

4. **You love to notice what's around you.** You can't tune people out; your brain won't let you do that. You're wired to gather information about what you see, hear, touch, and feel. Brain scans show increased activity in the ACG, also known as the "seat of consciousness" and where your moment-to-moment awareness comes into play.

   There's a lot to be said for being Brain Type 4. Not everyone can process information on a deeper level, connect with others with such empathy, and relate to those around them in meaningful ways.

If You Have Children . . .

Brain Type 4 parents are mothers and fathers full of empathy and love as they strive to nurture their children with love and kindness. Brain Type 4 children benefit from parents who understand their feelings, for the most part.

WHAT SPECT SCANS SHOW ABOUT THE SENSITIVE BRAIN

Brain imaging work shows that the Sensitive Brain Type often has increased activity in the brain's limbic or emotional areas.

NORMAL ACTIVE BRAIN SPECT SCAN

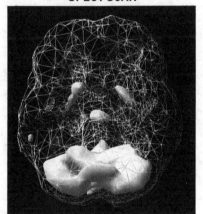

Most active areas in cerebellum at the back of brain

SENSITIVE BRAIN TYPE ACTIVE SPECT SCAN

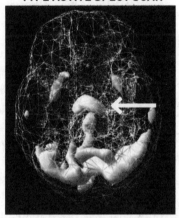

High deep limbic activity (arrow)

The limbic system is one of the most exciting and critical parts of being human and is power-packed with functions—all of which are critical for human behavior and survival. The primary functions of the limbic system include:

- **Setting the emotional tone of the mind:** Your overall emotional outlook highly depends on this brain region. Lower activity in the limbic system is associated with a sense of positivity and hopefulness. People with the Sensitive Brain Type who have increased activity in the limbic system have a tendency toward negativity and feeling hopeless and helpless.

- **Filtering external events through internal states (creates emotional coloring):** Emotional coloring, also known as emotional shading, is the way you interpret everyday events. Think of it like a camera lens filter that makes everything seem a bit brighter or a shade darker. When the limbic system is overactive, as it is in those with the Sensitive Brain Type, you're more likely to interpret events and conversations in a negative way.

- **Storing highly charged emotional memories:** Think of the best days of your life—college graduation, getting married, the birth of your first child—and the worst days—being in a horrific car accident, declaring bankruptcy, the death of your spouse. What do all these events have in common? The emotional component of these memories is stored in the limbic system. With increased activity in this brain region, certain memories may evoke strong emotional reactions in Sensitive types.

- **Modulates motivation:** The limbic system is involved in how much get-up-and-go you possess to achieve what you want out of life. Lower activity in this brain region is associated with a can-do attitude. However, greater activity in the limbic system is linked to decreased motivation and can make it hard for Sensitive types to get off the couch to pursue their dreams.

- **Controls appetite and sleep cycles:** The hypothalamus (part of the limbic system) is heavily involved in how much you eat and sleep. For those in the Sensitive camp, heightened activity in the limbic system can cause changes in daily food intake and sleep habits—either a suppressed appetite and sleepless nights or overeating and oversleeping.

- **Promotes bonding:** This brain region plays an important role in your ability to connect with other people. When you have strong social connections, they boost your mood and positivity about your life. When you have the Sensitive Brain Type, you may be more likely to isolate yourself from others, depriving yourself of mood-boosting social bonding.

- **Directly processes the sense of smell:** When you smell the roses, the scent goes directly from the olfactory system to the limbic system where it is processed. This helps explain why scents can have such a powerful influence on mood and emotions. If you have the Sensitive Brain Type, you may want to surround yourself with pleasing aromas.

- **Modulates libido:** Healthy sexual activity is a key component of a happy life. For example, lovemaking triggers the release of some of the chemicals of happiness that promote emotional bonding. Increased activity in the limbic system for Sensitive Brain Types means a likelihood of decreased sexual desire. Therefore, Sensitive people may miss out on those feel-good neurochemicals.

Our experience at Amen Clinics tells us that when the limbic system is less active, it generally creates a more positive and hopeful state of mind. However, when the limbic system is working too hard, it is often associated with problems.

Problems When the Limbic System Works Too Hard

- Sadness or clinical depression
- Increased negative thinking
- Negative perception of events
- Flood of negative emotions, such as hopelessness, helplessness, and guilt
- Problems with appetite and sleep
- Decreased or increased sexual responsiveness
- Social isolation
- Physical pain

BRAIN TYPE 4:
SENSITIVE NEUROCHEMICALS OF HAPPINESS

Sensitive Brain Types tend to be low in a combination of chemicals, including dopamine, serotonin, oxytocin, and endorphins. The key is to raise those levels. I've already devoted some time to discussing raising dopamine (see chapter 5: The Spontaneous Brain Type) and serotonin (see chapter 6: The Persistent Brain Type) levels. Here, I'll focus on oxytocin and endorphins.

Oxytocin—the molecule of trust

Produced by the hypothalamus, oxytocin has been called the cuddle or love hormone, but it is so much more. Studies have found that couples in the first stage of romantic love have higher levels of oxytocin as well as higher dopamine (pleasure) and lower serotonin levels (obsessions) than their unattached friends. Oxytocin is increased during sexual activity and linked to the intensity of orgasms.[3] It has been associated with increased trust, well-being, pair bonding, maternal behaviors, generosity, stress reduction, and social interactions. With bonding, oxytocin has also been associated with behaviors that protect the social group. It causes people to gravitate toward those who are similar to them, even lying to protect others in their group. It has been shown to decrease pain and promote wound healing (close relationships improve physical health). Oxytocin stimulates a sense of contentment, lowered anxiety, and feelings of calmness and security when with your mate—key elements in happy relationships. Oxytocin amplifies the effects of both positive and negative social interactions.

Low oxytocin levels have been associated with depression and feeling your survival is threatened—certainly not a recipe for happiness. Low levels of this neurochemical have also been linked to autism. Higher oxytocin levels can decrease cortisol and stress and increase the likelihood mates will be monogamous (it lowers testosterone).

Like the other chemicals of happiness, there may be a downside to too much oxytocin. It may be related to people becoming too attached, trusting, or codependent. Higher levels may be associated with overlooking the flaws of others or staying with abusive partners or friends because the bond is too strong. This is why I encourage my patients to be very careful about their sexual encounters. Increased oxytocin levels have been associated with envy, gloating, and "mama bear" aggression if anyone threatens your loved ones. It may also be involved in social contagion, groupthink, distrust of others who are not like you (it leads to in-group protection), and racial prejudice.

What lowers oxytocin? Testosterone, being apart from a loved one, isolation, betrayal, grief, and acute stress drain oxytocin. The pandemic was disastrous for many people's oxytocin levels and their levels of happiness.

Oxytocin can be prescribed as a drug. Researchers have shown that emotional trauma can benefit from oxytocin[4] and that it can calm the fear circuits in the brain and decrease the symptoms of post-traumatic stress disorder (PTSD).[5] I first learned about oxytocin's positive impact on grief while reading a book by Dr. Ken Stoller, who worked with us at Amen Clinics for several years. In *Oxytocin: The Hormone of Healing and Hope*, Ken writes about his own firsthand experience with oxytocin and grief:

> In 2007, my beloved 16-year-old son Galen was killed in a train accident, sending me into a chasm of what I came to view as pathological grief—where I was unable to modulate obsessive thoughts about how my son died, what he might have experienced, what if I had been able to be there, and so on. This collection of fear, anxiety, and panic took on a life of its own, as if it were a separate thought-stream that I had no control of. It was suffocating and debilitating.
>
> Although I had become adept at using oxytocin for treating fear and anxiety in children on the autism spectrum, it took me over three weeks after my son passed until I had the idea that it might help me too. . . . It took about ten minutes to experience the full effect, and with each passing minute a great sense of emotional equanimity took place. The panic and fear dropped away from me as if I were shedding clothing. If I wanted to think about my son's train accident, I could. But the moment I didn't want to think about it, the accident faded into the background of my mind. It wasn't there hammering away at me as if it had a life of its own. . . . I was able to process my grief without the interference of negative obsessions.[6]

Here are 13 ways to boost oxytocin:

1. **Develop social alliances.** When you're hanging out with your pals or crew, you feel socially supported and less alone in this world. That's why the pandemic was so difficult for so many people—they lost the oxytocin from meeting their friends for a Saturday morning bike ride or after-church brunch.

2. **Touch.** When you need an oxytocin boost, reach out to touch someone you love. The simple act of holding hands can crank up levels of the molecule of trust.

3. **Give (or get) a massage.** It makes sense that receiving a feel-good massage means that your brain will feast on an uptick of oxytocin, but researchers like Dr. Kerstin Uvnäs-Moberg, author of *The Oxytocin Factor*, state that oxytocin is also released when a person is giving a massage.[7]

4. **Give a gift.** If you want to encourage the release of oxytocin, surprise someone you care about with a gift. It doesn't have to be an extravagant present, just a little something that will make them smile. In turn, that will promote positive feelings in you.

5. **Make eye contact.** Gazing into the eyes of a loved one—even if it's just a furry four-legged friend—can trigger the release of oxytocin.[8] Maintaining eye contact has a calming effect and enhances connections, even when it's between two strangers.

6. **Listen to music you love.** Turns out that researchers are refining their ideas about how music alters the body and the mind during physical exercise. Not only does music raise oxytocin levels,[9] but listening to upbeat tunes also provides a distraction from pain and exhaustion, increases stamina, and enhances people's mood.[10] You think Rocky wasn't fired up when he ran up the 72 steps leading to the Philadelphia Museum of Art with "Gonna Fly Now" blaring in the background? While you're listening to music, sing along—even if the only time you sing is when you're standing in a shower stall—to increase oxytocin.

7. **Take a yoga class.** Decades of studies point to yoga's ability to reduce depression, anxiety, and stress while improving sleep and enhancing overall quality of life. Sounds like an ingredient for happiness, doesn't it? Additional research suggests that doing yoga increases oxytocin levels.[11]

8. **Practice loving kindness meditation.** To trigger the release of oxytocin, spend time with this form of meditation, in which you direct thoughts of love, compassion, and goodwill toward yourself, those close to you, and others with whom you have strained relations.

9. **Engage in positive social interactions.** Telling someone you love them or sharing your feelings with a trusted friend can spark an uptick in oxytocin production.

10. **Engage in random acts of kindness.** Did you volunteer at a food bank during the pandemic? Tutor young children in the neighborhood? Oxytocin levels spike in people who regularly volunteer.[12]

11. **Pet your animals.** There's a reason why dogs are known as a human's best friend—the simple act of stroking or caressing a dog's soft fur stokes the release of the molecule of trust, and it's documented.[13] Research has also found that cats—even with their sometimes persnickety and aloof temperaments—make us feel happy too![14]

12. **Eat with someone you care about.** Too many people dine alone or on the go these days when the act of sharing food can do wonders for oxytocin production. Think about the stimulating conversations you've had over the years or how you felt when someone you love and trust asked you, "So how was your day?"

13. **Make love.** The intimacy that comes from having sex is a crucial way to raise oxytocin levels and show affection for your significant other. Researchers have found that oxytocin is released during sexual contact and through gestures like hugging and holding hands.[15]

Endorphins—the molecule of pain relief

Another set of chemicals that is often low in the Sensitive Brain Type is endorphins, which are triggered to manage pain and severe stress. In blocking pain, endorphins help us escape dangerous situations that are potentially life-threatening, such as escaping after we have been bitten by a wild animal or getting out of a burning car, even if we have a broken leg. Endorphins are also released when we push ourselves to distress, such as a runner's high when athletes push their limits. They make us feel euphoric, which is why people can get addicted to intense exercise. These molecules are also involved in the pleasurable sensations of sex, listening to certain pieces of music, and eating delicious foods such as chocolate. Endorphins and opiate drugs help relieve pain, but unless prescribed with extreme caution, can kill people. Drugs such as oxycodone, hydrocodone, codeine, morphine, fentanyl, and heroin are some of the most addictive substances that are ravaging our society. The National Institute on Drug Abuse states that more than 100 people die each day in the United States from an opioid overdose.[16]

Low levels of endorphins have been associated with depression, anxiety, stress, mood swings, fibromyalgia, headaches, trouble sleeping—and, as one would expect, it sets people up for addictions, especially to opiate drugs.

The connection between pleasure and pain

Remember the discussion about wanting and liking? Wanting and pain are closely connected because of endorphins. Consider the word *tantalize*, which stems from the ancient story of the torture of Tantalus, mythical son of the Greek god Zeus, who was condemned for his faults by eternally being tempted with delicious food and drink just out of his reach. He was painfully tantalized.[17] Roller coasters, horror movies, extreme sports, running with the bulls, or chronically conflicted relationships are all examples of this connection. When endorphin levels are too low, the temptation is to look for extremes that will boost them.

Have you ever wondered why people become cutters (intentionally cutting themselves repeatedly), spend hours in tattoo parlors, or engage in sadomasochistic sexual behaviors? They are causing pain to trigger endorphins and the associated euphoria. When you understand the endorphin system and response, the unusual behavior begins to make sense. They may be seeking an endorphin rush to block emotional pain. When I put them on the opiate blocker naltrexone, which blocks the euphoric effect, they often stop the behavior. Naltrexone has also been used with alcoholics to decrease the buzz and thus decrease alcohol intake.

The *Dr. Phil* show recently reached out to me to scan the brain of a man who had become addicted to women hurting him. He would hire them to punch him, spit on him, and humiliate him. One time, he even asked a woman to run him over with her car. It started innocently as a child, when he would tease girls until they became angry with him, but it escalated to a dangerous level, which ruined his relationships and made him feel incredible shame. His brain had become addicted to the endorphins created by the pain of being physically hurt.

For Sensitive Brain Types, here are eight natural ways to balance endorphins and boost your overall happiness.

1. **Exercise.** Physical activity triggers the release of this pain-relieving neurochemical and can produce the "runner's high" that makes you feel great.

2. **Giving to others.** When it comes to increasing your levels of endorphins, it is better to give than to receive, so find ways to be of service to others.

3. **Yoga.** The stress-reducing effects of yoga are well-documented, but a lesser-known benefit is its ability to raise endorphin levels.[18]

4. **Meditate.** A regular meditation practice has been associated with increases in endorphins[19] as well as positive mood, which is helpful for people with the Sensitive Brain Type.

5. **Eat spicy foods.** The compound capsaicin—found in jalapeño, habanero, and other chili peppers that can make your head sweat—is associated with an endorphin rush and pain reduction.[20]

6. **Consume dark chocolate.** Why does eating chocolate reduce pain and enhance our moods? In part, it's because of anti-inflammatory ingredients in dark chocolate that also promote the release of endorphins.

7. **Laugh more.** You can thank endorphins for many of the benefits of laughter, including elevating the pain threshold. Simply watching a half hour of comedy clips with a few friends is enough to increase endorphin levels.[21]

8. **Try acupuncture.** The ancient therapy of acupuncture[22] has been shown to help with depression,[23] fibromyalgia,[24] and insomnia.[25] In fact, I've treated many patients with treatment-resistant depression (meaning that traditional treatments have not worked) who told me that when they took an opiate, such as hydrocodone for a dental procedure, they felt instantly better. Of course, I would never give them an opiate prescription for depression (addiction vulnerability makes them way too dangerous), but that piece of history triggered me to send them to an acupuncturist, and they often found relief. Acupuncture doesn't work for all depressions, but it is effective for Brain Type 4.

Happiness prescription for Brain Type 4: Sensitive

Support your brain type. Follow the suggestions above to boost oxytocin and endorphins and engage in brain healthy behaviors that protect your brain and calm your limbic system.

Understand your career path. The Sensitive Brain Type is common among nurses, therapists, health-care professionals, pastors, and others involved in ministry. Poets, painters, songwriters, and other artists also often fall into this camp.

Appreciate your learning style. You don't do well in a busy setting, whether it's a classroom or sitting in a coffee shop, working remotely while people line up for their lattes.

Know what you want in a relationship. Pick a partner who is positive and upbeat, who can also respect your need for peace and quiet. You want to be joined to someone else who has a sense of purpose.

When You're in a Relationship with the Sensitive Brain Type

People with the Sensitive Brain Type are the ones who can tune into what you're thinking and feeling and are there for you when you need a shoulder to cry on, someone to listen to your problems, or some chicken soup when you're sick. These people give you the opportunity to connect on a deep level, and romantic relationships, friendships, and work relationships can be very intense. In some cases, a Sensitive Brain Type's limbic system may be too overactive, which can lead to negativity, social isolation, and interpreting things the wrong way. You may feel powerless to help them regain their positive attitude or to spark their desire to hang out with friends or be social on the job. Encouraging them to try the BRIGHT MINDS therapy lamp or Happy Saffron Plus from BrainMD can promote a more positive mood so you can both feel happier.

What their romantic partners say:
"I love talking with him late into the night."
"Sometimes she takes things the wrong way."

What their coworkers say:
"She's like the 'office mom' who takes care of all of us."
"He's a loner."

What their friends say:
"We have so many fun memories together."
"Sometimes she brings me down with her negativity."

Watch for times when you get off track. Have you been listening to the ANTs (automatic negative thoughts) in your life—the self-talk that's telling you that you don't measure up or are going to fail? Make sure to pay attention to chapter 13 on Positivity Bias Training.

Know what makes you uniquely happy. Make a list of the things that bring you joy and look at it every day to remind yourself of the activities you love.

What makes people with the Sensitive Brain Type happy?

- Listening to calming music
- Having a strong sense of purpose
- Thinking deep thoughts
- Smelling scents of lavender
- Nursing others back to good health
- Practicing mindfulness
- Having some alone time during the day
- Close, meaningful relationships
- Walks among nature's beauty
- Journaling
- A good night's sleep
- Writing, painting, and other creative ways to express their emotions

What makes people with the Sensitive Brain Type unhappy?

- Negative thoughts that won't go away
- Thinking about past relationships that didn't work out
- Being socially disconnected from others
- Setbacks on the job
- Putting on weight
- Driving on busy boulevards
- Being surrounded by bright lights
- Hearing loud sounds
- Watching scary or violent movies
- Going to bed late

☺ **Look for the micro-moments of happiness.**

- Looking into your significant other's eyes and feeling a connection

- Hearing a happy song you love come on the radio
- That feeling you get when someone smiles because of something you did for them
- Hugs with your dearest friends
- Taking a walk with your lovable dog

CHAPTER 8

THE CAUTIOUS BRAIN TYPE

The Anxiety Centers and GABA

Happiness is not a brilliant climax to years of grim struggle and anxiety.
It is a long succession of little decisions simply to be happy in the moment.

J. DONALD WALTERS

One of the lessons I have learned in more than three decades of clinical practice is that comedians who spend their lives making others laugh are not necessarily the happiest people themselves. Take Brittany Furlan, for example. This Instagram influencer with 2.4 million followers produces laugh-out-loud content, but inside her head, it is full of anxious and worrisome thoughts. When Brittany came to see me at Amen Clinics to get her brain scanned, she told me everything was giving her anxiety.

"I keep telling myself, maybe I should just get a lobotomy," she said, and she was only half laughing.

From the outside, it looks like Brittany leads a charmed life. A social media megastar—*Time* magazine named her one of the most influential people on the internet in 2015—she's married to a famous musician with the financial means to take luxury vacations. But even that makes her nervous.

"Any other person would be like, 'Go to Bali, . . . yeah!'" she told me, but her mind immediately turns to what could go wrong.

"I'm like, where's the closest hospital? . . . What if I have a panic attack and have a heart attack?" she fretted. "What are they going to do? Airlift me?"

Her husband says she has a serious case of "Worst-Case Scenario Syndrome."

It's something I see in many patients who have the Cautious Brain Type. In the general population, having the Cautious Brain Type is associated with being prepared, thinking about the consequences of what you say or do before you do it, avoiding risks, and being on time. You're the type who likes to arrive early for meetings, did your school homework first and *then* went out to play with your friends, and starts work projects immediately so you can finish them long before the deadline.

Ask Brittany, and she'll say if she has something due in three months, she'll try to bang it out that first night just to be able to cross it off her list. "I can't have anything on my plate. It gives me anxiety," she said during our session, which can be viewed on our Facebook page.[1]

Like many Cautious Brain Types, Brittany has a busy mind that makes it difficult to relax, even while on vacation in a beautiful place like Bali.

BRITTANY'S ACTIVE SPECT SCAN

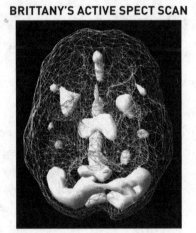

Increased anterior cingulate, limbic, and basal ganglia activity

COMMON TRAITS IN BRAIN TYPE 5: CAUTIOUS

People with this type tend to score high on the following traits:

- Preparation
- Caution
- Risk aversion
- Motivation
- Reserve
- Busy mindedness
- Moodiness
- Difficulty relaxing
- Anxiety

They tend to score low on:

- Lack of concern about preparation
- Risk taking

- Calmness
- Ability to relax
- Quiet mind
- Even temper
- Security

Cautious individuals have many strengths. You likely have high standards (for yourself and others), analyze issues in great detail before taking action, and are thorough and reliable. When you say you'll do something, you do it.

Security, safety, and predictability are important to you. You don't like taking big risks—no thank you to bungee jumping, cliff diving, or free climbing—and you are equally thoughtful about other areas of your life. Investing in an untested cryptocurrency isn't your style. Neither is signing up for an experimental surgical procedure or being the first person on your block to buy a self-driving car.

You're the type who gets things done and does them well. Someone who's on the extreme end of the Spontaneous Type and has ADD could never accomplish what a Cautious person can do in the same amount of time. I remember a CEO with ADD whom I was treating. She had trouble staying organized at work, so I urged her to hire an assistant who had Persistent and Cautious Brain Type traits to help her stay organized, be prepared, and stick with a job assignment from start to finish. The pairing worked! The CEO was able to focus on her strengths while the Persistent-Cautious assistant kept things humming along.

Cautious Brain Types often look to the future with trepidation, but when you are wrapped up in the future, it means you are missing out on the present and live with a baseline level of anxiety, which creates misery.

Some anxiety is a good thing. When kept in balance, anxiety keeps you safe because your brain is doing its part to protect you from making silly or tragic mistakes. When you have a healthy level of stress before a major test or an important assignment, you're engaged and primed to perform at your highest level. When you're mentally prepared, you understand the parameters and boundaries of the project, which lowers anxiety levels and allows you to perform at your best.

In some people with Brain Type 5, this anxiety can become exacerbated in stressful situations. Anton "Neels" Visser is a prime example. As this 22-year-old entrepreneur explains it, he grew up being "the least anxious, most confident" person. But that changed when his lifestyle shifted, and he started flying on planes every four days. In his opinion, it upended his homeostasis.

To learn more about why his anxiety levels had changed, he came to Amen Clinics to get a brain scan.

"I wanted to understand the anxiety and stress that kind of circulate in my brain daily," he said in his session with Dr. Daniel Emina, a wonderful psychiatrist who works with me at Amen Clinics.[2] In talking with Dr. Emina, Neels described how he had developed a "negative feedback loop" in his brain. That's when Dr. Emina posed an unexpected question:

"Are there any benefits to that feedback loop?"

After thinking about it for a moment, Neels responded, "The benefit is probably preparation. It's like me preparing to *not* do something I did previously, or it's me training myself that that thing caused harm or that it hurt me."

"You've pretty much described how neuroanatomy and neurophysiology kind of works," Dr. Emina said. "We have a thought pattern that eventually leads to emotion, that eventually leads to behaviors and [repetition]. Just like any other habit that we form—good or bad habits—you can strengthen them. So you may have benefits that may be good things about being able to overthink about a situation that allows you to prepare for something. The challenge is usually when you get to a situation where you feel like you can't improve or you can't fix [it]."

Neels nodded in agreement, admitting that for him, "That's the pain point for me—the things I feel I cannot fix."

Feeling a lack of control is a sticking point for many Cautious types. And nothing has left people feeling more out of control in recent history than the pandemic. Many Cautious types did not fare well in the era of COVID-19. Frightening news feeds, worries about health and safety, and economic uncertainty fueled their anxiety and caused them to worry even more, crushing their happiness.

Cautious types were the ones rushing out to buy up every last roll of toilet paper during the early days of the pandemic. I remember the scenes of panic buying and stripped store shelves, something you see whenever a hurricane is headed toward the Gulf Coast or a major blizzard is headed for New York City. Paul Marsden, a British consumer psychologist at the University of the Arts London, said that panic buying is our way of "taking back control" when the world is spinning off its axis. Panic buying plays to our fundamental psychological need for autonomy when the future is uncertain.[3]

People with Brain Type 5 are also more vulnerable to panic attacks, which are sudden episodes of intense fear based on perceived threats rather than imminent danger. To calm their nerves, some turn to alcohol, marijuana, or other substances. There are healthier ways to soothe stress and anxiety. The good news is that you can get control of your symptoms by following a simple four-step panic plan that I've taught to hundreds of patients.

DR. AMEN'S FOUR-STEP PLAN TO FIGHT PANIC

Step 1: Don't forget to breathe. When anxiety threatens to swallow you, your breathing becomes shallow, rapid, and erratic. Since the brain is the most metabolically active organ in the body, any mental state that lowers the inflow of oxygen will trigger more fear and panic. Stop this downward spiral in its tracks by being mindful that it's happening and taking slow, deep breaths to boost oxygen levels in your brain. The influx of fresh molecules of oxygen will help you regain control over how you feel.

How do you practice deep breathing? By learning how to breathe from your diaphragm, an area of the body that tends to "clench up" when you're anxious. To practice breathing from your diaphragm, try doing this:

- Lie on your back, and place a small book on your belly.
- As you take 3–4 seconds to slowly inhale air through your nose, watch the book rise. Hold your breath at the top of your inhalation for a second.
- When you exhale for 6–8 seconds, watch the book go down. Then hold your breath for a second before inhaling again.
- Repeat 10 times and notice how relaxed you feel.

Step 2: Don't flee even though everything within you says, "Run!" When anxiety feels like it's wrapping you in a bear hug, resist the temptation to flee for the hills. Do not ignore whatever is causing your anxiety. Leaving the situation, unless it is dangerous or life-threatening, allows the anxiety to control you.

Step 3: Write down your thoughts. Too often in panicked situations, our thoughts are distorted and need to be challenged. Pay attention to the automatic negative thoughts (or ANTs, as I call them), being sure to write down or record as many as you can. If you can show them to a therapist, great, but if not, take a closer look at what you've written. Can any of them be rewritten so that they are a more realistic version of the same thought? See chapter 13 for more tips.

Step 4: Consider a simple supplement, such as GABA or magnesium. Panic attacks often come from overactive anxiety centers, and these supplements can calm them down quickly.

Some people with the Cautious Brain Type feel like they are on high alert at all times. Clinical practice has taught me that this is often related to past emotional trauma. I'm familiar with and use several excellent therapeutic methods for helping people overcome anxiety symptoms brought on by traumatic experiences. One method I recommend is called eye movement desensitization and reprocessing, or EMDR. My patients, such as Troy and Shannon Zeeman, have found this form of therapy helpful in removing the emotional charges of traumatic memories.

The Route 91 Shooting and EMDR

On a clear and warm Sunday evening, October 1, 2017, country music fans Troy and Shannon Zeeman were tapping their leather cowboy boots to the bass-heavy country rock music being played by Jason Aldean and his band, the final act of the Route 91 Harvest music festival held in Las Vegas.

The Zeemans were among 20,000 happy concertgoers that evening. Troy and Shannon—who'd recently survived a serious bout of breast cancer—were hanging out with friends in front of the stage when a crazed gunman began firing an assault rifle from the 32nd floor of the Mandalay Bay Resort and Casino overlooking the venue. Hundreds of high-caliber rounds rained down on the audience. Some concertgoers fled for the exits. Others froze like statues, too afraid to move.

Troy and Shannon recalled the horrific event during an episode of the *The Brain Warrior's Way Podcast* with Tana and me.[4] Troy, a Newport Beach police officer, said that during the barrage, "You could see the impact rounds hitting everywhere around us so that it was just raining down on us." His experience as a police officer kicked in, and he quickly assessed the situation, determining that the shooter was not in the crowd.

For Shannon, however, who did not have that training, it was sheer terror. There was a point where they all thought the guy was walking toward them. That triggered her fight-or-flight response and she thought, *If this guy comes around the corner, I just fought for my life for the last year. He's not taking me.*

As Shannon described what had transpired, she could feel the energy in her body the way she had on that terrible night. "The whole experience, it was just so heightened," she said. "I feel that whole vibration goes through my body . . . you were just on autopilot like you say, just trying to survive and get out."

Troy took a bullet to the leg and was struck by shrapnel multiple times, but he had the presence of mind to lead about 20 people to safety.

When the deadliest active shooter incident in US history was over, 58 country music fans were dead and more than 700 were injured, including Troy, who survived but has bullet fragments inside his leg to this day.

The Zeemans, grateful to be alive, struggled with their emotions in the months after they came home, the memories of the blood and carnage never far away from their conscious thoughts. When they came to Amen Clinics for answers, their SPECT scans showed overactivity in the worry (anterior cingulate), mood (limbic system), and anxiety (basal ganglia) centers of the brain in what we call the "diamond pattern," often seen in people who have PTSD.

SHANNON'S ACTIVE SPECT SCAN

TROY'S ACTIVE SPECT SCAN

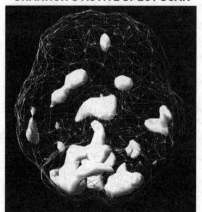 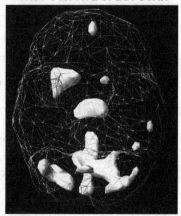

Diamond pattern of increased activity in the anterior cingulate (worry), limbic system (mood), and basal ganglia (anxiety), often associated with PTSD

When I sat down with the Zeemans, they told me that they had met with counselors who specialized in combat and traumatic events and followed their advice to try yoga classes, get into meditation, and take recommended nutritional supplements, which seemed to help. But Shannon and Troy were not entirely over the emotional hump.

"Did anyone ever explain EMDR to you?" I asked.

Shannon and Troy looked at each other. Clearly, they had never heard of it.

I explained that EMDR uses eye movements to stimulate both sides of the brain simultaneously to remove the emotional charges associated with traumatic memories.

The concept intrigued the Zeemans. I had them meet with one of our therapists, who directed them to hold specific memories in mind as they tracked her hand while she moved it back and forth across their field of vision. Bringing up traumatic memories while doing the eye movements tends to calm or soothe the overactive areas and decrease the emotional response connected to traumatic memories.

If you've gone through significant trauma, check out EMDR (emdria. org). While the brain is naturally wired to help you eventually recover from traumatic events, some circumstances can be so traumatic that they disrupt the normal flow of neural communication for a long time. In a sense, memories get stuck, making you feel like you are frozen in time. EMDR can help you get unstuck by restoring the communication process.

This is how much EMDR has helped the Zeemans: Troy says that when he started this form of therapy, his anxiety levels were an 8 on a scale of 1 to 10, 10 being worst. Today, he feels much calmer and says he's a 2, which is excellent progress. I'm pleased that Shannon and Troy determined that they weren't going to allow the emotional trauma of Route 91 to defeat them.

So far, they are victorious.

WHAT SPECT SCANS SHOW ABOUT THE CAUTIOUS BRAIN

A look at our brain-imaging work shows that the Cautious Brain Type often has high activity in the basal ganglia. On these SPECT images, heightened activity appears in the anxiety centers of the brain, such as the basal ganglia, insular cortex, or amygdala.

NORMAL ACTIVE BRAIN SPECT SCAN

CAUTIOUS BRAIN TYPE ACTIVE SPECT SCAN

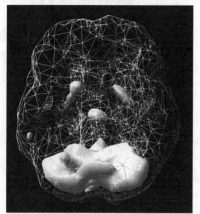 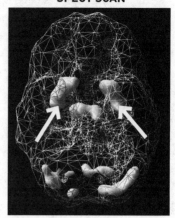

Most active areas in cerebellum at the back of brain

High basal ganglia activity (arrows)

The basal ganglia, which surrounds the limbic system, has many functions, including:

- **Integrating feeling and movement:** When there is balanced activity in the basal ganglia, it helps you think and react smoothly in any situation. Because people with the Cautious Brain Type have increased activity in this area, it means you're more likely to freeze in an emergency, shake when frightened, or get tongue-tied when you feel nervous in a job interview.

- **Shifting and steadying fine motor movements:** The basal ganglia is involved in motor coordination and is critical to handwriting. Heightened activity in this area, which is common in the Cautious crowd, is linked to better dexterity and a knack for detailed handiwork.

- **Suppressing unwanted motor behaviors:** Deficiencies in the basal ganglia are associated with two conditions that affect motor control: Parkinson's disease and Tourette's syndrome. These illnesses involve a lack of control over movements.

- **Helping to set the body's anxiety level:** Whether you're one of those people who feels relaxed and carefree or tense and nervous depends on the activity in your basal ganglia. Among Cautious types, heightened activity in this area of the brain makes you prone to anxiety, fear, increased awareness, and tension.

- **Forming habits:** Your everyday habits and decisions are foundational elements of happiness. The basal ganglia is instrumental in the formation of those habits, whether they are healthy ones that enhance happiness or unhealthy ones that steal your joy. People with the Cautious Brain Type may be prone to habits such as nail biting, teeth grinding, or skin picking.

- **Elevating motivation and drive:** In some cases, higher anxiety levels associated with increased activity in the basal ganglia can act as a motivator. For the Cautious Brain Type, this may make you strive for peak performance, increase your productivity, and energize you to tackle a long to-do list.

- **Mediating pleasure/ecstasy:** Happiness depends on the ability to feel pleasure. When there is underactivity in the basal ganglia, people tend to have difficulty feeling pleasure. Happily, this is not the case for Cautious Types who have increased basal ganglia activity.

Problems When the Basal Ganglia Works Too Hard

- Anxiety, nervousness
- Physical sensations of anxiety (such as headaches, upset stomach, and shortness of breath)
- Tendency to predict the worst
- Conflict avoidance
- Risk aversion
- Tourette's syndrome/tics
- Muscle tension, soreness
- Tremors
- Fine motor problems
- Low/excessive motivation
- Sensitivity to rejection
- Social anxiety

When Dr. Emina showed entrepreneur Neels Visser his brain scans, he pointed out that there was high activity in the basal ganglia. As Dr. Emina explained it, the basal ganglia is involved in many useful things, as you can see from the list above. Having extra activity in this brain region comes with some benefits, including heightened positive feelings from pleasurable activities and dexterity since the basal ganglia is associated with fine motor movement.

"I try to get patients to channel this extra activity into something," Dr. Emina said. That could be playing a musical instrument, knitting, making ceramics, painting, woodworking, or any other form of activity that involves some form of handiwork. Neels intuitively found a way to express that by producing music and being a DJ.

"We actually need anxiety," Dr. Emina continued. "Everybody thinks that anxiety is a bad thing, but you're not supposed to try to completely avoid anxiety. You're supposed to see it as your brain is trying to tell you something."

That anxiety is your brain warning you of potential danger. It may be reminding you of something you did that caused you to be injured physically or to be hurt emotionally. It is your brain's way of telling you, "Don't make that mistake again!"

As Dr. Emina shared with Neels, "I actually get concerned when people go too low in anxiety. Some people will try to get themselves to go really low in anxiety, whether it's with prescribed meds or with nonprescribed options like weed or alcohol. But if you dip your anxiety too low, you will eventually impact your motivation." What you need, and what the Cautious Brain Type can strive for, is a healthy amount of anxiety—enough to motivate you to get things done but not so much that fears and worries prevent you from feeling happy.

BRAIN TYPE 5: CAUTIOUS NEUROCHEMICALS OF HAPPINESS

In our clinical experience at Amen Clinics, we have found that people with the Cautious Brain Type tend to have low levels of the neurotransmitter GABA and high levels of cortisol. Let's take a closer look at how these chemicals influence Brain Type 5.

GABA—the molecule of calmness

Gamma aminobutyric acid (GABA) is the primary inhibitory neurotransmitter in the brain. GABA's primary role is to reduce brain cell excitability and slow down the firing of neurons. It helps balance more stimulating neurotransmitters, such as dopamine and adrenaline. Too much stimulation can cause anxiety, insomnia, and seizures; while too little nerve cell firing can cause lethargy, confusion, and sedation. Again, it is about balance.

A wide variety of cells in the brain and body make GABA. It has relaxing, antianxiety, and anticonvulsant effects, and it increases a sense of calmness in many of my patients. Low GABA levels have been found in patients with anxiety, panic attacks, alcoholism, bipolar disorder, tremors, and epilepsy. Deficiencies can be caused by poor nutrition; chronic, unremitting stress; or genetics (more likely if you have anxious family members).

GABA has been found to be helpful to reduce symptoms of anxiety, alcohol withdrawal, high blood pressure, overeating, premenstrual syndrome, and some cases of depression. I recently suggested a teenager take the supplement GABA. After a few weeks of trying it, his mother wrote, "GABA has helped my son! He had been struggling with racing thoughts. The pandemic seemed to have triggered something in him where his mind wouldn't calm down. He was having a hard time falling asleep. I noticed a significant positive difference in his disposition. He makes sure to take it every day."

One of my favorite GABA pandemic stories happened at home. Tana and I work together. We have recorded more than 1,000 episodes of *The Brain Warrior's Way Podcast* and four national public television specials. Initially, we struggled working together, as we both have strong personalities, but over time, we made it work for us. For the public television specials, I write the scripts, and she edits her sections as we read through them. Sometimes that can bring up tension or disagreements. During the pandemic, the societal unrest caused a lot of anxiety for Tana, and I suggested she take our GABA Calming Support supplement. A few weeks later, we were preparing for our latest public television special, "Overcoming Anxiety, Depression, Trauma, and Grief." During the script readings, she was thoughtful as usual but much mellower. There was no tension at all between us. When we finished, she looked at me and said, "That was so easy. I didn't feel the need to continuously say no." We both thought the GABA helped a lot.

Certain classes of drugs, such as benzodiazepines (e.g., Xanax, Valium, Ativan), increase GABA, but they can be addictive, so I generally avoid those drugs, as well as antiseizure medications, with patients.

Here are eight natural ways to balance GABA.

1. **Eat the building blocks of GABA.** Foods do not contain GABA, but your brain and body use compounds found in green, black, or Oolong teas, lentils, berries, grass-fed beef, wild-caught fish, seaweed, noni fruits, potatoes, and tomatoes to create GABA.

2. **Get adequate amounts of B6.** Vitamin B6, abundant in spinach, garlic, broccoli, brussels sprouts, and bananas, is a required cofactor for GABA synthesis.

3. **Consume fermented foods.** Beneficial bacteria in the gut can synthesize GABA. Fermented foods such as sauerkraut, kimchi, plain kefir, and coconut water kefir can increase GABA levels.

4. **Promote healthy GABA production with probiotics.** Probiotics, especially *Lactobacillus rhamnosus,* increase GABA. Other strains to consider include *Lactobacillus paracasei, Lactobacillus brevis,* and *Lactococcus lactis.*

5. **Try nutraceuticals.** Supplements such as GABA, lemon balm, l-theanine, magnesium, taurine, passionflower, and valerian have been shown to enhance levels of this critical neurotransmitter.

6. **Meditate.** Research suggests that meditation is linked to GABA production and enhances emotional regulation.[5]

7. **Practice your downward dog.** One study found a 27 percent increase in GABA levels among yoga practitioners after a 60-minute session as compared to participants who read for an hour.[6]

8. **Eliminate GABA robbers.** Caffeine, nicotine, alcohol, and chronic stress all deplete GABA. If you have the Cautious Brain Type, do your best to limit or avoid these.

Cortisol—the molecule of danger

Known primarily as the stress hormone, cortisol is so much more. Made in the adrenal glands that sit on top of your kidneys, its release is controlled by the brain, especially the hypothalamus and pituitary gland, when you feel danger. Because most cells in the body have cortisol receptors, it affects many functions. Cortisol is involved in the fight-or-flight response to threat, helps control blood sugar levels, regulates metabolism, decreases inflammation, and helps us form new memories, especially about possible threats. It also helps balance blood pressure and salt and water ratios. Cortisol is a crucial hormone to protect overall health and well-being. It is generally higher in the morning and gradually decreases throughout the day.

Cortisol is also released during periods of stress. If stress is too high or lasts too long (think the COVID-19 pandemic), cortisol can damage the body. High levels of cortisol are associated with anxiety, depression, irritability, grief, headaches, memory loss (shrinks the hippocampus), weight gain, especially around the belly and face, thin and fragile skin that's slow to heal, type 2 diabetes, easy bruising, a heightened vulnerability to infections, acne, and for women, facial hair and irregular menstrual periods—none of which contribute to happiness. Chronically low levels of cortisol are associated with fatigue, dizziness, weight loss, muscle weakness, areas of the skin that turn darker, low blood pressure, and an inability to manage stress. Balance is important.

In a study of 216 middle-aged men and women whose cortisol levels were measured eight times during the day, researchers found lower cortisol levels were associated with happiness.[7] In addition, the happiest group had lower heart rates and other signs of a healthier heart.

Stress, caffeine, nicotine, intense prolonged exercise, long commutes, sleep apnea and poor sleep quality, unsettling noises, and low zinc levels all raise cortisol. Sugar releases cortisol, so it helps you feel good in the moment, but in the long-term it increases inflammation and damages your immune system.

Here are 13 simple ways to balance cortisol.

1. **Get your zzz's.** Aim for at least seven hours of quality sleep each night to balance cortisol.

2. **Get moving.** Physical activity keeps cortisol in check. Just don't overdo it, and don't engage in intense exercise too close to your bedtime.

3. **Meditate.** Numerous studies have found that meditation lowers stress and cortisol levels.

4. **Try hypnosis.** Foundational research dating back to the 1960s shows that medical hypnosis sessions can lower cortisol levels.[8] (Medical hypnosis focuses on supporting and restoring the mind.) At Amen Clinics, we have found benefits in using hypnosis for overcoming anxiety, reducing pain, enhancing sleep, and more.

5. **Experiment with tapping.** Emotional Freedom Technique (EFT), which is often referred to as EFT tapping, is a natural treatment that has been used since the 1990s for anxiety, depression, PTSD, chronic pain, and other issues. Research shows EFT can lower cortisol.[9]

6. **Laugh more.** Getting a good chuckle can decrease levels of the molecule of danger.

7. **Engage in deep breathing.** Just a few deep belly breaths can almost instantly lower cortisol, along with heart rate and blood pressure, to help you relax.

8. **Turn on some relaxing tunes.** Music can soothe your soul and curb cortisol production.

9. **Practice tai chi.** This slow-moving form of martial arts can reduces mental and emotional stress and causes a dip in cortisol levels.[10]

10. **Get a massage.** A rubdown can do wonders for your neurochemicals of happiness—lowering cortisol while increasing dopamine and serotonin.[11]

11. **Adopt a furry friend.** Having a dog, cat, or other pet that you can cuddle has been shown to ramp up bliss and minimize the molecule of danger.

12. **Eat healthy foods.** Dark chocolate, pears, fiber, green and black tea, and water can help balance cortisol.[12] (More on this in chapter 11.)

13. **Try targeted nutraceuticals.** Supplements such as ashwagandha, rhodiola, phosphatidylserine, l-theanine, and fish oil can be beneficial in lowering the stress hormone.

Happiness prescription for Brain Type 5: Cautious

Support your brain type. Follow the suggestions above to boost GABA and calm cortisol and engage in brain healthy behaviors that protect your brain and soothe your basal ganglia.

Understand your career path. You like job security and tend to have an analytical mind, which makes careers in accounting, research, or data mining popular among Cautious types.

Appreciate your learning style. You like to tackle new subjects with gusto, starting early and putting in extra hours in the evenings or on weekends. Despite being well-prepared, jitters when you have a test or need to give a presentation can cause you to underachieve.

Know what you want in a relationship. You may have a fear of rejection and don't like being judged, so you tend to seek out someone who will give you ample reassurance and boost your confidence.

When You're in a Relationship with the Cautious Brain Type

Having a Cautious Brain Type in your life can keep you from doing unsafe, irrational, or unproven things. Count on these people to be prepared whether they're in charge of the slides for your work presentation, making reservations for your annual golf trip with the guys, or cooking a romantic dinner for you. They're never going to forget to preheat the oven, and they'll remember that you love asparagus but hate brussels sprouts. Sometimes all that preparedness can twist into anxiousness that makes it hard for them to relax. They may become clingy and needy, which may be a turnoff, or they may avoid any type of conflict. They can let issues fester until they become major problems.

To improve relationships with these people, make them feel safe, valued, and loved. And gently encourage them to relax—a foot rub after work, calming essential oils at the office, or going for a spa day with friends.

What their romantic partners say:
"I never have to worry that she'll be late."
"He cares too much about what other people think of him."

What their coworkers say:
"If you need some help organizing that project, he's the right guy for the job."
"She always shoots down new ideas and finds reasons they won't work."

What their friends say:
"I love being able to rely on him."
"I wish she could just relax and have fun for once."

Watch for times when you get off track. Pay attention to when you start to sink into worst-case scenarios. Don't allow anxiety to take charge. Put an immediate halt to rising anxious thoughts with deep breathing so you can reassess the situation.

Know what makes you uniquely happy. Make a list of the things that bring you joy and look at it every day to remind yourself of the activities you love.

What makes people with the Cautious Brain Type happy?

- Being surrounded by a calm environment
- Everything being in its place and having a place for everything
- A substantial hike in the great outdoors
- A warm bath at the end of the day
- Adding calming scents to bathwater
- Making a pros-and-cons list before a big decision
- Taking a vacation close to home
- Having an excellent dental checkup
- Balancing a checkbook to the penny
- Finishing an assignment on time

What makes people with the Cautious Brain Type unhappy?

- Being in a chaotic environment
- Living in the future with fear
- Being late for an appointment
- Having too much to do
- Physical stress symptoms that make them think something is seriously wrong
- Reading about or watching news disasters
- Hearing loud sounds or seeing bright lights
- Imagining worst-case scenarios
- Missing their daily calming routines

☺ **Look for the micro-moments of happiness.**

- That moment when you slip into a warm bath and stress melts away
- That first sip of chamomile tea as you wind down in the evening
- Feeling snug and secure in a blanket on your couch
- Having 20 minutes to yourself with a calming meditation
- A beautiful morning hike with your partner

BRAIN TYPES 6–16

It is common to have more than one brain type. As a reminder, Brain Types 6–16 are a combination of Brain Types 2–5:

Brain Type 6: Spontaneous-Persistent
Brain Type 7: Spontaneous-Persistent-Sensitive
Brain Type 8: Spontaneous-Persistent-Sensitive-Cautious
Brain Type 9: Persistent-Sensitive-Cautious
Brain Type 10: Persistent-Sensitive
Brain Type 11: Persistent-Cautious
Brain Type 12: Spontaneous-Persistent-Cautious
Brain Type 13: Spontaneous-Cautious
Brain Type 14: Spontaneous-Sensitive
Brain Type 15: Spontaneous-Sensitive-Cautious
Brain Type 16: Sensitive-Cautious

If you have a combination type, it means you may have some of the characteristic traits of each of those types. As the names above suggest, you may be Spontaneous in some ways and Persistent in others, or you may be Sensitive *and* Cautious. You may find that one set of traits is more dominant at certain times of your life and another set takes over at other times.

As an example, let's look at Brain Type 6: Spontaneous-Persistent. At Amen Clinics, we often see this type in children and grandchildren of alcoholics.

Spontaneous-Persistent people tend to be:

• Spontaneous
• Risk-taking
• Creative, out-of-the-box thinkers
• Restless
• Easily distracted
• Only able to focus if interested
• Persistent
• Relentless or strong-willed
• Stuck on thoughts

The SPECT scans of this type typically show lower activity in the PFC (executive function and decision making) as well as increased activity in the ACG (flexibility and attention). Spontaneous-Persistent types also tend to have lower dopamine and serotonin levels. The best strategies to balance

Brain Type 6 include natural ways to boost both dopamine and serotonin. Physical exercise boosts both dopamine and serotonin, as does using a combination of certain supplements, such as 5-HTP and green tea.

In terms of the happiness prescriptions for combination brain types, try a mix of the suggested interventions for types 2–5 based on which traits are most dominant. The key is finding balance for the neurochemicals of happiness and optimizing activity in your brain.

HAPPINESS HIGHLIGHTS FOR SECRET 1:
KNOW YOUR BRAIN TYPE

- Support your brain type: Balanced, Spontaneous, Persistent, Sensitive, Cautious, or a combination type.
- Understand your career path.
- Appreciate your learning style.
- Know what you want in a relationship.
- Watch for times when you get off track.
- Know what makes you uniquely happy, including micro-moments of happiness unique to you.

MAIN BRAIN TYPE SUMMARY

Low Score	Trait	High Score
Short attention span Impulsivity Undependability Worry Negativity Anxiety	BALANCED	Focus Good impulse control Conscientiousness Flexibility Positivity Resilience Emotional stability
Hatred of surprises Risk aversion Routine Affinity for sameness Convention Practicality Attention to detail Impulse control Feeling settled	SPONTANEOUS	Spontaneity Risk-taking Creativity, out-of-the-box thinking Curiosity Wide range of interests Short attention span Impulsiveness; careless mistakes Restlessness Disorganization Love of surprises Tendency toward ADD
Adaptability Timidity Spontaneity Flexibility Letting go of negativity easily Letting go of hurts easily Ability to see what is right Being noncritical Cooperation	PERSISTENT	Persistence Strong will Preference for routine Unbending Easily "stuck" on thoughts Holding on to hurts Tendency to see what is wrong Opposition/argumentativeness Obsessive-compulsive tendencies
Superficiality Consistent happiness Positive thoughts	SENSITIVE	Sensitivity Deep feelings Empathy Mood variability Pessimism Lots of ANTs (automatic negative thoughts) Depression
Lack of concern about preparation Risk taking Calmness Ability to relax Quiet mind Even temper Security	CAUTIOUS	Preparation Caution Risk aversion Motivation Reserve Busy mindedness Moodiness Difficulty relaxing Anxiety

PART 2

THE BIOLOGY
OF HAPPINESS

OPTIMIZE THE PHYSICAL FUNCTIONING OF YOUR BRAIN

QUESTION 2

Is this good for my brain or bad for it?

CHAPTER 9

BRIGHT MINDS ARE HAPPIER

11 Essential Strategies to Optimize Your Brain for a More Positive Outlook

---

I slowly learned that being happy comes down to making sure
you not only are using all parts of your brain in a balanced
way, but are also connecting your brain and your body.

WENDY SUZUKI, PHD, *HEALTHY BRAIN, HAPPY LIFE*

Brain health is the missing link to happiness, great relationships, and peak performance. My friend Tony Robbins and many other self-help teachers give useful strategies for optimizing the software of your mind, but if the hardware is not working right, you'll never be or feel your best. The foundational secret to happiness is that you must first optimize the physical functioning of your brain. When you do, you are much more likely to implement the other secrets of happiness and be happier on a consistent basis.

One of the most important lessons from our work at Amen Clinics over the last 30 years is if you want to keep your brain healthy, or rescue it if it is headed for trouble, you must prevent or treat the 11 major risk factors that steal your mind. The good news is that most of them are preventable or treatable. To help you remember these risk factors, I created the mnemonic BRIGHT MINDS. I have written extensively about these factors in my books *Memory Rescue* and *The End of Mental Illness*,[1] so I will only summarize the main points here and show you the intriguing ways these risk factors relate to your happiness.

HAPPINESS TRANSFORMATION IN 30 DAYS

I love the question, "Is this good for my brain?" I have stopped thinking about my brain as something that is just hardwired. I get to choose!

—JB

Blood Flow
Retirement and Aging
Inflammation
Genetics
Head Trauma
Toxins

Mental Health Issues
Immunity and Infections
Neurohormone Issues
Diabesity
Sleep

BLOOD FLOW

Blood brings nourishment to every cell in your body and takes away waste products. Research suggests that blood vessels age faster than brain cells. Anything that damages blood vessels also damages your brain and starves it of the nutrients it needs. Low blood flow is associated with depression, attention deficit hyperactivity disorder (ADHD), and schizophrenia. It is also the number one predictor of Alzheimer's disease. In my experience with our patients, I have found that when they improve blood flow to the brain, it can make them happier.

So how do you improve brain blood flow today?

- Hydrate. Your brain is 80 percent water. Any form of dehydration is bad for your brain.

- Limit caffeine and nicotine. Both constrict blood flow to the brain. A cup of coffee a day is not a problem, but more caffeine than that can be trouble.

- Be serious about treating high blood pressure. As blood pressure goes up, blood flow to the brain goes down.

- If you have any heart issues, make sure to address them—anything that damages your heart also damages your brain.

- Avoid being a couch potato. Exercise, especially with coordination exercises (people who play racquet sports live longer than everyone else) and walking like you're late. Did you know that people who are 80 who can walk 3.5 miles an hour have about an 85 percent chance of living to

90; but those who can only walk one mile an hour have a 90 percent chance of not living to 90?[2]

- Eating chili peppers, rosemary, and beets can help increase blood flow. In addition, eating dark chocolate, which is rich in blood flow–friendly flavanols, can support the oxygenation of brain cells and improve cognitive performance.[3]

- The supplement ginkgo biloba can help; the prettiest brains I've ever seen take ginkgo.

- I also like a treatment called hyperbaric oxygen therapy (HBOT) because I've seen it increase blood flow to the brain. We published a study using HBOT on veterans with brain injuries and showed it significantly increased blood flow and helped improve their memory and mood.[4]

- Practice happiness. Exciting research using brain SPECT imaging shows that happiness training—which involves positive psychology interventions (see chapter 13 for more information)—increases blood flow to the frontal regions of the brain.[5]

- Think about happy memories. Something as simple as remembering happy events from your life activates many areas of the brain.[6]

- Watch a comedy. Laughing while viewing funny movies increases vascular function.[7]

RETIREMENT AND AGING

The older you get, the more serious you need to be about doing the right things for your brain. Brain imaging work reveals that your brain typically becomes less and less active with age. I hate that! Below are SPECT scans of a healthy 35-year-old compared to a 55-year-old man with mild memory problems and an 82-year-old woman who suffered from depression and memory problems.

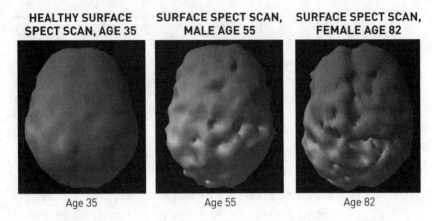

HEALTHY SURFACE SPECT SCAN, AGE 35   **SURFACE SPECT SCAN, MALE AGE 55**   **SURFACE SPECT SCAN, FEMALE AGE 82**

Age 35   Age 55   Age 82

Now, compare these to my grandmother's scan at 92. She lived to 98 with a completely clear mind.

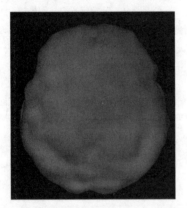

Dr. Amen's grandmother's brain scan

Dr. Amen's grandmother (right)

One of the most astonishing things I've discovered from looking at SPECT scans is that your brain does not have to degenerate. The right plan can delay or even reverse the aging process. Now, that should make anyone feel happier. To decrease the risks from retirement and aging, avoid anything that accelerates it, such as:

- Loneliness, which is associated with depression and dementia. A 2019 study found that three in five Americans report feeling lonely,[8] and loneliness exploded during the pandemic.

- Dropping out of school early or having a limited education.

- Being in a job that does not require new learning or being retired and not challenging your brain. When you stop learning, your brain starts dying.

- High ferritin levels; a ferritin blood test measures iron storage. High ferritin promotes aging.

- Short telomeres. Telomeres are the end caps of chromosomes, like plastic caps on shoelaces. They protect your genes. Shorter telomeres are associated with aging and memory problems but are not an inevitable sign. Four years ago, I had my own telomeres tested. I was 63, but my telomere age was 43. I'm not bragging much, but I live the message. HBOT was found to also lower telomere age.

To slow retirement and aging, research shows that these strategies can help:

- Lifelong learning and memory training programs.

- Being socially connected and volunteering.

- Meditating.

- Being engaged in life but taking time to rest, too. Older adults who integrate activities with rest and relaxation are happier.[9]

- Taking a daily multivitamin.

- Eating foods that contain vitamin C, such as strawberries and red bell peppers, is associated with increased telomere length.

- One of my grandmother's secrets was that she kept her mind active and spent thousands of hours knitting blankets for those she loved. Knitting is a coordination exercise that activates the cerebellum, which is involved with processing speed and memory.

INFLAMMATION

Inflammation comes from a Latin word meaning "to set a fire." If inflammation is high in your body, it's as if a low-level fire is destroying your organs, which increases your risk of depression and dementia. Blood tests for inflammation include measuring C-reactive protein and the omega-3 index. Having rosacea and joint pain are also signs of inflammation. You may know that too much inflammation is associated with cancer and arthritis, but did you know that it is also linked to depression, autism, and dementia?

You can control a number of important and surprising causes of chronic inflammation, such as:

- A diet high in sugar and processed foods. The Standard American Diet is killing us, making us fatter and more inflamed than ever (more on this in chapter 11). Get your food right, and your mind will follow.

- Gum disease is a major cause of inflammation, and poor oral health has been linked to depression and anxiety.[10] You must floss and take care of your teeth. I was always too busy to floss until I saw the research showing gum disease was a major cause of inflammation, depression, and memory loss. Now I floss every day. I was recently at the dentist, and he told me my mouth looks better than ever. I was like a seven-year-old kid, so happy that I wanted to put a sticker on the refrigerator. I even called Tana to tell her, and she was like, "Seriously? That's what makes you happy?"

- Low levels of omega-3 fatty acids are another common cause of inflammation that affects 97 percent of the population. No wonder we have an epidemic of brain health issues. Taking omega-3s has been found to help with mood, focus, memory, and weight. In a new study we published in the *Journal of Alzheimer's Disease*, the hippocampus (memory and mood) was healthiest in people who had the highest omega-3 levels.[11]

- Gut problems are also a major cause of chronic inflammation and have been associated with depression. What do the gut and brain have to do with each other? Everything. Three-fourths of your neurotransmitters are made in your gut. It is often called the second brain because it is loaded with nervous system tissue. This is why you may feel excited and have butterflies in your stomach or wind up with loose stools when you feel anxious or stressed. Taking care of your gut is critical to lowering inflammation, and that's why probiotics have been shown to help your brain.

- Perceived unhappiness. Just thinking that you aren't a very happy person is associated with increased levels of pro-inflammatory cytokines (proteins).[12] On the flip side, people who consider themselves to be happy tend to have lower levels of these harmful compounds.

- Lack of positivity. People who say they have few positive experiences on a daily basis have higher levels of inflammation. Being able to point to frequent moments of positivity throughout the day is associated with lower levels of inflammation.[13]

GENETICS

Depression, anxiety, ADHD, Alzheimer's disease, and other mental health and cognitive issues run in families the same way heart disease does. Emerging research shows that your overall sense of well-being—aka happiness—also has a genetic component. A 2015 study in *Behavior Genetics* found that genetics accounted for about one third of a person's life satisfaction.[14] Does this mean if you grew up in a family with negativity, anxiousness, or unhappiness that you are doomed to experience it too? No! Despite what most people think, genetic risk is not a death sentence; rather, it should be a wake-up call to get serious about all of your risk factors, including the genetic ones, and be diligent about prevention as soon as possible.

- If you think you're at genetic risk for brain issues, early screening is essential. At Amen Clinics, we use brain SPECT imaging in addition to psychological assessments and other testing as brain health screening tools. Sadly, brain imaging is not standard practice in psychiatry or in the medical field. When I turned 50, my doctor told me I should have a colonoscopy. I asked him why he didn't want to look at my brain as well. Weren't both ends just as important? As a society, we screen our hearts, bones, breasts, and prostate glands, but very few people ever look at their brains. In the future, that will change.

- Test your genes with 23andMe or other genetic testing services to know your vulnerabilities, and meet with a medical professional to help you interpret the results.

- The most important thing to do if you have genetic risk factors is to be serious about prevention as soon as possible. Stop making excuses, like it's too hard, too expensive, or you don't want to feel deprived. Trust me, losing your memory and independence is hard and expensive, and you and your family will feel deprived!

- Take responsibility for your life and your happiness. If 40 percent of your sense of well-being lies in genetics, that means 60 percent is in your hands. You are in control of your outlook on life.

HEAD TRAUMA

Your brain is about the consistency of soft butter, while your skull is hard with sharp bony ridges inside. Head injuries, even mild ones that occurred decades ago, are a major cause of depression, addictions, and memory problems. A study from the Mayo Clinic found that one-third of people who played football at *any* level had lasting brain damage.[15] I played football in high school, and it showed when I first scanned my brain, but my scan was much better 20 years later because I'd taken the same steps I'm telling you to take.

If you've had a head injury, the good news is that many things can help it heal, even years later. Amen Clinics did the first and largest brain imaging study on active and retired NFL players. The level of damage was alarming, but what really excited us was that on our BRIGHT MINDS program, 80 percent of our players showed significant improvement in blood flow, mood, memory, attention, and sleep. When you feel better, have better recall, and sleep better, you are more likely to be on top of your game, and that makes you happier.

Mercedes Maidana is another great example. She is a famous big-wave surfer, motivational speaker, and life coach from Argentina. She suffered a serious concussion surfing a 30-foot wave off the coast of Oregon. Subsequently, she suffered from anxiety, depression, and memory problems. Her scan showed low activity in her brain, but by changing her diet, taking targeted supplements, and doing HBOT, today she is happier, thriving, and leading health retreats for women. If you put your brain in a healing environment, it can get better, but it is critical to protect it, especially for developing brains. So if you have children and want them to grow up to be happy adults, encourage them to stick with brain healthy sports.

TOXINS

Your brain is the most metabolically active organ in your body. It makes up only 2 percent of your body's weight, but it requires 20–30 percent of the calories you take in and 20 percent of your blood flow and oxygen. Exposure to any toxin can damage your brain and your happiness. Toxins are some of the most common causes of depression, anxiety, brain fog, irritability, sleep disorders, confusion, memory loss, and aging. But the root cause of these issues—toxic exposure—often goes undetected.

When I first started performing SPECT scans, I noticed a toxic pattern on the brains of substance abusers (alcoholics, cocaine addicts, and marijuana users). At Amen Clinics, we published a study on nearly a thousand pot smokers compared to nonusers. As a group, the pot smokers showed lower blood flow in every area of the brain, especially the hippocampus (mood and memory).[16] This is clear evidence that getting stoned can cause lasting damage.

The scans taught me another important lesson. Besides drugs and alcohol, many other things are toxic to your brain, such as:

- Smoking, even secondhand smoke

- Mold exposure, from water damage

- Carbon monoxide

- Chemotherapy and radiation. As they kill cancer cells, they also kill healthy cells

- Heavy metals, including mercury, aluminum, and lead. Did you know that when the government took lead out of gasoline, they left it in small airplane fuel? We did an in-house analysis on 100 pilots and found 70 percent had toxic-looking brains. Lead is also found in 60 percent of lipstick sold in the US. Be careful who you kiss, or it could be the kiss of death.

At Amen Clinics, our patients who have been exposed to toxins are some of the unhappiest because they feel like they have lost their personality. Look at Pamela. She came to us because she could no longer finish a sentence, sometimes forgot her children's names, and was spending her days in bed.

"This wasn't the person I was before," she said. "I was a vibrant, successful businesswoman. I had it all together and then all of a sudden, I was falling apart." For Pamela, things kept getting progressively worse as the years went by. "I ended up getting depressed because it seemed like nobody really understood," she said.

After extensive testing, we discovered Pamela had been exposed to toxic mold in addition to having Lyme disease and other issues. With targeted treatment, she was able to start feeling like herself again.

If you have any of these risk factors, such as mold exposure or chemotherapy, it means you need to be even more serious about taking care of your brain just like you would if you have a genetic risk or head trauma.

To decrease your toxic risk:

- Limit your exposure whenever you can.

- Buy organic foods to decrease pesticide consumption.

- Read labels! If a product lists ingredients such as phthalates, parabens, or aluminum, don't buy it. What goes on your body goes in your body and affects your brain.

Also support the four organs of detoxification, including your:

- Kidneys—drink more water

- Gut—make sure to eat plenty of fiber

- Skin—sweat with exercise and take saunas. Saunas have been found to help depression in cancer patients,[17] increase feel-good endorphins,[18] and lower the stress hormone cortisol.[19]

- Liver—Eat more brassicas, which are detoxifying vegetables, such as broccoli, cauliflower, cabbage, and brussels sprouts.

One thing you can do today is download one of the many free apps, like Think Dirty, to scan your personal products and see how toxic they are. They'll tell you on a scale of 1–10 how quickly they're killing you. When I first used one, I threw out half the products in my bathroom.

MENTAL HEALTH ISSUES

Untreated mental health issues, such as depression, anxiety, bipolar disorder, obsessive-compulsive disorder (OCD), ADHD, addictions, and chronic stress can hurt the brain and make you unhappy. Exposure to stress hormones over time has been shown to shrink the hippocampi involved with mood and memory. If you struggle with any of these issues, it's critical to get them treated. In a 2015 study, researchers found that average happiness appears to be higher in countries that invest more in mental health care.[20] Be aware, however, that mental health treatment does not necessarily mean medicine. In a 2016 article in the *American Journal of Psychiatry*, researchers wrote that nutraceuticals (supplements with medicinal effects) were a low-cost option that should be considered in the treatment of depression.[21]

In making recommendations for our patients at Amen Clinics, we always try to keep a number of principles in mind, and you should too whenever you go to the doctor, such as:

- Use the least toxic, most-effective treatments.

- Don't start something you will have a hard time stopping just to deal with the anxiety of the moment. For example, many people are prescribed antianxiety or antidepressant medication in very short office visits, and doctors rarely tell them these pills may be hard to stop.

- Medications should never be the first and only treatment.

- Skills, not just pills. Once we optimize the physical functioning of the brain, we then need to give people the skills they need to program it properly.

If I am dealing with someone who has severe depression, bipolar disorder, or schizophrenia, I usually start with medication to stabilize their situation while I'm trying to figure out what may have caused it. At the same time, I am always trying to support the patient's nutritional status to be able to lower any medications that may be needed. In my book *The End of Mental Illness*, I share our method for dealing with many brain health issues, such as depression, addictions, bipolar disorder, and ADHD. But for now, let me show you just six things I recommend for anxiety before prescribing medications:

1. Check for low blood sugar, anemia, and hyperthyroidism, as these can cause anxiety.

2. Meditation and slow, deep belly breathing can immediately increase a sense of calmness.

3. Medical hypnosis and visualization exercises can be powerful to calm anxiety.

4. Calming exercises such as yoga or qi gong can help.

5. Kill the automatic negative thoughts (see chapter 13) that make you feel awful. You do not have to believe every stupid thought you have.

6. Start with nutritional supplements like l-theanine, GABA, and magnesium before resorting to antianxiety medications that are hard to stop.

All of these strategies have research showing they may help you, and *none* of them will ever hurt you. We cannot always say that about medications.

Let me tell you about Terry,[22] who had a hard time keeping up in school. His parents and teachers made him believe that he was "lazy, stupid, and irresponsible." He felt an incredible amount of shame his whole life. He eventually dropped out of school, fell into depression, and lived in isolation. He didn't believe he could ever have a family and worked very hard just to get by. When he was 46, his mental health worsened, and he believed something must be wrong with his brain, but his MRI was normal, which it often is. An MRI looks at the brain's structure, when the problem is often with how the brain functions.

When he came to our clinic in New York, his SPECT scan showed severe damage to his frontal lobes, which was consistent with a traumatic brain injury. He later learned from his mother that his injury had happened when he was a small child. When he talked to his mother about the scan, they both cried together for hours when they realized he didn't have a bad attitude but a troubled brain.

Terry got serious about rehabilitating his brain, using our BRIGHT MINDS program, including diet, supplements, and HBOT. Months later, his scans showed dramatic improvement, as did his life. His mood, energy, and hope have soared, and he now sees a much brighter future for himself, including the possibility of a family.

TERRY

Terry (right) with Dr. Sandy Lowe from our New York City clinic

TERRY'S SPECT SCANS BEFORE AND AFTER

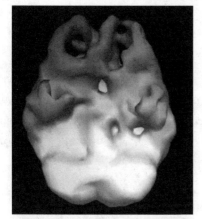

Severe damage to frontal
and temporal lobes

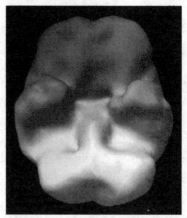

Marked overall improvement

IMMUNITY AND INFECTIONS

Your immune system protects you from outside invaders, such as viruses like COVID-19, and internal troublemakers, such as cancer cells. When your immune system is weak, you're more likely to get infections or cancer. When it's overactive, you are more likely to have autoimmune disorders, such as rheumatoid arthritis or multiple sclerosis, as well as increasing your risk for depression, anxiety, and even psychosis. Having any kind of illness saps the joy out of your life.

Take COVID-19 long haulers, for example. Most people who were infected with COVID-19 found that their symptoms eventually subsided after a period of several weeks. However, medical practitioners became aware of a subset of patients who had symptoms that persisted even long after their COVID-19 tests were negative. One might expect that problems such as shortness of breath, lingering cough, and body aches—among others—could take a while to subside after catching the virus, especially if a person had been hospitalized with COVID-19. But surprisingly, a significant number of people—even if they only had mild or moderate cases—experienced ongoing brain-related symptoms, such as:

- Depression
- Anxiety
- Intense fatigue
- Brain fog or difficulty thinking clearly
- Concentration and memory problems

- Headaches
- Sleep problems
- Loss of taste and smell

These lingering symptoms from the infection robbed people of their zest for life. At Amen Clinics, we are seeing a growing number of patients with ongoing symptoms. Their post-COVID-19 SPECT scans show a number of abnormalities, including overall decreased blood flow, which is a pattern often seen with infections and is associated with brain fog and memory problems, and heightened activity in the emotional centers of the brain, which is common in depression.

ACTIVE SPECT SCANS BEFORE AND AFTER COVID-19

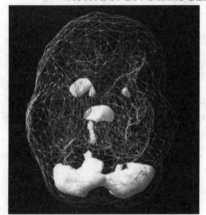

Before COVID-19 infection

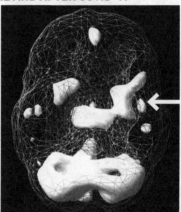

After COVID-19 infection, heightened activity in the limbic system

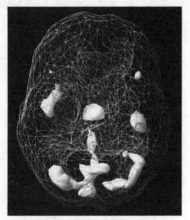

Before COVID-19 infection

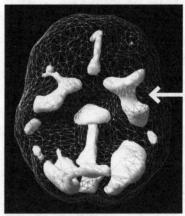

After COVID-19 infection—heightened activity in the limbic system

ACTIVE AND SURFACE SPECT SCAN OF LONG-HAUL COVID-19 PATIENT

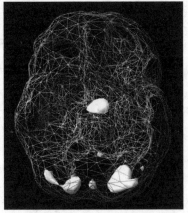 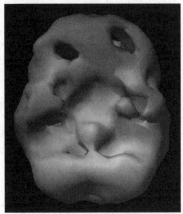

Low activity in cerebellum, and
lower overall activity

Lower overall activity

Sometimes infections can masquerade as other health problems. You may have read in the news that country music legend Kris Kristofferson was diagnosed with Alzheimer's disease. He saw one of the doctors who works with us, Mark Filidei, DO, who discovered Kris actually had Lyme disease. On antibiotics and HBOT, his memory improved, and he was back on the road touring again, although he has since retired at the age of 84. If you're struggling with your memory or a mental health issue that does not respond to typical treatments, ask your physician to explore infectious diseases.

Some of the best ways to strengthen your immunity include:

- Knowing and optimizing your Vitamin D level.

- Taking probiotics, because gut health is critical to your immunity.

- Eating foods in the allium family, such as garlic and onions, as well as antimicrobial, anti-inflammatory mushrooms.

- Trying an elimination diet for a month to see if food allergies may be damaging your immune system (eliminate gluten, dairy, corn, soy, sugar and artificial sweeteners, dyes, and preservatives).

- Avoiding hiking where deer ticks live (Lyme disease).

- Watching a comedy to boost your immune system. During the pandemic, Tana's mom, Mary, spent the night with us before her vaccine appointment the next day. She's in her seventies and usually falls asleep whenever we watch movies together. I picked a movie I thought would keep her awake, *The War with Grandpa* with Robert De Niro. It was heartwarming and absolutely hysterical. Mary not only stayed awake, but she also laughed the entire time, which boosts immune system function. And Tana couldn't help but laugh seeing her mom chuckling like that. Laughter is contagious. That's the kind of contagion you want.

- Adopting a positive outlook. Did you know that having a negative outlook—what psychiatrists call a negative affective style—is associated with poor recruitment of the immune response and a possible heightened risk for illness? By contrast, people who are happier may have a more effective immune response.[23]

NEUROHORMONE ISSUES

Neurohormones are like Miracle-Gro for your brain and essential for stable moods, a strong memory, and a healthy mind. Without healthy hormones, you feel temperamental, tired, and foggy, and your hippocampi will become smaller and weaker, further impacting your mood.

- Testosterone helps you feel happy, motivated, sexual, and strong.

- Thyroid gives you energy and mental clarity. My friend Dr. Richard Shames says, "Low thyroid doesn't kill you. It just makes you wish you were dead."

- DHEA (a hormone produced in the adrenal glands and available as a supplement) helps fight aging.

- In women, estrogen and progesterone work to prevent mood swings, help boost blood flow, and keep your brain young.

To keep your hormones healthy:

- Test them every year after the age of 40.

- Avoid hormone disruptors, such as pesticides, phthalates, and parabens in personal care products.

- Avoid animal proteins that were raised with hormones or antibiotics.

- Add fiber to decrease unhealthy estrogens.

- Lift weights and limit sugar to boost testosterone.

- For women, optimize estrogen and progesterone levels.

- Use hormone replacement when needed.

- Work with your doctor.

- Try laughter yoga. It may sound silly, but laughter yoga, in which you giggle your way through your sun salutations, reduces cortisol, the stress hormone.[24]

Mercedes, the big-wave surfer I mentioned earlier who had suffered a concussion, had low thyroid, which is common in people who have had head injuries. This is new information and something the Amen Clinics also found in football players. Optimizing Mercedes's thyroid improved her energy and focus. Who doesn't feel happier when that happens?

DIABESITY

Diabesity is a double-barreled threat to your brain. It involves being over-weight or obese and/or having a high blood sugar level (being prediabetic or diabetic). I've published three studies showing that as your weight goes up, the physical size and function of your brain goes down.[25] With 72 percent of Americans overweight (including 42 percent who are obese), and nearly 50 percent diabetic or prediabetic, we are experiencing the biggest brain drain in our country's history.

The excessive fat on your body is not innocuous. It disrupts your hormones, stores toxins, and produces chemicals that increase inflammation. When obesity is combined with diabetes, the risk is worse. High blood sugar levels damage your blood vessels. A wealth of research shows that obesity increases the odds of depression,[26] and some studies indicate that the risk of depression doubles for those with diabetes.[27] Diabesity does not lead to happiness.

To get diabesity under control, you have to get your food right. (See chapter 11 to learn the rules of eating for happiness.)

SLEEP

An estimated 60 million Americans have sleep-related issues. Chronic insom-nia, sleeping pills, and sleep apnea significantly increase the risk of brain health problems and make you feel moody, irritable, and foggy. Here is a scan of someone with sleep apnea. We often see low activity in areas that die early in Alzheimer's. If you snore and stop breathing at night, or someone tells you that you do, get assessed.

SLEEP APNEA SCAN

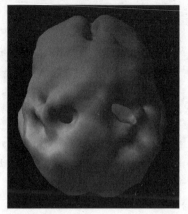

"Holes" indicate areas of low activity

When you sleep, your brain cleans or washes itself. If sleep is disrupted, trash builds up in your brain, which damages your memory. Getting less than seven hours of sleep each night is associated with weight issues, hypertension, accidents, and even trouble in your marriage, because you are more likely to say something you wish you hadn't. If you want to improve your brain and feel better tomorrow, improve your sleep tonight.

Do this by avoiding:

- Caffeine (no caffeine after lunchtime)
- A warm room
- Light and noise, especially from your gadgets
- Alcohol. Yes, it will put you to sleep, but when it wears off, your brain will rebound and wake you up a few hours later.

To sleep better:

- Make your room cooler, darker, and quieter.
- Turn off your gadgets so they don't disturb you.
- Listen to music with a slow, relaxing rhythm (about 60 beats per minute).
- Try medical hypnosis. (Amen Clinics has a powerful program to help you retrain your brain to sleep.)
- Take magnesium and melatonin, which are often very effective, as is 5-HTP if you're a worrier.
- If you have bad thoughts that keep you awake, journal to get them out of your head.

To be happy, you must keep your brain healthy. Use the BRIGHT MINDS approach to get and keep your brain healthy.

TEST YOUR BRAIN

A final thought on brain health and happiness is that it is important to test your brain on a regular basis. We screen many other organs (skin, heart, lungs, breasts, cervix, colon, kidneys, liver, and thyroid) but virtually never screen the most important organ of all—your brain. There are a number of ways to screen for brain health, including:

- Brain SPECT imaging
- Quantitative EEG
- Cognitive tests

All these tools are available at Amen Clinics, but brain imaging is not routinely available in conventional medicine or traditional psychiatry. You can ask your health-care provider about cognitive assessments. Everyone could benefit from a SPECT scan after the age of 50 (40 if you have Alzheimer's disease or dementia in your family). I also recommend that you take the Brain Health Assessment (brainhealthassessment. com) you read about in part 1 on a regular basis. Not

HAPPINESS TRANSFORMATION IN 30 DAYS

This has been a REMARKABLE 30-Day Challenge. I LOVED every minute of it. The daily challenge has something I can really put into practice. The MOST gratifying thing is to be HAPPY EVERY DAY, LOVE MY BRAIN, and pass the word on.

—FD

only does this quiz help identify your brain type, but it also assesses mood, memory, executive function, and flexible thinking.

HAPPINESS HIGHLIGHTS FOR SECRET 2:

OPTIMIZE THE PHYSICAL FUNCTIONING OF YOUR BRAIN

- Improve **B**lood Flow
- Slow **R**etirement and Aging
- Reduce **I**nflammation
- Know **G**enetics
- Avoid **H**ead Trauma
- Reduce exposure to **T**oxins

- Treat **M**ental Health Issues
- Build **I**mmunity to prevent infections
- Balance your **N**eurohormones
- Prevent **D**iabesity
- Get good **S**leep

NOURISH YOUR UNIQUE BRAIN

QUESTION 3

Am I nourishing my unique brain?

CHAPTER 10

HAPPY NUTRACEUTICALS

Natural Ways to Feel Good

If you're too happy, you must've had saffron.

PERSIAN FOLKLORE

Early in the pandemic, our youngest daughter came to Tana and me in tears telling us she was feeling hopeless and depressed. It was common for teenagers during that historically stressful time, when depression had tripled nationwide in just a few months. Just prior to the shutdowns, Chloe had gotten her driver's license, landed her first job as a hostess at Zinc Cafe in Laguna Beach, and was feeling like her life was expanding in ways she had looked forward to for years. In the span of a few days, fear was everywhere, she couldn't go anywhere, and Zinc Cafe closed, so she lost her job.

Often a string of stresses like those stacked together causes depression, and 2020 was filled with stress after stress. Using the strategies of meditation; killing the ANTs (the automatic negative thoughts you will learn about in chapter 13); infrared sauna (shown to be a treatment for depression[1]); and taking the supplements vitamin D, omega-3 fatty acids, and Happy Saffron Plus (which has saffron, zinc, and curcumins), Chloe bounced back within a few weeks to be her usual self. She went on to thrive during that difficult time, graduating from high school with high grades, getting another job later at The Beachcomber, a world-famous restaurant in Newport Coast, and being accepted into college. During the pandemic, everyone in our home (Tana, Chloe, my two nieces who live with us, and I) took Happy Saffron, among a number of other supplements, to promote a more positive mood.

In 2010, I founded BrainMD, a nutraceutical company, initially for patients at Amen Clinics and then for the general public. I'd been following the science of nutraceuticals (supplements with a pharmaceutical effect) since first ordering brain SPECT scans in 1991. The scans surprised me by showing that a number of psychiatric medicines that I had been taught to prescribe—such as benzodiazepines for anxiety, sleeping medications, and opiates for pain—had toxic effects on brain function, making brains look older and less healthy than they should be. This deeply concerned me. *Primum non nocere*—Latin for "first, do no harm"—had been drilled into me in medical school, and doing anything that could potentially harm my patients upset me, so I started looking for science-based natural supplements as an alternative.

My book *The End of Mental Illness* summarizes much of the science of nutraceuticals and major mental health conditions.[2] Here, I'll focus on nutraceuticals that are specifically associated with happiness and mood:

1. The four basics everyone needs to be happy
2. The nutrients that, according to research, support each of the main chemicals of happiness and your brain type
3. The nutraceuticals that have shown overall effectiveness in boosting mood

THE FOUR BASICS EVERYONE NEEDS TO BE HAPPY

1. Multivitamins/minerals

Everyone should take a broad-spectrum multivitamin/mineral supplement daily. According to recent reviews,[3] vitamin and mineral deficiencies are rampant. Look at the list below to see the percentage of Americans who are low in the following vitamins:

- Vitamin D—over 93 percent
- Vitamin E—over 90 percent
- Magnesium—over 54 percent
- Vitamin C—over 37 percent
- Vitamin A—over 45 percent
- Vitamin K—over 31 percent
- Vitamin B6—over 12 percent
- Zinc—over 10 percent
- Folate—over 10 percent

Why are we lacking in so many vital nutrients? According to the Centers for Disease Control and Prevention (CDC), about 90 percent of Americans fail to consume five servings of fruits and vegetables a day,[4] the bare minimum required to get adequate amounts of nutrients. And because most adults aren't getting enough vitamins in their diet, an editorial in the *Journal of the American Medical Association*[5] recommended that everyone take a daily vitamin supplement because it helps prevent chronic illness.

My friend Mark Hyman, MD, the head of strategy and innovation at the Cleveland Clinic for Functional Medicine, explains that people who "eat wild, fresh, organic, whole, local, nongenetically modified food grown in virgin mineral- and nutrient-rich soils that has not been transported across vast distances and stored for months before being eaten . . . and work and live outside, breathe only fresh unpolluted air, drink only pure, clean water, sleep nine hours a night, move their bodies every day, and are free from chronic stressors and exposure to environmental toxins" might not need supplements.[6] However, in our fast-paced society where we skip meals, pick up food on the fly, and eat lots of sugary treats and chemically treated or processed foods, we could all benefit from a multivitamin and mineral supplements.

What do nutrients have to do with mental health and happiness? Dozens of studies in the past few decades have reported mental health benefits from multivitamin/mineral formulas consisting of more than 20 minerals and vitamins.[7] In a 2020 review of the science on broad-spectrum nutritional supplements for the treatment of certain mental health issues, 16 of 23 studies showed positive effects for symptoms of depression, anxiety, or stress.[8] In addition, researchers have shown that multivitamin/mineral complexes can help with mood,[9] aggression,[10] and attentional issues.[11]

Research suggests that multivitamin/mineral supplements may also benefit people in times of great stress, which is one of the reasons why I strongly recommended them to my patients during the pandemic. In two interesting randomized, placebo-controlled trials, people taking a broad-spectrum multivitamin/mineral reported decreased levels of anxiety and stress. One followed the 2011 6.3 magnitude earthquake in New Zealand.[12] Another came on the heels of the 2013 catastrophic flooding in Alberta, Canada.[13] In the New Zealand earthquake study, participants taking the supplements reported greater improvements in mood, anxiety, and energy. After one month of supplementation, the rate of post-traumatic stress disorder (PTSD) dropped from 65 percent to 19 percent, while the rate among those who took no supplements did not change. The researchers on the flooding study suggested a potential benefit "if such formulas were distributed as a post-disaster public health measure."[14]

Other scientific studies on nutraceuticals have found they may be mood boosters. Check out this 2010 study involving 215 men ages 30 to 55 who were split into two groups—one group took a multivitamin for a month while the other group took a placebo.[15] The results? The men who took the multivitamin reported better mood, more vigor, and improved cognitive performance as well as less stress and mental fatigue. Basically, they felt happier and got smarter.

Dr. Hyman calls the B vitamins—folate, vitamin B6, and vitamin B12—the "mighty methylators for mental health."[16] In light of a study in the *American Journal of Psychiatry* that found that 27 percent of severely depressed women over the age of 65 were deficient in B12, he wrote, "If you think about it, this suggests that more than one-quarter of all severe depression can be helped with B-12 shots."[17]

Are Your Medications Making You Sad?

Many medications can cause nutrient depletions and put you at risk for sadness. While you shouldn't stop taking necessary medicines without checking with your doctor, it is important to be aware of potential nutritional pitfalls so you can replace vital nutrients. Some (or all) of the following medications may cause problems:

- Antacids: Decrease stomach acid, calcium, phosphorus, folic acid, and potassium. Also, dysbiosis, or small bowel overgrowth of unhealthy bacteria, can cause vitamin K deficiency and low mineral absorption.

- Antibiotics: Decrease vitamins B and K

- Antidiabetics: Decrease CoQ10, vitamin B12

- Antihypertensive medications: Decrease vitamins B6 and K, CoQ10, magnesium, and zinc

- Anti-inflammatories (Aleve, ibuprofen, etc.): Decrease vitamins B6, C, D, and K, folic acid, calcium, zinc, and iron

- Cholesterol-lowering medications (especially statins): Decrease CoQ10, omega-3 fatty acids, and carnitine

- Female hormones: Decrease folic acid, magnesium, B vitamins, vitamin C, zinc, selenium, and CoQ10

- Oral contraceptives: Decrease B vitamins, magnesium, folic acid, selenium, zinc, tyrosine, and serotonin. Roughly 16 to 52 percent of women taking oral contraceptives experience depression; antidepressants are typically the first-line treatment. Nutritional deficiencies are rarely considered. A recent study found that oral contraceptives can double the risk of suicide in teenage girls and significantly increase the risk in adult women.[18]

2. Vitamin D

This vitamin is critical for building bones and boosting the immune system, but it also is essential for a healthy brain, mood, and memory. Low levels have been associated with depression, Alzheimer's disease, heart disease, diabetes, cancer, and obesity. Ninety-three percent of the population is low in vitamin D because we are spending more time indoors and using more sunscreen (your skin absorbs the vitamin from the sun).

One study examined vitamin D supplementation in subjects who were between 18 and 43 years old and found that those who took vitamin D reported higher positive emotions, such as being enthusiastic, excited, and determined.[19]

You should know your vitamin D level like you should know your blood pressure on a regular basis. It is a simple blood test. If it is suboptimal, take between 2,000 and 5,000 IUs a day and recheck after two months to make sure it is in the healthy range.

3. Omega-3 fatty acids

When it comes to overall health and well-being, omega-3 fatty acids are essential. In fact, they are so critical that researchers at the Harvard Chan School of Public Health have pointed to low levels of omega-3s as one of the leading preventable causes of death.[20] Insufficient levels of two of the most important omega-3s—eicosapentaenoic acid (EPA) and docosahexaenoic acid (DHA)—have also been linked to:

- Depression and bipolar disorder[21]

- Suicidal behavior[22]
- Inflammation[23]
- Heart disease[24]
- ADHD[25]
- Cognitive impairment and dementia[26]
- Obesity[27]

These are conditions that get in the way of feeling good about yourself and about life in general. This could apply to you—at least, if you are among the 95 percent of Americans who, according to research, do not get enough dietary omega-3 fatty acids. The human body doesn't produce omega-3s on its own, so you have to get them from outside sources. If you aren't getting enough of this essential nutrient from your diet, it's bad news for your brain. That's because omega-3s contribute to about 8 percent of your brain's weight.

Unless you are taking omega-3 supplements, you have a high chance of having low levels of EPA and DHA.[28] At Amen Clinics, we tested the levels of 50 consecutive patients who were not taking fish oil supplements (the most commonly used source of EPA and DHA). The results were even worse than I expected. A shocking 49 out of 50—that's 98 percent!—had suboptimal levels. I began thinking we have an omega-3 crisis on our hands.

In a subsequent study, our research team analyzed the SPECT scans of 130 patients along with their EPA and DHA levels. Not surprisingly, the people with the lowest levels of EPA and DHA had lower blood flow in the brain, which is associated with depression and is the number one predictor of future brain problems. When we had these same patients undergo cognitive testing, the ones with lower omega-3 scores also had lower scores in mood.

Now, for the happier news. Increasing your intake of omega-3s promotes a more positive mood. For example, studies show that eating fish with high levels of omega-3 fatty acids is correlated to a lower risk of depression and suicide.

Even better, having higher levels of EPA is associated with happiness. That's according to exciting research out of Japan, where researchers enlisted 140 female nurses to assess happiness (measured by the Subjective Happiness Scale), a sense of fulfillment, and omega-3 levels.[29] The research team found that subjective happiness significantly correlated with a sense of fulfillment— being purposeful equated with being happy—as well as the levels of EPA and DHA. The correlation was particularly strong with the levels of EPA. Other studies have also suggested that EPA is more effective in treating depression and other disorders.[30]

Most adults should take between 1 and 2 grams of omega-3 fatty acids, with a 60 percent EPA to 40 percent DHA ratio.

4. Probiotics (means "for life")

If you're not happy, the reason may not be related to your brain or mind. Remember that your gut is often referred to as the "second brain." You have about 30 feet of tubing (including your stomach) that goes from your mouth to the other end. This tubing is lined with a single layer of cells with tight junctions that seal the tubing and allow you to digest your food efficiently without partly digested stuff seeping into your abdomen. Big trouble happens when the cell junctions widen and the lining becomes excessively porous, a condition known as leaky gut. Leaky gut is associated with depression, bipolar disorder, anxiety disorders, and even Alzheimer's disease. It is also linked to chronic inflammation and autoimmune diseases.

Considering the nearly 100 million neurons in your GI tract and the direct communication it has with the brain, the health of your gut is tightly linked to the health of your brain. In large part, the health of your gut depends on bugs. That's right, your GI tract is host to an estimated 100 trillion micro-organisms (bacteria, yeast, and others), roughly three times the total number of cells in the rest of the human body. This community of "bugs" is collectively known as the microbiome. The microbiome plays a vital role in the synthesis of neurotransmitters (brain chemicals you learned about in part 1), such as serotonin, which has a strong influence on mental well-being.

Some of those bugs are beneficial to your health and well-being while others are harmful. And in a classic "good guys vs. bad guys" scenario, they are all trying to wrestle for control of your microbiome. When the ratio of good bugs to bad bugs is about 85 percent good guys to 15 percent troublemakers, it creates a healthy gut. When the bad guys outnumber the good ones, the bad bugs cause trouble that can lead to intestinal and mental problems. Many everyday things can kill off the good bugs and tip the balance in favor of the bad guys, such as:

- Medications (antibiotics, oral contraceptives, proton pump inhibitors, steroids, NSAIDS)
- Low levels of omega-3 fatty acids
- Stress
- Sugar and high fructose corn syrup
- Artificial sweeteners
- Gluten

- Allergies to the environment or food
- Insomnia (especially among soldiers and those involved in shift work)
- Toxins (antimicrobial chemicals in soaps, pesticides, heavy metals)
- Intestinal infections (H. Pylori, parasites, Candida)
- Low levels of vitamin D
- Radiation/chemotherapy
- Excessive high-intensity exercise
- Excessive alcohol

By avoiding the things that fuel the growth of bad bugs, you can enhance the health of your gut, improve your mental well-being, and increase your chances of feeling good. Other strategies to grow the good army of bugs include:

- **Consuming prebiotics:** Prebiotics are dietary fibers that promote gut health, such as those found in apples, beans, cabbage, psyllium, artichokes, onions, leeks, asparagus, and root veggies (sweet potatoes, yams, squash, jicama, beets, carrots, and turnips).

- **Adding probiotics:** Eat more fermented foods that contain live bacteria, such as kefir (look for brands with no added sugar), kombucha (choose low-sugar varieties), pickles, unsweetened yogurt (goat or coconut), kimchi, pickled fruits and vegetables, and sauerkraut.

- **Taking probiotic supplements:** In particular, *Lactobacillus helveticus* (strain R52) and *Bifidobacterium longum* (strain R175), in a very specific ratio, were shown in two placebo-controlled clinical trials to help mood and lower anxiety over four to eight weeks.[31] In one study, with this specific probiotic strain combo, 86 college students who consumed probiotics daily for one month showed improvements in panic anxiety, neurophysiological anxiety, worry, and mood regulation.[32] In another probiotic study, 111 adults consumed *Lactobacillus plantarum* daily for 12 weeks, which resulted in a significant reduction in stress and anxiety within as little as 8 weeks.[33]

NUTRIENTS TO SUPPORT THE SIX CHEMICALS OF HAPPINESS

1. **Dopamine, especially important for the Spontaneous Brain Type:** Probiotics, such as *Lactobacillus plantarum* PS128,[34] nutrients such

as vitamin D[35] and omega-3 fatty acids,[36] and herbals such as rhodiola,[37] panax ginseng,[38] Bacopa monnieri,[39] green tea extract,[40] and Ginkgo biloba extract[41] have been found to increase dopamine levels to promote improved focus and increased energy while enhancing endurance and stamina. L-tyrosine, magnesium,[42] curcumins,[43] l-theanine,[44] and berberine[45] also increase dopamine.

2. **Serotonin, especially important for the Persistent Brain Type:** Probiotics, such as *Lactobacillus plantarum* PS128,[46] nutrients such as l-tryptophan, 5-HTP, magnesium, vitamin D, vitamins B6 and B12, methylfolate, and herbals such as saffron, St. John's wort, and curcumin can all boost serotonin.

3. **Oxytocin, especially important for the Sensitive Brain Type:** To produce oxytocin, the body needs Vitamin C.[47] Magnesium is required for oxytocin to function effectively. The probiotic *Lactobacillus reuteri*, which is available in supplement form, improves levels of both oxytocin and testosterone.[48] Research shows that sage, anise seed, and fenugreek boost oxytocin in pregnant women.[49] Even a small dose of the sleep hormone melatonin increases the secretion of oxytocin within an hour after ingestion.[50]

4. **Endorphins, especially important for the Sensitive Brain Type:** The amino acid L-phenylalanine blocks enzymes that degrade endorphins, thereby increasing them.[51] St. John's Wort,[52] *Lactobacillus acidophilus* probiotic,[53] and melatonin can also be beneficial.[54]

5. **Gamma aminobutyric acid (GABA), especially important for the Cautious Brain Type:** Oral GABA, magnesium, vitamin B6, l-theanine, taurine, and probiotics (especially *Lactobacillus rhamnosus, Lactobacillus paracasei, Lactobacillus brevis*, and *Lactococcus lactis*) support healthy GABA levels. Lemon balm, l-theanine, taurine, passionflower, and valerian can also support GABA.

6. **Cortisol, especially important for the Cautious Brain Type:** The herbals ashwagandha and rhodiola, and the nutrients l-theanine and EPA + DHA omega 3s, lower the stress hormone.

RESEARCH-BASED NUTRACEUTICALS TO ENHANCE HAPPINESS

Saffron: beneficial for all brain types

Of all the supplements to enhance happiness, my favorite is saffron. Saffron has been the happiness spice in the Middle East for at least 2,600 years. An Assyrian text from about 668–633 BCE recommended it for medicinal use that dated back as far as the 17th century BCE. Saffron flowers are depicted with reverence in Bronze Age wall paintings on the Mediterranean island of Thera.[55] Saffron is made from the *Crocus sativus* flower by handpicking and drying the female parts (stigmas), the three thin red structures in the middle of each flower.

Saffron

Modern science has validated many of saffron's traditional applications. Randomized controlled trials have confirmed its benefits for the brain,[56] eyes,[57] circulation,[58] lungs,[59] joints,[60] reproductive system,[61] and the body's antioxidant defenses.[62] But saffron's most proven application is mood enhancement.[63]

Saffron is an excellent mood enhancer and antidepressant, as documented by a number of double-blind, placebo-controlled clinical trials. In fact, some studies have compared saffron with the antidepressants fluoxetine (Prozac), imipramine, or other drugs. Saffron's degree of benefit was comparable to fluoxetine's [64] and partially restored male and female sexual function that had been impaired by fluoxetine.[65] Saffron was found similarly effective to imipramine and didn't have imipramine's adverse effects such as dry mouth and sedation.[66]

These studies show that the effects of saffron on mood were comparable to those seen with antidepressants.

Additional brain benefits of saffron. Scientific evidence shows that saffron has also proven useful for a variety of issues that are happiness robbers, such as:

- Reduced anxiousness, the most commonly reported of all mental problems.[67]
- Improved memory and other measures of cognitive functions in older adults.[68]
- Improved attention and behavior problems in children after only three weeks, as judged by both parents and teachers.[69]

The means by which saffron generates its impressive brain benefits are not clearly worked out, but saffron has considerable antioxidant power, coming from crocin, crocetin, picrocrocin, and safranal as well as from the flavonoids quercetin and kaempferol. In animal studies, these constituents help account for saffron's protection of the brain against toxic damage.

BrainMD makes Happy Saffron Plus with 30 mg of saffron, plus zinc and curcumins, which have both been found to help with mood. Dr. Parris Kidd, the Chief Science Officer at BrainMD who has been specializing in brain-focused nutrients for more than 35 years, helped me develop Happy Saffron Plus. We first released it in February 2020, right before the pandemic hit. One of the first reviews called it "Viagra for women" because the reviewer reported it enhanced desire and function. I gave it to my assistant Kim, who started humming the next day. Her son asked her why she was humming, and she said she didn't know why; she just felt happier. Given the benefits above, it is one supplement I just don't skip.

Curcumin: beneficial for all brain types

The turmeric root (really a rhizome or underground stem) parallels saffron in being revered as a panacea for at least 2,600, perhaps as many as 4,000 years.[70] It also is traditionally associated with positive mood and happiness, even being used for ritual skin adornment at some weddings in India. Turmeric's most active constituents are its three curcuminoids, which commercially are called curcumin. These excellent antioxidants promote healthy inflammatory (healing) response.[71] The problem is that they are poorly absorbed when taken by mouth and only work if their absorption is technologically enhanced. The Longvida curcumin extract has enhanced absorption.[72] In one study, healthy participants received either Longvida or a placebo and then had to take a difficult computerized cognitive test.[73] After taking the test, the Longvida group reported less frustration and other negative mood changes related to the test's difficulty. After 28 days, they had to take the test again. Again the curcumin group had fewer negative mood changes, better alertness, and less physical fatigue. Though curcumin has fewer trials for mood compared to saffron, a meta-analysis of six randomized controlled trials concluded curcumin improved mood and anxiousness.[74]

Zinc: beneficial for all brain types

The body needs zinc to make energy, DNA and proteins, and antioxidant enzymes; to make new cells; for immunity, healthy growth, and development. Low zinc predicts problems with mood.[75] Results from several trials suggest zinc can improve mood, both in healthy and overweight individuals and as part of a comprehensive personal program for participants with mood problems.[76] Zinc is fundamentally involved in regulating serotonin and dopamine receptors.[77] The CDC reports that 11–20 percent of Americans (varying with ethnic group) aren't getting sufficient zinc in their daily diets. The elderly population, pregnant or lactating women, vegetarians and vegans, sickle cell anemia sufferers, and alcohol abusers all have greater vulnerability to zinc deficiency.[78] Because the body doesn't absorb plant-based zinc as well as that from other sources, vegetarians may need up to 50 percent more zinc than nonvegetarians.

Magnesium: especially beneficial for the Cautious Brain Type

This important nutrient maintains and protects the body's health in hundreds of ways. Deficiency can lead to irritability, fatigue, mental confusion, anxiety, and stress, which is often seen in the Cautious Brain Type. Over 50 percent of Americans do not get enough magnesium in their diets. It also works as a treatment for depression in those who are low in magnesium.[79]

SAMe: especially beneficial for the Sensitive Brain Type

S-Adenosyl-Methionine (SAMe) is necessary to produce several neurotransmitters—including serotonin and dopamine, as well as epinephrine—and supports proper brain function. Normally, the brain creates all the SAMe it needs from the amino acid methionine. Sadness or depression, which is a vulnerability for Sensitive Brain Types, can impair the synthesis of SAMe from methionine. Many studies show SAMe can help enhance mood.[80] For people who have the Sensitive Brain Type, SAMe is often a good fit. SAMe has also been found to suppress appetite and reduce joint inflammation and pain.[81] I often use it as a first-line treatment for my patients who have mood issues and joint pain. The typical adult dose is 200 to 400mg 2–4 times a day. Caution: For people with bipolar disorder, SAMe may trigger mania.

St. John's Wort: especially beneficial for the Persistent Brain Type

St. John's wort (*Hypericum perforatum*) is a plant located in the subtropical regions of North America, Europe, Asia, India, and China and has been used for centuries in the treatment of mood disorders and depression.[82] The biologically active ingredient in St. John's wort is hypericin, thought to increase the availability of various neurotransmitters—including the chemicals of happiness, serotonin, dopamine, and GABA, as well as glutamate. St. John's wort acts similarly to that of popular prescription antidepressants, including Prozac, Paxil, and Zoloft. These drugs and the herb maintain elevated levels of serotonin, which has a mood-enhancing effect.

Stress depletes serotonin levels. St. John's wort offsets that and may actually be the most powerful supplement for boosting serotonin. I have seen dramatic improvement for many of my patients on St. John's wort; SPECT scans of before and after treatment document its effectiveness. In many patients, St. John's wort reduces hyperactivity in the anterior cingulate gyrus, which can make you inflexible and stressed when situations don't go as you want (common in Persistent Brain Types). This supplement also reduces moodiness.

Unfortunately, it can also decrease activity in the PFC. One of our patients said, "I'm happier, but I'm dingier." Keep in mind that St. John's wort inhibits the efficacy of other drugs, including birth control pills.

The typical dose is 300 mg a day for children, 300 mg twice a day for teens, and 600 mg in the morning and 300 mg at night for adults. It is important that the preparation of St. John's wort contains 0.3 percent hypericin, which is one of the active ingredients.

The American Journal of Psychiatry says, "Nutraceuticals are low-cost options that are worthy of clinical consideration."[83] I agree. The following chart provides a quick reference for the nutraceuticals that support the five primary brain types. If you have a combination brain type, check the recommendations in your results from the Brain Health Assessment at brainhealthassessment.com.

NUTRIENTS TO MAKE YOU HAPPY BASED ON BRAIN TYPE

BRAIN TYPE	BALANCED	SPONTANEOUS	PERSISTENT	SENSITIVE	CAUTIOUS
All brain types: multivitamin/mineral, omega-3s, probiotics, vitamin D, saffron, zinc, curcumins					
Type-Specific Happiness Nutrients	L-tyrosine, rhodiola, ginseng, green tea extract	5HTP, St. John's wort, vitamins B6, B12, methylfolate	SAMe, DL phenyl-alanine, vitamin C, magnesium	GABA, magnesium, vitamin B6, l-theanine, valerian

---

HAPPINESS HIGHLIGHTS FOR SECRET 3:
NOURISH YOUR UNIQUE BRAIN

- Take the four basics to support your brain health: high-quality multivitamin/mineral, vitamin D, omega-3 fatty acids, and probiotics.
- Support the chemicals of happiness for your brain type with targeted nutraceutical supplements.

CHOOSE FOODS YOU LOVE THAT LOVE YOU BACK

QUESTION 4

Do I choose foods today I love that love me back?

CHAPTER 11

THE YOU, HAPPIER DIET

Happy Foods vs. Sad Foods

One cannot think well, love well, sleep well, if one has not dined well.
VIRGINIA WOOLF

Eating crappy food isn't a reward—it's a punishment.
COMEDIAN DREW CAREY

The Super Bowl is one of the biggest eating days of the year, when Americans consume an estimated 1.33 billion chicken wings, 11 million slices of Domino's pizza, and $227 million worth of potato chips.[1] There's nothing "super" about consuming mass quantities of foods that sap your energy and contribute to depression and obesity. In fact, I think it should be called the "Unhappy Bowl." It's part of the reason why I have an ambivalent relationship with football.

As a child, teen, and young adult, I loved it. I was a huge Los Angeles Rams fan and played flag football in middle school, tackle football in high school, and intramural football in college and medical school. I loved watching football, like many boys and young men. That all changed when I started to look at the brain in my thirties and saw the damage football did to high school, college, and professional football players. Then my relationship with the game became very uncomfortable. It's hard to watch a game where I know it can be ruining the brains of players and subsequently causing emotional stress and pain in their families. I've scanned and treated more than 300 NFL players and have had many long discussions with their wives and children about the stress they have experienced. I would never support my grandchildren playing the game. Yet I still treat active players and make the excuse that I have to watch a few games a year to keep up with them (it's a rationalization, I know). I tell my active players, "If you are going to have a brain-damaging job [own it], you must do everything else right. You should always be rehabilitating your brain." Tom Brady is an incredible example of what to do if you decide to play a brain-damaging sport.

Like nearly 100 million other people, I sat down on February 7, 2021, to watch the Super Bowl between the Tampa Bay Buccaneers and the Kansas City Chiefs. It was billed as the greatest quarterback in the game (Patrick Mahomes) versus the greatest quarterback of all time (Tom Brady). Forty-three-year-old Brady clearly outplayed the 25-year-old Mahomes, and the Buccaneers won 31-9. In football years, 43 is considered ancient, but I knew Brady's secret. In his book, *The TB12 Method*, Brady explains that, on most days, he wakes up around 5:30 a.m. and downs 20 ounces of electrolyte water followed by a smoothie filled with bananas, blueberries, nuts, and seeds. After a morning workout (the first of several), he guzzles more water infused with electrolytes and a protein shake to help with post-workout muscle recovery. Breakfast consists of eggs and avocados. Lunch is usually fish and either vegetables or a salad with nuts. When the football legend snacks, he reaches for guacamole, hummus, or mixed nuts. For dinner, it's chicken and more vegetables. By the end of the day, he's consumed up to the equivalent of 25 glasses of water—keeping his body and brain well-lubricated. On game days, he switches things up with an almond butter and jelly sandwich—fast energy for explosive movements during the game.[2]

To most people on first glance, that might seem like a restrictive or even a sad diet. Some people have even called it insane, and one of his New England Patriot teammates said he would never eat Brady's bird food (although that player did not have a long career). One of Brady's most important strategies to long-term success and happiness—especially for someone who plays a contact sport that is notorious for concussions and the resulting cognitive and psychological problems that destroy happiness—is the food he consumes. He eats foods he loves that also love him back, not for momentary pleasure but for long-term health and success, which are associated with lasting happiness. He is doing everything he can to help keep his brain, body, and moods at their best.

This shows that even if you have been bad to your brain—think head injuries, bad habits like smoking and poor sleep, and more—eating well can go a long way to increase performance and happiness.

For Brady, fish, vegetables, and blueberries make him happy. What about you? What foods make you happy? Grab a sheet of paper or tap on the notes app on your phone and start listing them. Jot down the first 20 things that pop into your head. I do this exercise with some of my patients, and some of the most common foods that end up on their happy list include the same ones that made it into a survey conducted by the Harris Poll in 2015.[3] The pollsters asked more than 2,000 adults to name their favorite comfort food (comfort foods tend to make us feel better when we're feeling down, stressed, or depressed), and the winner was . . . *drumroll please* . . . pizza!

The full list of the top ten comfort foods from the Harris Poll included the following feel-good-fast fare:

1. Pizza
2. Chocolate
3. Ice cream
4. Macaroni and cheese
5. Chips
6. Hamburgers
7. Steak
8. Popcorn
9. Pasta
10. Mexican food

How many of these comfort foods made it onto your list? If you're anything like my patients, your list probably looks similar to the one above. Your list may also include foods like bread, cheese, cookies, doughnuts, candy, or mood-enhancing beverages like wine, soda, or coffee. However, there's one big problem with these so-called happy foods: They might give you a fleeting lift, but in the long run, they are all more likely to contribute to mood problems, stress, anxiety, and depression. In the same way I have to break it to my patients, I have to let you know that your happy foods are actually sad foods that are draining your joy.

One of the seven secrets to happiness is to enjoy the real happy foods (and beverages) that will make you feel better, not just in the moment but for the long run. I have written about some of these brain-healthy eating basics in all of my books, but in this book I am going to point you to specific foods with scientific evidence showing that they elevate moods, boost energy, and calm anxiousness and stress—the necessary ingredients for happiness. I will also share the sad foods to avoid—the ones that dampen your mood, zap your energy, and ramp up tension.

The following general rules apply to all brain types, but I will also break down targeted recommendations for each of the five primary brain types. Not all diets are right for all brain types. Take it from Rachael Ray, who took our Brain Health Assessment and discovered she has the Persistent Brain Type. After going on one of those high-protein, low-carb diets, she told me, "I was so mean that I wondered why my husband didn't leave me." She was on the wrong eating plan for her brain type. Knowing how to eat for your brain is one of the keys to feeling happier.

1. Choose foods that make you happy now *and* later.

The real happy foods are the ones that make you feel good in the moment but also enhance your mood, energy, and physical well-being in the long run. This one simple eating strategy is the most important with respect to happiness. Think of those comfort foods I mentioned earlier. They may give you a quick boost now but rob you of feelings of contentment later. In general, they are low-quality foods that have been scientifically engineered to taste so good that they trigger your brain's "bliss point" and the release of some of the neurochemicals of happiness—such as dopamine—causing you to become addicted to them.

The Standard American Diet (aptly referred to as "SAD") is filled with foods that are loaded with unhealthy ingredients and artificial chemicals that are detrimental to mental, emotional, and physical well-being. A growing body of research shows that the SAD diet increases your risk for depression, anxiety disorders, ADHD, and dementia, as well as diabetes, hypertension, heart disease, and cancer.[4] As a psychiatrist who has met with tens of thousands of patients over more than three decades, I can tell you that having any of those issues steals your *joie de vivre*.

Happy Foods: Foods that make you happy now . . . *and* later include:

- Organic colorful fruits and vegetables, especially berries and leafy greens
- Sustainably raised fish and meat
- Nuts and seeds
- Healthy oils
- Eggs
- Clean protein powders (sugar-free, plant-based)
- Dark chocolate
- Unprocessed foods
- Organic foods
- Low-glycemic foods (they don't spike blood sugar)
- High-fiber foods

Sad Foods: I call these the weapons of mass destruction because they are destroying the health of America, and we are exporting these food patterns around the world. These are foods that make you happy now but make you feel bad, tired, anxious, or stressed later, including those that are:

- Highly processed
- Sprayed with pesticides
- High-glycemic foods (they spike blood sugar)
- Low fiber
- Food-like substances
- Artificially colored and sweetened
- Laden with hormones
- Tainted with antibiotics
- Stored in plastic containers

2. Make your calories count toward happiness, not depression.

From an Amen Clinics patient:

> This morning, I met a friend at Starbucks, and I could hear Tana in my head saying, "Don't drink your calories." And Chloe saying, "Just because I like it doesn't mean I have to have it."
>
> So I didn't indulge. Yay, me! Instead I came home and had a smoothie for lunch. And I feel good!
>
> I even got more steps yesterday than my husband did, and he's a farmer! I also am looking at rotund people differently. I used to be condemnatory, but now I know they are in the grip of their diet—it has them. I've changed my thoughts about heavy people.

Calories count! The calories you consume can either fuel good moods or dampen your outlook. Supersizing your meals can lead to supersizing your body, and obesity is strongly linked to depression, lower self-esteem, and poor body image, as well as psychiatric issues such as ADHD, bipolar disorder, panic disorder, and addictions.[5] Among women, increased body mass index (BMI) is also linked to a rise in suicidal thoughts,[6] a sign of deep unhappiness. And a 2021 brain imaging study shows that as your weight goes up, blood flow to your brain goes down.[7] As you saw in the BRIGHT MINDS chapter, low blood flow is associated with depression and other issues that steal your joy.

A growing body of scientific evidence backs up the calorie-happiness connection. Restricting calories can even lead to a happier marriage, according to a 2016 study in *JAMA Internal Medicine*.[8] This research included 218 nonobese adults. One group was asked to cut their calorie intake by 25 percent while the other group ate as much as they wanted. At the end of the two-year trial period, participants completed a series of self-reports regarding their moods, quality of life, sleep, and sexual activity. The results showed that the calorie-cutting group experienced improvements in all areas—significantly enhancing moods while increasing sleep duration as well as sexual drive and relationship satisfaction. The calorie restriction group also lost an average of over 16 pounds. The folks who ate whatever they desired? They didn't see these same benefits.

Other scientific studies have found that calorie restriction has an antidepressant effect. In a 2018 review of existing research, scientists pointed to studies showing that calorie restriction reduces risk factors for psychiatric illnesses, such as depression, as well as neurodegenerative diseases.[9] Trimming calorie consumption also increases longevity, memory, and quality of life. Now that's something to get happy about!

How does cutting calories cue the brain for happiness? Researchers are still diving into the specific mechanisms at play, but they suggest that the answers may lie in:

- Increasing blood flow to the brain (as you saw in the BRIGHT MINDS chapter, boosting cerebral blood flow enhances mood)
- Increasing stem cell production (new cells) in the hippocampus (responsible for mood and memory)
- Increasing brain-derived neurotrophic factor (BDNF), which enhances learning
- Promoting autophagy (a process that eliminates the toxic waste buildup in the brain)

Happy Foods: The highest-quality foods you can find that are also calorie smart

Sad Foods: Low-quality, high-calorie foods that increase your risk of depression, anxiety, and other mental health issues

3. Hydrate to be happier.

Your brain is composed of approximately 80 percent water, and it needs adequate hydration for you to feel your best. Being even slightly dehydrated can mess with your mood and more, making you feel more depressed, anxious, tense, angry, or hostile in addition to draining your energy, increasing pain, and lowering your ability to concentrate.[10]

In a 2013 study on dehydration and mood in the *British Journal of Nutrition*, 20 healthy women went without fluids for 24 hours.[11] The intentional dehydration produced fatigue, confusion, and decreased alertness, as well as a trend toward greater anxiety. Other research on the effects of dehydration on brain function reveals that it widely impairs mood.[12]

Outside the science lab, dehydration can occur for many reasons, such as:

- Intense exercise—even 30 or 40 minutes on the treadmill can drain your fluid reserves
- Extreme heat
- Lack of fluid intake
- Consuming too much caffeine or alcohol (which are dehydrating)
- Eating a high-sodium diet
- Taking diuretics

To stay properly hydrated, drink eight to ten glasses of water a day. But guzzling isn't the only way to ensure you are keeping your brain well-lubed. Consuming water-rich foods, such as vegetables and fruits, can help you reach your fluid needs.

Happy Foods: Water, plain sparkling water, water flavored with slices of fruit (spa water), water with flavored stevia from Sweet Leaf, coconut water, herbal tea, green tea, and black tea (in small amounts if caffeinated), water-rich veggies and fruits: cucumbers, lettuce, celery, radishes, zucchini, tomatoes, bell peppers, strawberries, melon, raspberries, and blueberries

Sad foods: Alcohol, highly caffeinated drinks (coffee, energy drinks, sodas), high-sodium foods

4. Power up feel-good neurochemicals with high-quality protein.

If you want to be happier, include protein in your diet. After water, protein is the most abundant substance in your body, and it plays a major role in the healthy growth and function of your body's cells, tissues, and organs. What may be surprising to you is that protein can greatly impact happiness levels too. Here are some of the many ways protein influences moods:

- Helping avoid blood sugar imbalances that are associated with anxiety and depression
- Preventing food cravings that make you feel bad
- Providing the building blocks for many of the neurochemicals of happiness

When blood sugar levels spike and crash, it puts you on an emotional roller-coaster ride associated with low mood and irritability. Stabilizing your blood sugar by including small amounts of protein with every meal keeps your mood on an even keel. At Amen Clinics, we think of protein as medicine that should be taken in small doses with every meal and snack, at least every four to five hours, to help balance your blood sugar levels.

Balancing those blood sugar levels by consuming protein also helps ward off cravings, which have been linked to depression. Anyone who has been a slave to cravings—whether it is for ice cream, doughnuts, or potato chips—knows that they tend to make you feel tense, anxious, and irritable. Saying so long to cravings helps you say hello to better moods.

Proteins contain important amino acids that your body needs but is unable to produce on its own. These are called essential amino acids, and they are precursors (necessary for production) for neurotransmitters, including serotonin and dopamine, which play an important role in mood and emotional health. For example, the body needs a protein called tryptophan in order to produce serotonin, the molecule of respect I wrote about in part 1. Serotonin is important for all of the brain types but can be especially beneficial for people with the Persistent Brain Type. And an amino acid called tyrosine that is found in dietary protein is essential for the production of dopamine. As you may recall, dopamine is typically low in people with the Spontaneous Brain Type, so it is even more critical for these people to get enough protein in their diet.

For optimal feel-good neurotransmitter production, you need to fuel your body and brain with 20 essential amino acids. Be aware that plant foods—such as nuts, seeds, legumes, some grains, and vegetables—often contain protein, but unless they are combined properly they do not provide all 20 of the essential amino acids you need. Only animal sources, such as fish, poultry, and most meats contain all of them.[13]

Take note that small amounts of high-quality protein are crucial for happiness, but eating large amounts can contribute to unhappiness. That's because overconsumption of protein can lead to increased stress and inflammation in the body, which is associated with low moods and anxiousness.

What do I mean by high-quality protein? Proteins that are free of pesticides if plant-based and those that are free range, grass fed, and free of hormones and antibiotics if animal-based.

Adding protein powders to smoothies can also boost your protein intake. Look for plant-based protein powders that are sugar-free but have fiber, branch chain amino acids, and enzymes to aid in digestion. BrainMD makes delicious chocolate and vanilla plant-based protein powders (brainmd.com). I love starting the day with a protein smoothie.

Tana's "Happy Smoothie": My Daily Way to Start the Day

Every morning I start my day by making my wife, Tana, what she calls her "Happy Smoothie." I start by putting some water and ice in a blender, then I add BrainMD's chocolate-flavored high-quality, plant-based protein powder. I add a scoop of a prebiotic powder that is great for gut health—remember that good gut health is tightly linked to happiness, while poor gut health is associated with depression. Next, I sprinkle in a scoop of NeuroGreens, which includes dried veggies and fruits that are loaded with antioxidants. And as you will see in this chapter, every serving of veggies and fruits you eat increases happiness levels, so this is a very happy morning routine.

I also like to use a scoop of Smart Mushrooms, which contains six species of mushrooms known to enhance immunity and cognition. I feel happier and more secure knowing I am better equipped to fight off viruses (take that, COVID-19!). After a scoop of BRIGHT MINDS Powder—a powdered multivitamin/mineral/brain complex—goes into the mix, I toss in about a cup of frozen, organic mixed berries for yet another burst of joy. Finally, I add a few drops of chocolate-flavored stevia, a natural sweetener that does not impact blood sugar levels. This breakfast drink tastes amazing—like chocolatey, berrylicious goodness—and thanks to all the mood-boosters, it deserves the name "Happy Smoothie."

If you want to start your day with a mood lift that will promote positivity all day long, I highly recommend it.

INGREDIENTS

Water

Ice

Mixed frozen berries

Chocolate OMNI Protein Powder (BrainMD)

Smart Mushrooms (BrainMD)

NeuroGreens (BrainMD)

BRIGHT MINDS Powder (BrainMD)

Prebiotic Fiber for gut health

Chocolate Stevia (Sweet Leaf)

Happy foods: High-quality animal protein (fish, lamb, turkey, chicken, beef, pork), beans and other legumes, raw nuts, high-protein veggies (broccoli, spinach), high-quality protein powder (plant-based, sugar-free)

Sad foods: Low-quality proteins raised with pesticides, hormones, or antibiotics. Excessive protein, which sparks inflammation.

5. Keep your brain happy with healthy fats.

Although 80 percent of the brain is composed of water, 60 percent of the solid weight of your brain is fat. For decades, the medical community demonized dietary fat and touted low-fat diets as a primary strategy for good health. But they were wrong. When it comes to brain health and emotional well-being, fat is not the enemy. In fact, dietary fats are essential for optimal brain function and for positive mood.

For example, compelling research in the *Journal of Psychiatry and Neuroscience* shows that low levels of cholesterol—possibly caused by shunning fats in the diet—are associated with an increased risk of major depression and suicidal thoughts and behaviors. In fact, people with the lowest levels of cholesterol in this study had a 112 percent increased risk of suicidality.[14] On a more positive note, certain fats, such as omega-3 fatty acids, can help fight depression and reduce symptoms associated with the mood disorder.[15] Read into the research on omega-3 fatty acids and you will see that these fats promote positive mood and emotional balance. And that makes you happier.

A word of caution, though—not all dietary fats are created equal. I always tell my patients to avoid trans fats—the fats that are sometimes used in foods like store-bought baked goods, microwave popcorn, and frozen pizza—because they have been linked to depressive symptoms. For any of my patients who struggle with mood, I also recommend eliminating fats that are higher in omega-6 fatty acids (e.g., refined vegetable oils)—as they have also been associated with inflammation and depression.

Happy foods: Focus on healthy fats, such as avocados, nuts (walnuts are associated with less depression[16]), seeds, sustainable clean fish, and oils (avocado, coconut, flax, macadamia nut, olive, sesame, and walnut)

Sad foods: Vegetable oils (canola, corn, safflower, soy), industrial farm-raised animal fat and dairy, processed meats, and trans fats (any hydrogenated fats)

6. Opt for mood-boosting carbs that last.

When you first think of carbohydrates, your mind may immediately jump to bread, chips, or cookies. These foods fit into the feel-good-now-but-not-later category. In fact, refined carbs like pretzels, crackers, and doughnuts are linked to depression. Just look at the findings of a 2015 paper in the *American Journal of Clinical Nutrition*:[17] Researchers analyzed data from nearly 70,000 women who had no history of depression, other mental health disorders, or substance abuse. Over a three-year period, they found that women eating a high-glycemic diet (high levels of refined carbs) had an increased risk of depression. Those are sad carbs.

Now I want to introduce you to the happy carbs that lift your mood and keep you feeling good. First up are fresh vegetables and fruits. Notice that I put vegetables first. That's because I recommend a two-to-one ratio of vegetables to fruits thanks to their lower sugar content and higher nutrient levels. A study out of the University of Warwick found that the number of vegetables and fruits you eat has a linear correlation to your level of happiness. For each serving of vegetables or fruits you eat (up to eight servings a day) the happier you become, and it happens almost instantly. Prescription antidepressants don't work that fast![18] Think of the produce section at your grocery store as your "happy place."

Why is produce so beneficial for our moods? Research shows that vegetables and fruits support production of the neurotransmitters GABA, dopamine, and serotonin.[19] Eating foods that fuel healthy production of these neurochemicals of happiness helps you achieve a positive mood. Colorful vegetables and fruits also provide many nutrients, vitamins, and minerals that are beneficial for overall brain health, and with a better brain come better moods.

Other happy carbs include high-fiber foods like legumes and gluten-free whole grains, such as quinoa. These carbs have a positive effect on blood sugar levels and on overall physical well-being. They can support your mental health too. An interesting study from the University of Toronto found that older adults whose dietary intake included at least two to three sources of fiber had significantly decreased risk of post-traumatic stress disorder (PTSD).[20]

Happy foods: Colorful low-glycemic, high-fiber vegetables, fruits, and legumes that promote healthy neurotransmitter levels

Sad foods: High-glycemic, low-fiber foods, such as breads, pasta, potatoes, rice, and sugar, that increase your risk of mood disorders, anxiousness, irritability, and stress

7. Find happiness in your spice cabinet.

Wanna get happier? Cook with aromatic, flavorful herbs and spices. Certain items in your spice cabinet have natural antidepressant properties. Here are a few mood lifters that I personally love—*and they love me back!*

- **Saffron:** Fragrant and delicious, saffron is considered the most expensive spice in the world. Multiple studies[21] show that a saffron extract was as effective as antidepressant medication in treating major depression.

- **Turmeric:** Found in curry, turmeric triggers the release of serotonin, one of the neurochemicals of happiness. Turmeric holds a special place in my heart because it also contains a compound that reduces the plaques in the brain that are associated with Alzheimer's disease.[22]

- **Cinnamon:** This fall favorite is high in antioxidants and has been shown to help improve attention and blood sugar regulation, which helps with mood. In addition, it is a natural aphrodisiac, which can improve your love life, and that can definitely make you happier.

- **Rosemary:** Extracts of this aromatic herb have been shown to have antidepressant effects[23] that may be helpful for burnout and mental fatigue.

Try Tana's Cinnamon Latte

I enjoy making the most delicious cinnamon latte for Tana. It's her recipe, but she swears that I make it better. I start with half-caf coffee (half caffeinated, half decaf) so it gives her a little happiness boost without being dehydrating. Then I warm up organic, unsweetened, vanilla-flavored almond milk. Next, I add a little stevia—sometimes vanilla, other times chocolate or hazelnut flavored—then I top it all off with a tiny bit of erythritol (a natural sweetener) and a dash of cinnamon, which helps with moods. I put it all in a blender, which makes it get really frothy just like a cappuccino from your favorite coffee bar. It smells intoxicating and tastes divine. I think it's the perfect way to wake up. My latte is about 30 calories, while the ones you get at those major coffee shops are north of 600 calories. Who needs to waste that many calories when you can have something just as yummy for a fraction of the calories?

Happy foods: Lots of herbs and spices

Sad foods: Artificial colors and flavors geared to hijack your brain and deteriorate your joy

8. Say yes to sexy foods.

Having sex makes people happier. Sexual intimacy with the love of your life is one of life's greatest pleasures. Some of the benefits of sex include improved brain health, immune system, and overall physical health. Emotionally, sex promotes greater trust and deeper love in committed relationships. It also enhances our ability to handle emotional conflict. Having happier relationships makes you happier overall.

To support a fulfilling sex life, add aphrodisiacs to your diet. Here are six sensual foods that can boost your sex life and your happiness.

- **Fruits** (especially pomegranate, berries, watermelon, apples, citrus, cherries, and dark-colored grapes) promote greater blood flow, which is necessary for healthy sexual function.

- **Oysters** are high in zinc, which is necessary for healthy testosterone levels.

- **Veggies** (like spinach, watercress, mustard greens, arugula, kale, beet greens, Swiss chard, lettuce, beets, turnips, and carrots) are rich in nitrates that get your blood pumping.

- **Dark chocolate** (with a 70 percent or greater cocoa content) contains phenethylamine and tyrosine, two compounds associated with increased levels of the feel-good hormones serotonin and dopamine, which have mood-lifting effects. Be sure to eat just a small square to maintain maximum desire.

- **Salmon** and other fatty fish that are high in omega-3s boost blood flow and are also good sources of vitamin D, which is essential for optimal testosterone levels.

- **Spice** up your romance with sex-boosting herbs like ginger, ginseng, and garlic that enhance blood flow.

9. Eat clean to keep your body happy.

When your body and organs are being assaulted by pesticides, food additives, preservatives, and artificial dyes and sweeteners, they can't function at optimal levels. These food saboteurs can kill your mood and lead to feelings of depression, anxiety, and fatigue. To avoid these culprits, start reading food labels. I know it can be a bit like trying to learn a foreign language, and food industry executives intentionally make it more difficult, but it is worth it! If you can't pronounce an ingredient listed on a label, it's probably not a happy food.

Eating organic, whenever possible, can help. I understand that it's more expensive to eat organic foods that are raised humanely and sustainably. If you want to keep your budget in mind, check out The Environmental Working Group's (www.ewg.org) list of foods with the highest levels of pesticides. These are the ones that are generally worth the extra cost.

Eating clean isn't just about being aware of the pesticides and chemicals that manufacturers and the agricultural industry are pumping into our foods. It also means understanding that some foods, such as fish, may contain toxins that attack our bodies and brains. For example, some types of fish are high in mercury, and exposure to heavy metals has been linked to depression, anxiety, and other conditions.[24] In general, the larger the fish, the higher the mercury content, so opt for smaller types of fish. Learn more at www.seafoodwatch.org.

Happy foods: Clean whole foods, sustainably raised, and organic whenever possible

Sad foods: Food raised with pesticides, hormones, and antibiotics, or containing artificial sweeteners, dyes, and preservatives

10. Fight depression and other happiness-draining issues with a monthlong elimination diet.

Scientists are increasingly recognizing that food sensitivities can get you down. Many of the patients we see at Amen Clinics have undetected subtle food allergies that contribute to depression, anxiety, bipolar conditions, fatigue, brain fog, slowed thinking, irritability, agitation, aggression, ADHD, dementia, and a host of other issues that make people unhappy. What makes these under-the-radar allergies so tricky to identify is that they often don't trigger immediate reactions. In many cases, it can take several days for symptoms to arise. By then, you aren't putting it together that the corn in a seemingly "healthy" salad you ate three days ago is linked to your current down-in-the-dumps mood.

One of the most powerful strategies we use with our patients at Amen Clinics—especially people who have not responded to traditional treatment—is an elimination diet. This involves ditching the following common allergenic foods—sugar, artificial sweeteners, gluten, soy, corn, dairy, and food additives and dyes—for one month.

Here is how these everyday foods can zap your zest for life.

- **Sugar:** Scheming food manufacturers may try to convince you that the sweet stuff delivers happiness, but it's actually a mood killer. All forms of sugar—even natural honey or maple—cause blood sugar levels to spike and then crash. This negatively impacts mood; increases anxiousness, irritability, and stress; makes you feel fatigued; and causes cravings. Diets that are too high in sugar also promote inflammation, which is associated with depression and other issues that make you unhappy.

- **Artificial sweeteners:** Do you think artificial sweeteners are giving you a quick boost of happiness without the downsides of sugar? Wrong! Aspartame (NutraSweet, Equal) has been linked to depression, anxiety, irritable moods, and insomnia, as well as a host of other neurophysiological issues.[25] Artificial sweeteners—including aspartame, saccharine (Sweet'N Low), and sucralose (Splenda)—can also lead to high insulin levels, which is associated with a higher risk for depression in addition to Alzheimer's disease and a variety of physical ailments.

- **Gluten:** When I first started talking to my patients about gluten sensitivity and how it can negatively impact mood and overall sense of well-being, most of them had never heard the word before. These days, "gluten-free" has become a ubiquitous marketing buzzword. Even so, gluten continues to be found in breads, cereals, granola, tortillas, and pasta, and it is pumped into foods like barbecue sauce, soy sauce, salad dressings, soups, processed meats, and veggie burgers. This is bad news for the one percent of the US population who have celiac disease, an autoimmune disease in which eating gluten causes damage to the small intestine, as well as the estimated 6 percent (almost 20 million) of Americans who have gluten sensitivity.[26]

   What do gluten sensitivity and celiac disease have to do with happiness? Research has linked them to depression, anxiety disorders, mood disorders, ADHD, and other issues that rob you of joy.[27] The good news is that going gluten-free has been found to decrease symptoms of depression, ADHD, and more. In fact, a 2018 review of 13 studies on gluten and mood symptoms involving 1,139 participants found that eliminating gluten from the diet significantly improved depressive symptoms.[28] The researchers suggested that nixing gluten from the diet may be an effective treatment strategy for mood disorders.

- **Soy:** Head to the grocery store, and you will find the shelves lined with soy-based products—milk alternatives, tofu, tempeh, and edamame, for example. But soy, which is a protein derived from soybeans, is also found in dozens of other food products, such as canned soup, canned tuna, baked goods, cereals, processed meats, protein bars, energy snacks, sauces, and even baby formula. This is problematic because soy contains components that can drain your glass-half-full outlook on life and turn it into a glass-half-empty view. Some of the happiness-robbing compounds in soy include high levels of inflammation-causing omega-6 fatty acids, as well as lectins, which are carbohydrate-binding proteins that can also be toxic. As you have seen, inflammation is linked to depression.

- **Corn:** News flash! Corn is not a vegetable; it is a grain. And its fatty acid profile—high in omega-6 and very low in omega-3—ranks among the worst of all grains. This makes it a sad food that can trigger inflammation and bad moods.

- **Dairy:** The scientific jury is still out on whether there is a connection between dairy consumption and mood issues.[29] However, in my practice, I have seen many patients whose symptoms of depression and anxiety worsen when they eat dairy products and who feel better when they cut it out of their diet. Plus, most dairy cows are raised with hormones and antibiotics.

- **Food additives and dyes:** Artificial dyes, preservatives, flavoring, and other additives have been associated with mood disorders as well as other issues. You may not realize that these culprits might be sucking the happiness out of you because these ingredients hide in so many common food products. Over 10,000 food additives are allowed in the US food supply.[30] And our consumption of artificial food dyes has increased fivefold, according to a 2010 article by the Center for Science in the Public Interest.[31] If you want to be happier, it's worth temporarily eliminating these from your diet. Here's why: Studies on monosodium glutamate (MSG) show that it can trigger depressive and anxious symptoms among other disturbances.[32] The evidence about Red Dye 40 is even more alarming.[33]

  Take a look at Robert, a 15-year-old who came to Amen Clinics. His parents brought him in due to recurring episodes of confrontational and belligerent behavior. He often got aggravated and angry for seemingly no reason. He was not a happy teen. With further investigation, it became apparent that these aggressive tendencies were happening after he consumed red foods or beverages. We suspected his emotional instability and bad behavior might be related to Red Dye 40, one of the most common food dyes that has been linked to temper outbursts and other issues. After exposure to Red Dye 40, Robert's brain SPECT scan showed excessive activity overall. Removing Red Dye 40 from his diet dramatically improved Robert's behavior and his moods.

ROBERT'S ACTIVE SPECT SCANS

WITHOUT RED DYE

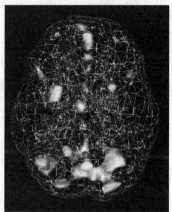

WITH RED DYE

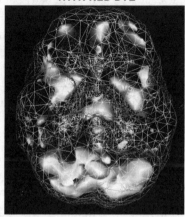

Marked activation with Red Dye 40

After eliminating these foods for one month, notice how you are feeling. Do you feel more upbeat? Calmer? Less tense? More emotionally stable? More energized? More alert? If so, chances are that one or more of these foods has been causing problems for you.

To find out which food is the culprit, reintroduce each of them to your diet one at a time every three to four days. Eat the reintroduced food at least two to three times a day for three days to see if you notice any physical or psychological reactions. Physical reactions may include headaches, aches and pains, congestion, skin changes, and changes in digestion or bowel functioning. Psychological reactions can include:

- Depression
- Anxiousness
- Anger
- Suicidal thoughts
- Brain fog
- Forgetfulness
- Fatigue

If you notice an issue immediately after consumption, stop eating that food at once. If you notice a reaction over the next few days, eliminate that food for 90 days to give your immune system a chance to calm down and your gut a chance to heal. You may want to eliminate that food forever.

When our patients follow an elimination diet, it often makes a dramatic difference. Except for artificial sweeteners, additives, and dyes, you don't have to lose all of these foods forever, unless you are sensitive to them.

Happy foods: Foods that don't cause any form of allergic reaction

Sad foods: Any food that makes you feel bad—either instantly or over time

11. Disrupt hedonic adaptation with intermittent fasting.

In chapter 5, I wrote about the concept of "hedonic adaptation." That's when something stimulates the brain's pleasure centers and a tolerance subsequently develops, driving you to need more and more of it to get the same feeling. That "something" can be food. For example, if you eat a scoop of ice cream after dinner, you may graduate to eating two scoops in order to get the same feeling of satisfaction. Then you want to add hot fudge to keep your pleasure centers humming at that bliss point. Then you start sprinkling broken-up pieces of brownies on top . . . *and then . . . and then . . . and then*. It's a never-ending quest for more, particularly for Spontaneous Brain Types who are low in dopamine.

Intermittent fasting, in which you take a break from eating for at least 12 hours between dinner and your next meal, can interrupt hedonic adaptation. A period of fasting can lower the hedonic pleasure point associated with food. Instead of needing more, more, more, your brain's pleasure centers are recalibrated to a lower set point. As a result, you may feel happier with just a few nibbles of ice cream (or a single bite of a more brain-healthy dessert). After 12 to 16 hours without any food, you may feel extremely grateful for foods you previously found less palatable.

In addition to reversing hedonic adaptation, intermittent fasting can also boost your mood. A 2013 study in the *Journal of Nutrition, Health and Aging* showed that fasting and calorie restriction significantly decreases anger, tension, confusion, and other mood disturbances while increasing vigor.[34]

12. Develop a happier mindset about your relationship with food.

Here is one of my favorite all-time testimonials about mindset and food. It's unfortunately accurate and funny:

I visited Costco for the first time ever this weekend.
There was death everywhere, every corner.
Samples of death covered in death.
I just kept hearing Dr. Amen in the back of my mind.
So I walked past it all! Got my organic goods and left, which is saying a lot because it was nearly lunch time and it all smelled so good!
Thank you for giving me the tools to make good choices.

Food is a relationship. Have you ever been in a bad relationship? I have several times, and it was painful. Too many people have a bad relationship with food, where they love foods that are high calorie, obesogenic, diabetes-promoting, and proinflammatory. Be smart, and begin to change to a new routine, where you only love foods that love you back.

If you had a million-dollar racehorse, would you ever feed it junk food? Only if you were an idiot. You would want to protect your investment with high-quality nutrition. Aren't you worth so much more?

We are all creatures of habit. Work to change your habits to ones that serve you rather than hurt you. For example, learn to make one decision, not 30. Think of every time you go to a Mexican restaurant and the server brings you a basket of chips. If you're hungry and those chips are sitting on the table, you could be having an argument inside your head. Your undisciplined mind will be taunting you, saying, "Go ahead, just eat one chip. It's not that bad." Meanwhile your PFC will have to be putting on the brakes, telling you, "Don't do it. If you eat one, then you're going to eat the whole basket." And which one usually wins out? To avoid this, simply tell the server, "No chips, please." That way, you can more easily avoid the temptation.

Look at this example of a patient who put this concept into action:

I said no once instead of 30 times. My wife and I invited friends over for a BBQ. Right away, my wife was talking about having hot dogs, hamburgers, buns, chips, etc. I insisted we have a BBQ that had good food. She pushed back, so I said we would forget about the BBQ. It was better for me to say no once instead of 30 times.

When it was all said and done, with much discussion, we had the BBQ and served appropriate food. No one complained that we didn't have junk food.

Here's a great way for you to start creating a happier relationship with your food. Go back to the list of comfort foods I asked you to create at the beginning of this chapter. Now, with the rules I have just shared with you in mind, cross out the foods you love that do not love you back. Replace the ones you delete with brain-healthy foods that fuel happiness. By focusing your diet on these 20 foods, you will feel more positive and upbeat for the long haul.

Try the World's Best Brain Healthy Hot Chocolate

I love hot chocolate, but the traditional form of this sweet treat does not love me back. Typical hot chocolate is full of sugar, bad fats, and low-quality chocolate—yuck! I decided to do a quick recipe rehab for a brain-healthy version that tastes just as good as—or even better than—the stuff you buy in the store. It makes you feel good too.

Here's how I make it: I start with organic raw cocoa powder that has no sugar. Real cocoa is a superfood and a powerful antioxidant that acts as a natural mood booster. I use about 1 teaspoon of cocoa and add it to about 16 ounces of warm almond milk that is organic, unsweetened, and vanilla flavored. Next, I add a few drops of chocolate-flavored stevia and stir it really well. Then, for the pièce de résistance, I use almond milk whipped cream that only has 1 gram of sugar. It's so delicious and it puts me in a great mood in the evening right before bedtime. What a happy way to end the day!

13. Eat for your brain type.

As I mentioned earlier, the final and most life-changing concept in the You, Happier Diet is eating foods that are targeted to your brain type. When you tailor the general rules to your specific brain, it will help you feel better than ever. Use the following chart to find the foods that will help optimize your brain to make you happier. If you have a combination brain type, eat for the one that's most prevalent.

Brain Type: BALANCED

DIET TYPE

Eat a balanced diet

HAPPY FOODS	SAD FOODS
Fruits and vegetables: Eat up to eight servings a day to boost levels of happiness; tomatoes, beets, and green leafy vegetables have been shown to lift mood	Sugar
	Artificial sweeteners
	High-glycemic carbs
High-quality protein: Fish, seafood, turkey, chicken, beef, lamb, pork	Foods that cause allergenic reactions
Flavonoid-rich foods: Blueberries, strawberries, raspberries, cocoa	Alcohol
	Too much caffeine
Omega-3-rich foods: Flaxseeds, walnuts, salmon, sardines, beef, shrimp, walnut oil, chia seeds, avocados, and avocado oil	
Probiotic-rich foods: Brined vegetables, kimchi, sauerkraut, kefir (no added sugar), miso soup, pickles, spirulina, chlorella, and kombucha tea (low-sugar)	

Brain Type: SPONTANEOUS

DIET TYPE

Eat a higher-protein, lower-carbohydrate diet, such as a ketogenic diet or paleo diet

HAPPY FOODS	SAD FOODS
Dopamine-rich foods for focus and motivation: Turmeric, green tea, lentils, fish, lamb, chicken, turkey, beef, eggs, nuts and seeds, high-protein veggies (such as broccoli and spinach), and protein powders	Sugar
	Artificial sweeteners
	High-glycemic carbs
Tyrosine-rich foods: Almonds, bananas, avocados, eggs, beans, fish, chicken, and dark chocolate	
Flavonoid-rich foods: Blueberries, strawberries, raspberries, cocoa	
Omega-3-rich foods: Flaxseeds, walnuts, salmon, sardines, beef, shrimp, walnut oil, chia seeds, avocados, and avocado oil	
Probiotic-rich foods: Brined vegetables, kimchi, sauerkraut, kefir (no sugar added), miso soup, pickles, spirulina, chlorella, and kombucha tea (low-sugar)	
Beets	
Green leafy vegetables	

Brain Type: PERSISTENT

DIET TYPE

Eat a diet that is higher in complex carbohydrates and lower in protein

HAPPY FOODS

Fruits and vegetables: Eat up to eight servings a day to boost levels of happiness; tomatoes have been shown to lift mood; MACA (a root vegetable native to Peru)

Serotonin-rich foods: Combine tryptophan-containing foods (eggs, turkey, seafood, chickpeas, nuts, and seeds) with healthy carbohydrates like sweet potatoes and quinoa to drive insulin into the brain

Omega-3-rich foods: Flaxseeds, walnuts, salmon, sardines, beef, shrimp, walnut oil, chia seeds, avocados, and avocado oil

Probiotic-rich foods: Brined vegetables, kimchi, sauerkraut, kefir, miso soup, pickles, spirulina, chlorella, and kombucha tea

Prebiotic-rich foods: Dandelion greens, psyllium, artichokes, asparagus, beans, cabbage, raw garlic, onions, leeks, and root vegetables (carrots, jicama, beets, turnips, and more)

SAD FOODS

Too much protein
High-glycemic carbs
Alcohol

Brain Type: SENSITIVE

DIET TYPE

Eat a balanced diet

HAPPY FOODS

Foods that spark endorphins: Spicy foods (jalapeño, habanero, chili, and other peppers) and dark chocolate

Fruits and vegetables: Eat up to eight servings a day to boost levels of happiness; tomatoes have been shown to lift mood; MACA (a root vegetable native to Peru)

Serotonin-rich foods: Combine tryptophan-containing foods (eggs, turkey, seafood, chickpeas, nuts, and seeds) with healthy carbohydrates like sweet potatoes and quinoa to drive insulin into the brain

Omega-3-rich foods: Flaxseeds, walnuts, salmon, sardines, beef, shrimp, walnut oil, chia seeds, avocados, and avocado oil

Probiotic-rich foods: Brined vegetables, kimchi, sauerkraut, kefir, miso soup, pickles, spirulina, chlorella, and kombucha tea

Prebiotic-rich foods: Dandelion greens, psyllium, artichokes, asparagus, beans, cabbage, raw garlic, onions, leeks, and root vegetables (carrots, jicama, beets, turnips and more)

SAD FOODS

Simple carbs, such as bread, rice, pasta, and potatoes, which increase inflammation and the risk of depression and negativity

Brain Type: CAUTIOUS

DIET TYPE

Eat a balanced diet

HAPPY FOODS

GABA-rich foods: Green, black, or Oolong teas, lentils, berries, grass-fed beef, wild-caught fish, seaweed, noni fruits, potatoes, and tomatoes

Vitamin B6-rich foods: Spinach, garlic, broccoli, brussels sprouts, and bananas

Magnesium-rich foods: Pumpkin and sunflower seeds, almonds, spinach, Swiss chard, sesame seeds, beet greens, summer squash, quinoa, black beans, and cashews

Omega-3-rich foods: Flaxseeds, walnuts, salmon, sardines, beef, shrimp, walnut oil, chia seeds, avocados, and avocado oil

Probiotic-rich foods: Brined vegetables, kimchi, sauerkraut, kefir, miso soup, pickles, spirulina, chlorella, and kombucha tea

L-theanine: Drink green tea

SAD FOODS

Alcohol
Caffeine
Sugar

PUTTING IT ALL TOGETHER

One of my young patients, Jude, age 9, came to see me for severe anxiety, depression, and both motor and vocal tics. When I first saw him, he couldn't sit still, cried easily, whined, and had more head jerks than I could count. He made odd grimaces, clucking sounds, and whistled at inappropriate times. I could see his suffering and diagnosed him with Gilles De La Tourette's Syndrome. Jude had no friends, and other children teased him daily. The first thing I recommended was an elimination diet. The parents thought I would prescribe medication, which I was willing to do, but I was able to convince them to give the diet a month. Plus, I added low-dose GABA and magnesium to help calm the anxiety and tics. When they came back a month later, his tics had decreased by 90 percent. Everyone was happy except Jude. He told me he didn't like any of the foods his parents were giving him to eat.

"None of the foods at all? Not even one?" I said.

Being a bit oppositional, common in kids with Tourette's Syndrome, he replied, "No, not even one."

"Then your job between now and the next time I see you is to find 20 foods you love that love you back. I'm not sure you will be able to do it." I added that last sentence to use his oppositional behavior to my advantage.

His mother and I discussed a plan where she would take him on a shopping trip to a healthy grocery store and go up and down each aisle to see if he could find 20 foods he loved that also loved him back.

When I saw Jude a few weeks later, he had a big smile on his face and showed me a list of 43 foods he loved that also loved him. He is currently happy, thriving in school, has friends, and the tics are completely gone. By the way, his list has grown to nearly 200 foods.

The right foods can make you very happy, while the wrong ones can steal your mind. You choose. Here is just a partial list:

Beverages
Water

Sparkling water (add a splash of chocolate or orange stevia [brand: Sweet Leaf] for a refreshing, calorie-free and toxin-free "soda")

Spa water (sparkling water with berries, a sprig of mint, or a slice of lemon, orange, peach, or melon)

Herbal tea

Unsweetened almond milk (for amazing taste, add a few drops of flavored stevia)

Coconut water

Lightly flavored waters, such as Hint

Vegetable juice or green drinks (without added fruit juice)

Water with cayenne pepper to boost metabolism

Beet juice (to increase blood flow)

Cherry juice (to help sleep)

Nuts, Seeds, Nut and Seed Butter, and Meal
Almond butter

Almond flour

Almonds, raw

Brazil nuts

Cacao, raw

Cashews

Cashew butter

Chia seeds

Coconut

Flax meal

Flax seeds

Hemp seeds

Pistachios

Pumpkin seeds

Quinoa

Sesame seeds

Walnuts

Legumes (small amounts, all high in fiber and protein, help balance blood sugar)
Black beans

Chickpeas

Green peas

Hummus

Kidney beans

Lentils

Navy beans

Pinto beans

Fruits (choose low-glycemic, high-fiber varieties)
Acai berries

Apples

Apricots
Avocados
Blackberries
Blueberries
Cantaloupe
Cherries
Cranberries
Figs
Goji berries
Goldenberries
Grapefruit
Grapes (red and green)
Honeydew melon
Kiwi
Kumquat
Lemons
Lychee
Mangosteen
Nectarines
Olives
Oranges
Passion fruit
Peaches
Pears
Plums
Pomegranates
Pumpkin
Raspberries
Strawberries
Tangerines
Tomatoes

Vegetables
Artichokes
Arugula
Asparagus
Bell peppers
Beets and beet greens
Broccoli
Brussels sprouts

Butter lettuce
Butternut squash
Cabbage
Carrots
Cauliflower
Celery
Celery root
Chicory
Chlorella
Collard greens
Cucumber
Garlic
Green beans
Horseradish
Jicama
Kale
Leeks
Maca root
Mustard greens
Okra
Onions
Parsley
Parsnips
Red or green leaf lettuce
Romaine lettuce
Scallions
Seaweed
Spinach
Spirulina
Summer squash
Sweet potatoes
Swiss chard
Turnips
Watercress
Wheatgrass juice
Zucchini

Prebiotic Foods
Artichokes
Asparagus

Beans
Cabbage
Chia seeds
Dandelion greens
Garlic, raw
Leeks
Onions
Psyllium
Root vegetables, including sweet
    potatoes, yams, squash,
    jicama, beets, carrots, turnips

Probiotic Foods
Brined vegetables (not pickled
    with vinegar)
Chlorella
Kefir
Kimchi
Kombucha tea
Miso soup
Pickles
Sauerkraut
Spirulina

Mushrooms
Black Truffles
Chaga
Chanterelle
Maitake
Oyster
Porcini
Reishi
Shiitake
Shimeji
White button

Oils
Avocado oil
Coconut oil (stable at high
    temperatures)
Macadamia nut oil

Olive oil (stable only at room
    temperature)

Eggs/Meat/Poultry/Fish
Arctic char
Chicken or turkey
Eggs
King crab
Lamb (high in omega 3s)
Rainbow trout
Salmon, wild caught
Sardines, wild caught
Scallops
Shrimp

Brain Healthy Herbs and Spices
Basil
Black pepper
Cayenne pepper
Cinnamon
Cloves
Curcumin
Garlic
Ginger
Marjoram
Mint
Nutmeg
Oregano
Parsley
Peppermint
Rosemary
Saffron
Sage
Thyme
Turmeric

Special Category
Shirataki noodles (the root of
    a wild yam plant—brand
    name Miracle Noodles—to
    replace pasta noodles)

———————————— ☺ ————————————

CHOOSE FOODS YOU LOVE THAT LOVE YOU BACK

- Choose foods that make you happy now *and* later.
- Make your calories count toward happiness, not depression.
- Hydrate to be happier.
- Power up feel-good neurochemicals with high-quality protein.
- Keep your brain happy with healthy fats.
- Opt for mood-boosting carbs that last.
- Find happiness in your spice cabinet.
- Say yes to sexy foods.
- Eat clean to keep your body happy.
- Fight depression and other happiness-draining issues with a month-long elimination diet.
- Disrupt hedonic adaptation with intermittent fasting.
- Develop a happier mindset about your relationship with food.
- Eat for your brain type.

PART 3

THE PSYCHOLOGY
OF HAPPINESS

MASTER YOUR MIND AND GAIN PSYCHOLOGICAL DISTANCE FROM THE NOISE IN YOUR HEAD

QUESTION 5

Is it true? What went well today?

CHAPTER 12

ANCHORING HAPPINESS INTO YOUR NERVOUS SYSTEM

Practices That Train Your Brain to Be Happy

As you think, so you feel,
As you feel, so you do, and
As you do, so you have.

JOSEPH McCLENDON, III, *BE HAPPY NOW*

Start this chapter by writing down the next sentence, then post it where you can see it every day:

Where you bring your attention always determines how you feel.

If you focus on loss, you will feel grief.
If you focus on fear, you will feel afraid.
If you focus on being belittled, you will feel small.
If you focus on those who have hurt you, you will feel angry.

If you focus on gratitude, you will feel grateful.
If you focus on those who love you, you will feel loved.
If you focus on those you love, you will feel loving.
If you focus on the times you have felt joy, you will feel joyful.

That's why one of the secrets to happiness is about using your mind to help you rather than hurt you. Unfortunately, many people focus on their worries and fears, which makes them feel awful. Negative thoughts raise cortisol, which makes you feel anxious and depressed. Positive thoughts release dopamine and serotonin, which help you feel so much better. Once you get your brain healthy, you then have to program it to be happy; and there are specific science-based processes to do this.

Twenty years ago, CNN asked me to participate in a chat room discussion about the brain.[1] (You're dating yourself if you can remember what a chat room was back before smartphones, apps, texting, and social media.) The questions from participants that evening were all over the map, but a couple stood out to me:

> **Chat participant:** *What is the measurement of happiness? When do I know that I'm happy enough?*
>
> **Dr. Amen:** *Well, that's really for you to decide. I think some people are happy if they're going to eat today, and others aren't happy until they find the perfect mate. It really depends on you and your personal definition of happiness. For me, it's doing something I love, and I'm blessed because I do that in my work, and [by] surrounding myself with people I love and who love me back.*
>
> **Chat participant:** *What about people who have everything in life but are still never happy with one thing or the other . . . is it their attitude or some physical defect in the brain?*
>
> **Dr. Amen:** *It's probably both. It's hard to know unless you look, and I talk to my colleagues about that all the time. If you have everything in life, and you're still unhappy, it may be your attitude, or it may be your brain. For example, you might have a hot limbic system that you inherited, and it's not your fault. Changing your attitude won't help. It may be something you need medicine for.*

What I meant by that last part is there's a difference between *will-driven behavior* (your attitude) and *brain-driven behavior*, which you cannot just will away. The name of the CNN chat that evening was "Happiness and Good Brain Function,"[2] which shows you that the quest for happiness is timeless and the desire to understand, heal, and optimize the brain is never quenched. Regarding the latter, correctly reprogramming the brain is more than reminding yourself to think happy thoughts. I prefer that you adopt a mindset of "accurate thinking" with a positive or optimistic can-do spin to stay in the right frame of mind—happy. However, that's not easy to do because the default setting on the brain—set back in prehistoric times—is negativity.

Back when our earliest ancestors were scratching out an existence in a pre-agrarian society, they came out of their caves or primitive shelters each morning looking for danger, just like tourists stumbling into Jurassic Park. Their early evolutionary minds were used to anxiety and fear, which protected them from the harsh elements and wild animals seeking to devour them.

One can hardly blame our ancestors for going through life with their heads on a swivel: They never knew when a lion, tiger, or bear would pounce on them. Because our forefathers and foremothers were preoccupied with thoughts of surviving wild beasts, a marauding army, a blanket of pestilence, or a poor harvest, their brains were wired for negativity. They automatically paid attention to what could go wrong—and its catastrophic results—instead of defaulting to what they could do to improve their lot in life.

Today, you still need to pay attention to what lies ahead because that's how you protect yourself and survive, although my experience is that most people overdo forward-looking thoughts and make themselves miserable. Thousands of years later, we know more about the mind-body connection, which can be summed up in this way: The body responds to every thought, feeling, belief, and attitude you have, which can positively or negatively affect your biological functioning as well as your happiness. As you would expect, negative, angry, and hostile thoughts are the worst.

There is also a gut-brain connection that works in two directions: Anxiety can be linked to stomach problems, and stomach problems can be linked to anxiety. If you've ever had a "gut-wrenching" experience, butterflies in your stomach, or felt ready to throw up before a big test, then you were reminded that feelings of anger, anxiety, sadness, and stress coming from the brain can trigger ill symptoms in the gut—and wipe the smile off any face. As Jordan Rubin, author of *Patient Heal Thyself* and *The Maker's Diet*, writes, "If you take care of your gut, it will take care of you."[3]

Taking care of the gut starts in the brain, where annoying, exasperating, enraging, or furious thoughts gather like storm clouds and cause a rise in your sympathetic nervous system. This invariably leads to muscle tension, higher blood pressure, sweaty palms, cold hands and feet, irregular heart rhythm, confused thinking, and gut and immune system problems. Our research shows that negative thoughts disrupt brain function in the PFC (decreasing activity), the temporal lobes (impacting your ability to learn), and the cerebellum (meaning less coordination).

On the other hand, positive, happy, and hopeful thoughts lead to a parasympathetic response: relaxed muscles, lower blood pressure, healthier heart rhythm, warmer hands and feet, clearer thinking, a healthy PFC, and a calmer limbic brain. Those are characteristics of happy, contented individuals.

Learning to direct your mind is a critical secret to happiness. While it would be easy for me to say, "Just think positive thoughts" and wish you the best, our minds are too clever—and too active—to stay there very long because the next negative event or pessimistic thought is just around the corner. At the same time, entertaining irrational positive thoughts can be as counterproductive as giving safe harbor to negative thoughts.

The key is to "take every thought captive,"[4] as the apostle Paul wrote to the Corinthian church nearly 2,000 years ago. *Taking your thoughts captive* means gaining control over what you think about yourself and your life. You do this through:

- Accepting responsibility for your thoughts
- Working on disciplining your mind, from which behaviors stem
- Carefully thinking through your problems rather than reacting to them
- Choosing to focus your thoughts on true and noble things

An example would be those who were laid off from their jobs during the pandemic and told their friends, "I'll never find a job again," "I'm worthless," or "I should have worked more hours."

When you move your mind to the happy side of things, though, you raise rational thoughts that leave the door open to something positive happening or something good coming out of a challenging situation, like getting laid off. If you were let go, you might entertain more hopeful thoughts, such as:

- *I don't know if I'll find a job again, but I'll do my best to find something I like.*
- *Just because I got let go doesn't mean I'm a worthless employee. They were losing money and had to let people go. It wasn't personal.*
- *Sure, I could have worked more hours, but working overtime wouldn't have saved my job.*

When it comes to moving your thoughts toward a happier perspective and away from the negative, I recommend four simple strategies to put into your daily life, starting by pushing your mind to look for what's right first.

1. PLAY THE "GLAD GAME."

I was just starting elementary school when Walt Disney Studios released *Pollyanna*, a feature film adapted from a popular novel about an orphan daughter of missionaries sent to live with her wealthy, stern, and unmarried aunt in the fictional town of Beldingsville, Vermont. Hayley Mills, a 14-year-old British actress with adorable blonde curls and a button nose, played the role of the title character.

Pollyanna was one of my favorite Disney films growing up. She told her friends that her departed father devised the Glad Game after she received a pair of crutches in the mail instead of the doll she wanted for Christmas—obviously a mix-up that wasn't easily rectified in 1913. What was she glad about? Well, Pollyanna said she was thankful that she didn't need the crutches.

When she went to live with Aunt Polly, Pollyanna was punished for being late for dinner and relegated to eating bread and milk in the kitchen with one of the maids. No problem—bread and milk became her favorite meal. When the spinster Aunt Polly banished her to a bedroom in the attic with no pictures, rugs, or mirror, she looked outside and decided she wouldn't have noticed the beautiful willow trees outside her window if she had pictures on the wall.

Pollyanna is quickly introduced to a grouchy old miser, a self-pitying invalid, a hypochondriac, a recluse, and a fire-and-brimstone preacher. They share one trait: They are always complaining about something. Pollyanna, however, mirrors what her missionary parents taught her: It's better to focus on the goodness of life and look for something to be glad about, no matter how dire or bleak the situation is.

One Sunday afternoon, Pollyanna is hanging out in the backyard of Aunt Polly's Victorian mansion, listening to Tillie (the house cook), Angie and Nancy (a pair of maids), and Mr. Thomas (the gardener) bellyache about Reverend Ford's fiery sermon earlier that morning while they shell green peas in preparation for Sunday supper.

Nancy says, "I hate Sundays. Oh, I just hate them." Pollyanna counters by looking on the bright side and pointing out that they get to have roast chicken that day. Nancy glumly asks if Pollyanna is going to start up again with all of her "glad this and glad that." Angie pipes in, asking about all this "glad" business.

Pollyanna explains that it's just a game she plays that she learned from her father. The others in the group keep moaning about why they hate Sundays, but Pollyanna insists this is when they need to play the Glad Game. Angie challenges her by saying, "Alright, Miss Smarty-Pants. What's so good about Sunday?" Pollyanna thinks for a moment then replies, "Well, there's always something. You can be glad because . . . because it will be six whole days before Sunday comes around again."[5]

The group chuckles and sends Pollyanna on her way, and she gradually transforms the entire community with her Glad Game and cheerful attitude.

It's a shame, though, how our perception of Pollyanna has changed in 60 years. Being called a "Pollyanna" has become an almost derogatory term to describe someone who's naively optimistic, intentionally blind to unpleasant truths, and woefully out of touch with the harsh realities of life. Today, the *Merriam-Webster Dictionary* defines "Pollyanna" as "a person characterized by irrepressible optimism and a tendency to find good in everything."

Eleanor H. Porter, the author of *Pollyanna*, which became a huge best-seller during the dark days of World War I, even experienced a backlash from reviewers and readers regarding Pollyanna's "unsophisticated reputation" a century ago. "You know, I have been made to suffer from the Pollyanna books," she said in an interview before her death in 1920. "I have been placed often in a false light. People have thought that Pollyanna chirped that she was 'glad' at everything. I have never believed that we ought to deny discomfort and pain and evil; I have merely thought that it is far better to 'greet the unknown with a cheer.'"[6]

Pollyanna's philosophy about finding something to be glad about in any situation is an excellent way to go through life. If there were ever a good time to play the Glad Game, then today would undoubtedly qualify. But no matter what situation or setback you find yourself in, I urge you to ask yourself this question: *What is there to be glad about?*

When it comes to being happy, it's critical to have a healthy brain and train it to look for what makes you happy rather than continually seeking whatever makes you sad, anxious, or afraid. What Pollyanna did was adopt a central happiness principle: *Push your mind to look for what's good around you rather than seeking out what's wrong.*

Did You Play the "Glad Game" During the Pandemic?

Some positives came out of the terrible COVID-19 pandemic. I know people who, after getting the virus, decided they were glad they got it. Their reasoning: Now they would have immunity to it, at least for a time. I guess that's one way of playing the Glad Game.

Here are some other positive things my patients told me they experienced during the pandemic:

- Feeling closer to their children because there was more time together
- Rediscovering the after-dinner walk
- Eating more home-cooked meals and less fast food
- Playing board games together
- Taking up new hobbies, like woodworking or knitting
- Practicing a musical instrument that had been gathering dust for years
- Going to bed earlier
- Binge-watching shows they never had time to watch before
- Playing table tennis with their children
- Rediscovering reading
- Going on local hikes
- Less traffic
- Time to re-evaluate values

2. GIVE YOUR MIND A NAME: PSYCHOLOGICAL SELF-DISTANCING.

Another exercise you can use comes from a friend of mine, Steven C. Hayes, PhD, author of *A Liberated Mind*, who says that most of us live with a constant stream of internal thoughts, criticisms from the past, and commands from bosses and authority figures bouncing around our brains. We can decide not to let them define us, Steven says, by cultivating a "psychological flexibility" that keeps us from fully buying into what our thoughts are telling us or allowing them to over-direct our actions and choices.[7]

Steven gave an example of the thoughts pinging around the recesses of his brain while he was writing his book:

It's time to get up. No, it isn't; it's only 6 o'clock. That's seven hours of sleep. I need eight—that's the goal. I feel fat. Well, birthday cake, duh. I have to eat cake on my son's birthday. Maybe, but not such a big piece. I bet I'm up to 196 lbs. Shoot . . . by the time I run the Halloween candy/Turkey Day gauntlet, I'll be back over 200. But maybe not. Maybe more like 193. Maybe exercise more. Anything would be "more." I've gotta focus. I have a chapter to write. I'm falling behind . . . and I'm getting fat again. Noticing the voices and letting them run might be a good start to the chapter. Better to go back to sleep. But maybe it could work. It was sweet of Jacque to suggest it. She's up early. Maybe it's her cold. Maybe I should get out of bed and see if she is okay. It's only 6:15. I need my eight hours. It's close now to seven and a half hours. Still not eight.[8]

Hayes calls these unwanted thoughts intrusive, and they come in all shapes and sizes, provoking feelings of shame, fear, and disgust in those who let them linger. An intrusive thought might start when you're sitting next to your spouse or a close friend and you have a fleeting thought that you could stab that person with your steak knife. You're not seriously thinking of committing murder, but for some reason, the morbid thought zips into your mind. Hayes says these intrusive thoughts, while often unsettling, are entirely normal and ordinary. According to researcher Adam Radomsky, in a study of more than 700 college students from 13 countries, nearly all (94 percent) of the students reported having an intrusive thought in the preceding 3 months.[9]

We can train ourselves to dismiss intrusive thoughts and the unhappy thoughts taking up parking spaces in our brains. During an episode of *The Brain Warrior's Way Podcast* that Tana and I did with Steve, he gave a helpful strategy that I have used with many of my patients. It's called "Give Your Mind a Name," and it involves giving your internal voice a name that you don't call yourself. If your mind has a different name, then it's different from "you."

Years of research show that "distanced self-talk" can help someone gain some psychological distance from intrusive thoughts, helping them better regulate their emotions, self-control, and wisdom.[10] People are better able to handle negative emotions and intense situations, even if they previously struggled to manage their feelings or behavior.

As humans, we have the ability of self-reflection, which helps us plan for the future and solve complex problems, but when we perceive bad experiences are happening, self-reflection can turn into the darkness of negativity, rumination, or obsession. Distancing ourselves from the negative chatter in our minds by giving our minds a name—or talking to ourselves in the third person—can bring in more reality and light and positively change our brains. When research-ers used imaging studies to assess the efficacy of self-distancing techniques on the brain, they discovered that

HAPPINESS TRANSFORMATION IN 30 DAYS

My mind's name is Mickey, and it is fun to yell at her when she is trying to make me think junk food is happy food.

—ME

these techniques calmed the emotional centers in the brain and enhanced self-control.[11]

Hayes calls his alter ego "George." When Steven noticed that his mind was starting to chatter, he'd answer back, "Thanks for the thought, George. Very thoughtful of you." He wasn't trying to act dismissively to his mind; he was totally sincere. When he catches himself having an obsessive thought—*How come I got a one-star review on Amazon today?*—he can defuse that thought by saying to himself, *I notice that I'm thinking about those poor Amazon reviews instead of all the five-star reviews I received.* This creates some space between him and the downer moment, making the negative thinking lose some of its punch. You can do the same, informing your mind that you've heard the intrusive thought, and now you're deciding to let it go.

As I listened to Steven talk about "George," I wondered, *What name would I give the part of my brain that sends me unhappy thoughts?* My mind didn't hesitate to provide an answer, as I wrote before: Hermie! Remember the name I gave my pet raccoon when I was 16 years old?

My parents had asked me to drive to the local pet shop in the San Fernando Valley to pick up a new collar for our dog. While I was browsing through the store, I felt something crawling up the back of my leg. I stopped and watched a baby raccoon climb up my torso, reach my shoulders, and tousle my hair. She was the cutest animal I'd ever seen, which meant I had to buy her.

My parents were furious when I came home with a pet raccoon in a cage. I soon fell in love with her and decided to name her Hermie. At the time, I did not know Hermie was a female and named her after a male character in one of my favorite movies that year: *Summer of '42.*

Hermie was fun, smart, and devious, much like my mind. When the telephone rang, she would knock it off its cradle and make raccoon noises into it; she would repeatedly flush the toilet just to watch the water swirl; and one day she TP'd my mother's bathroom. I remember that day because when my father came home from work, my mother announced to him, "Louie, it's either me or the raccoon!" Without tact, he replied, "Don't let the door hit you in the behind." (My father was not one to let anyone tell him what to do.) Hermie was causing trouble in their marriage, and she was not finished with her mischief.

She liked watching the guppies and goldfish swim in the aquarium in my sister Renee's bedroom. One day, I caught Hermie on her tippy-toes with one paw in the fish tank, playing with the fish. I shooed her out of the room. A few days later, I heard a terrible scream from Renee, who'd gone into her room only to discover an aquarium without any fish in it. When I found Hermie, she had a satisfied smirk on her face. I figured Hermie's days were numbered. Another time, when I was running late for work, I hurriedly put on a pair of sneakers, and . . . *squish*! My nose confirmed my worst fear: I had stepped into a shoe full of raccoon poo. Then there was the day when Hermie met my girlfriend for the first time. I was so excited for them to meet, but when my girlfriend put Hermie on her lap, Hermie defecated right there, which she had never done. I guess Hermie didn't want any competition for my affection.

So, when it came time to find a name to call the part of my brain that causes mischief and trouble, the name Hermie seemed to be a perfect fit. Hermie, like my mind, was always talking. Have you ever heard a raccoon? They are loud creatures with more than 200 noises, including purring, chittering, growling, hissing, snarling, whimpering, and even screeching. Baby raccoons often mew, cry, and whine,[12] which sort of sounds like my mind. How about yours?

These days, my mind (Hermie) will randomly speak up about my failures, fears, and frustrations. She will tell me I'll lose someone or something important to me. She can play nice on occasion, but left unchecked, she can scare or terrorize me with a wide range of issues.

When Hermie shows up causing trouble, I metaphorically put her in her cage after assessing these thoughts and then quickly dismissing them—if they are irrational or unhelpful—which is what you should do. Then I go about my day. Don't allow those negative thoughts to linger and marinate in juices of fright and fearfulness, alarm and agitation.

Consider giving your mind a name. Some names my patients have given to their minds include the villain Ursula from *The Little Mermaid*, the shield maiden Lagertha from the History Channel drama series *Vikings*, and the actress and comedian Melissa McCarthy because you cannot take her characters seriously. One NHL player I treated named his mind Johnny because that was the name of his nemesis on the ice, and he knew he would never allow Johnny to beat him.

A woman I work with gave her mind the name Rita. This is how she explained it: "I'm giving my mind the name Rita. When I was in grade school, Rita was the first girl that I remember feeling less than, jealous of, and sort of competed with . . . for no other reason than insecurity. She got to eat Cheetos every day. They were always in her lunchbox, which my mom wouldn't allow because we didn't eat unhealthy foods growing up. I was so jealous of those Cheetos and wanted them so badly. That's how it started, anyway. Now, when I'm feeling insecure or depressed or hopeless, guess what I automatically crave and eat until I feel like garbage: CHEETOS! I am going to tell Rita to take a hike."

Bottom line: Don't let those negative thoughts live rent-free in your mind. Tell Hermie you're on to her—or him!

3. INTERRUPT UNNECESSARY UNHAPPY MOMENTS.

I learned this strategy from my friend Joseph McClendon III. When he was a teenager, a racially motivated attack by three white men left him injured and eventually homeless. After hitting rock bottom, he somehow transformed his mindset to become a doctor of neuropsychology, a best-selling author, and a spellbinding orator who often teaches at Tony Robbins's seminars. Joseph says that when unnecessary unhappy moments come up, he takes a simple, four-step process to get back on track:

a. **Feel bad on purpose.** Spend a few seconds feeling bad. Go to the dark place. Let the bad feeling wash over you. Sounds sort of crazy, doesn't it? But a few seconds can be empowering because, if you know how to make yourself feel bad, you can also decide to interrupt it.

b. **Interrupt the pattern.** If the bad feelings are unnecessary or unhelpful, which they often are, then interrupt them. I say "unnecessary" because some bad feelings are necessary. For me, those feelings surfaced when my grandfather and father died and when I unintentionally said something hurtful to my wife. I needed to feel bad at those moments, and it would be inappropriate *not* to allow myself to feel that way. Yet, most times when I feel bad, it *is* unnecessary and needs to be interrupted and replaced, such as when I was attacked on the internet after a "Why I Got the Vaccine" live chat.

  After you practice feeling bad, say, "Stop," stand up, and take three deep breaths. By doing this, you create space where a void will take shape. Careful, though: Voids always want to be filled, so your mind will default to negativity if you allow it; instead, direct it toward something better and more useful for yourself.

  For many of my patients, I have them wear a rubber band around their wrists (like one of my favorite Lakers players Wilt Chamberlain did[13]). When they feel bad, I ask them to stand up, say "Stop," snap the rubber band against their wrist, and then do several deep-breathing exercises. The physical act of standing up, creating a physical distraction, and intentionally focusing on breathing interrupts the pattern of feeling bad.

c. **Purposefully focus on happy memories.** Fill the void with happy memories so you can feel good on purpose. Remember, where you focus your attention determines how you feel. I ask all of my patients to write down 10 to 20 of their happiest life memories. (See the following sidebar of some of the happiest memories I return to.) Focus on one of those nice memories until you can truly feel happy or joyful. Imagine the memory with all of your senses: See what's there, hear any sounds, feel the sensations, and smell and taste what is in the air. Do this for several minutes until you can feel the memory in your soul.

Happy Moments from the Four Circles That I Use to Replace Bad Thoughts

Biological
- Doing 12 pull-ups with 25 pounds of weight around my waist on national TV at the age of 60
- Getting to a healthy weight
- Eating delicious foods I love that love me back
- Petting Aslan and Miso
- Playing table tennis at a high level

Psychological
- Making fudge when I was four years old with my grandfather at his kitchen stove
- Being my college commencement speaker
- Being the commencement speaker 40 years later at my alma mater
- Speaking at the American Airlines Center in Dallas to 26,000 people for 90 minutes and feeling like the audience loved every word
- Speaking to 7,500 high school students in Massachusetts at the conference for future physicians
- Having *Change Your Brain, Change Your Life* be a *New York Times* bestseller for 40 weeks
- *Discover Magazine* listing my research as the top neuroscience story and one of the top 100 science stories of 2015
- "Love Your Brain Week" on CNN

Social
- Marrying Tana
- Waking up next to her every day and going through our routines
- Being a grandfather—so many great memories, especially reading to Haven, who is just like her mom and now three years old
- Getting an unexpected present of a blanket with images of Tana, the kids, and grandkids on it

- Watching my teams—the Lakers and the Dodgers—win world championships within weeks of each other in the fall of 2020
- Watching my daughter Kaitlyn perform Pocahontas when she was seven years old
- Having my daughter Breanne get accepted to veterinarian school at the University of Edinburgh

Spiritual
- Focusing on my life's purpose
- Having patients say our work changed their lives
- Working hard to change how psychiatric medicine is practiced
- Creating *The Daniel Plan* with Pastor Rick Warren and Dr. Mark Hyman, which is a program to get the world healthy through religious organizations that has been done in thousands of churches worldwide

d. **Celebrate.** Last, wire the good feeling into your nervous system by celebrating your ability to interrupt the unnecessary unhappy moments. Joseph McClendon III likes to clench his fist, smile, and say, "Yes!" I like to raise my arms like Kobe Bryant did at the end of a Lakers game when he made a three-point shot to win. Celebrating is essential to making new habits stick.

☺ **Micro-Moments of Happiness**
- The instant you interrupt an unnecessary unhappy moment
- Having a tough day but finding something to be glad about anyway
- Talking back to your mind and calling it by the name you gave it
- The minute you walk through your front door and recall a happy memory
- Making your list of the best memories of your life

If you practice feeling bad, go through this simple process and begin to gain mastery over your happiness.

Joseph is so keen on dealing with unnecessary unhappy moments that he sets a timer on his smartphone so that a ringtone goes off at the top of the hour, reminding him that it's time to "visit" a bad feeling, just for an instant.

"You don't want to get mired in it or bogged down with it," he told me. "You just feel it for a couple of seconds, then stand up, put a smile on your face, snap out of it, and pat yourself on the back. Do that ten times, and it's really going to be hard to find that negative emotion again."

The step of standing up is more important than you think. When you rise to your feet, you create a scotoma—a blind spot—in the brain. It's like when you're sitting on the couch in the living room and decide that you want to read the local newspaper that's sitting on the kitchen counter. You stand up, make your way to the kitchen, and walk in—and immediately ask yourself, *What am I looking for again?* What happened is that you interrupted a pattern—sitting on the couch—and created a scotoma or blind spot. The same principle applies when you have a bad feeling: Stand up, create a scotoma for the brain, replace it with something positive, celebrate, and move on.

When you move on physically, your brain opens up, allowing you to put something else in its place—like something positive that you can "anchor" into your mind.

I included Joseph's quote at the beginning of the chapter. It is so powerful I want you to read it again:

As you think, so you feel.
As you feel, so you do.
As you do, so you have.

In other words, thoughts create feelings like happiness or anger. Feelings create our behaviors, and our behaviors create our successes or failures in our relationships, work, money, and health. It starts with brain health and then getting your thoughts to serve you rather than hurt you.

Of course, it is okay to feel bad now and then. The Hermies of the world inevitably want a hearing. But now you have the tools you need to replace negative, bad thoughts with happy memories.

4. FEEL GREAT ANYTIME, ANYWHERE.

The last tool is an exercise I use with my patients to anchor your happiest memories to specific places in your brain that you already know, such as rooms or objects in your home, so you can easily recall them. It is based on a technique known to the ancient Greeks. The Greek poet Simonides[14] was said to have left a banquet just before the roof collapsed and killed all those inside.

Even though many bodies weren't recognizable, Simonides was able to identify them by their place at the table. The practical use of this technique involves placing what you want to remember into a specific location. Then by going back in your mind to the location, the object or fact should come back to you.

For example, in memorizing a speech that is organized and outlined, choose the ideas or the major subdivisions and associate them in some way with the different rooms in your home. As you are delivering the speech, imagine yourself walking from room to room, discovering the associations you have made in the proper order.

In order to make this effective, use these two tips:

> a. **Make it active.** Your brain does not think in still photographs, so the more action there is, the more details you can employ in a scene.

> b. **Make the picture as crazy and disproportionate as possible.** It will be easier to remember the details as you recall the strange or unique things in the room.

Your memory powers will be limited only by the number of locations you can think of. I think of walking in my front door, then the living room, then the family room, kitchen, guest room, and so on. You can literally associate hundreds of things with the insides of most homes. This is how many "memory athletes" become so good at memorizing long lists. They use this anchoring technique.

Here's the exercise I want you to try: Write down 10 to 20 of the *best* memories of your life and then anchor them to specific places in your home, using all of your senses. Whenever you feel upset, imagine walking through your home, reliving your happiest memories. With a little practice, you can train your brain to feel great, almost in an instant.

Let me show you how I do this with five of my best memories. In my mind:

- **I start at the front door.** Carrying Tana across the threshold after our wedding as she pleads with me not to drop her. She had good reason to be concerned: I lost my footing and almost dropped her when we practiced our wedding dance the night before we were married. We still laugh about it. (Remember, make the image as vivid as you can.)

- **I move to the family room, next to the kitchen.** I see my daughter Kaitlyn as a seven-year-old in front of the TV, performing her part in the play *Pocahontas*. Not only did she love to perform, but being in front of the TV, blocking our view, was never a problem for her.

• **I go into the kitchen, which smells amazing.** My mom is making dinner and wants to hear all about my day. She's always been like that, and I know how blessed I am to still have her.

• **I stand at the stove.** I see myself as a child standing on a stool next to my grandfather, who is making fudge. He was a professional candy maker and my best friend when I was growing up. (But now we're making a sugar-free version so I can keep him around longer.)

• **I walk upstairs.** I see Chloe's room and imagine the zebra-hooded sweater she wore as she sat on my shoulders at a Lakers game, where she kissed my bald head and told me she loved me for the first time.

What happy memories can you anchor? With a little practice, this exercise can help you feel amazing anytime, anywhere. People who do it tell me they love it, especially when they share their memories with others.

CHAPTER 13

POSITIVITY BIAS TRAINING

Directing Your Mind to What's Good

When you appreciate the good, the good appreciates.

TAL BEN-SHAHAR, *CHOOSE THE LIFE YOU WANT:*
THE MINDFUL WAY TO HAPPINESS

I'll never forget the morning of May 5, 2020, a Tuesday. I was in my bathroom, brushing my teeth and getting ready for a day that would begin with me driving my 90-year-old father, Louis Amen, to an appointment with his pulmonologist. In early February, while COVID-19 was establishing a beachhead in this country, my father had suffered a gastrointestinal bleed and lost a lot of blood. We had taken him to the hospital, where doctors could not find the source of the bleed. His medical team should have given him a transfusion, but since they felt his anemia was not quite severe enough, they had discharged him after a week, even though he was still in a weakened state. At the time, I noticed he also had a new cough.

In the middle of March, his cough was getting worse. We were just starting the first nationwide lockdown—called "15 Days to Slow the Spread"—so this novel coronavirus was on everyone's mind. I had COVID-19 test kits at Amen Clinics and sent my niece Krystle, who was the clinic director for our Costa Mesa office, to my parents' home to have them tested.

Two days later, we discovered that both my parents tested positive. Paramedics whisked them to the hospital, where the staff arranged for my parents to share a room. We weren't allowed to visit them, however, and wondered if we would ever see them again this side of heaven. This happened at a time when images of forklifts loading dead bodies into refrigerator trucks parked outside New York City hospitals were dominating the news coverage.

My parents were put on a regimen of hydroxychloroquine, azithromycin, and zinc. My mom was part of a clinical trial where she was randomized to receive either hydroxychloroquine and azithromycin or remdesivir. Tana and I laughed with Mom when she told us over the phone that she had to sign an agreement not to get pregnant during the treatment. Perhaps my mother's playful sense of humor was one of the reasons she recovered almost immediately. Five days later, they were both released from the hospital and became local celebrities when the *Orange County Register* put them on the front page as an elderly success story.

Yet my dad's recovery lagged. He never gained back his energy or vitality and was sleeping up to 16 hours a day. Doctors ordered chest X-rays and put him on an antibiotic, but he was clearly not himself.

I was getting ready to leave the house on May 5 when Mom called me on my cell. She was in a panic.

"He's stopped breathing!" she cried out.

"Stay on the line. I'll call 911!" I replied.

After describing the situation to the local emergency services and giving them my parents' address, I jumped into my car and raced to their home, listening to Mom on speakerphone.

"Louie, get up," I heard her say to my father. "Louie, wake up."

I've never driven the four miles between our homes any faster. I arrived just after the paramedics pulled into their driveway. When I rushed into the family room, I saw Dad lying on his back with an intubation tube down his throat.

"He has no heart rate," an EMT told me. "Do you want us to revive him?"

I didn't hesitate. "Of course," I said, fully expecting the paramedics wouldn't be able to resuscitate him.

Meanwhile, Mom was obsessing. "He was fine and having a great day. I went to get dressed, and when I came back, he wasn't breathing."

"How long?" I asked my mother.

My mother shook her head. She didn't know.

While paramedics conducted CPR without success, a Newport Beach Police Department (NBPD) officer entered the house. I recognized him— Officer David Darling, an NBPD veteran. I'd met him and many of the fine policemen and policewomen during my monthly visits to the (NBPD) headquarters, where I volunteered my time giving two-hour seminars on brain health. I wanted our police force to have healthy brains because they have a chronically stressful occupation. My friend Jon Lewis, the NBPD Chief, had the same vision as I did.

Officer Darling pulled my mother and me to the side. In a voice filled with compassion, he said, "I'm sorry to tell you this, but when someone dies at home, we have to do an investigation."

Mom's eyes got big. "Do you think I killed him? That I was cheating on him?" My mother knew she was being ridiculous; her sly smile gave her away. We all knew that a police investigation of a 90-year-old man who stopped breathing inside his home during a worldwide pandemic didn't make sense, but those were the rules.

"Mrs. Amen, we just have to follow procedure."

That was the start of a terrible, horrible, no good, very bad day, which went by in a blur. Even though we were under California's severe lockdown orders, within 90 minutes, three dozen people arrived at Mom's house to comfort her and our family, including nearly all my siblings and their spouses and partners.

That evening, after a long, emotional day of dealing with the mortuary and then watching my father's body being taken away on a gurney, I showered and got ready for bed.

For the last three or four years, I had a ritual of putting myself to sleep by saying a prayer and then asking myself, *What went well today?* This was the bookend to how I started every day by saying to myself, as soon as my feet hit the floor in the morning, "Today is going to be a great day." I had embraced these twin measures of positivity bias training because I had programmed my mind to look for what is right more than what is wrong. I want to focus on why it will be a great day each morning and *what went well* when my head hits the pillow. Training my brain to search for the good things that happened during the day was kind of like making my own highlight show. It's my habit, ritual, and routine. It is what I do.

When it was time to fall asleep that night, I said a prayer, and then my mind went to *What went well today?* Then, all of sudden, my mind objected. Hermie (my mind), said, *Seriously, you are going to do that tonight, on the worst day of your life in 38 years? The worst day since you lost your grandfather in 1982? If you loved your father, isn't that disrespectful?*

Yet, because it was my habit, I thought about the interaction between Officer Darling and my mother. A smile creased my lips because, even in tragedy, my mother hadn't lost her sense of humor. Then I thought about the dozens of texts I got that day from my friends and my father's friends. Both he and I were loved. And before I drifted off to sleep, I remembered Tana and I sitting alone with my father in the family room saying goodbye. I was holding his hands and noticed how soft they were just before the mortuary staff took him away. Even with the tragedy, I slept well that night because I had been training my mind for years.

A couple of days later, we decided to cremate my father. Somebody went to the mortuary to retrieve his clothes, wedding ring, and paperwork. At my parents' house, I was going through the paperwork with my mother and came across a picture, randomly inserted in the stack of papers, of my father laying at the mortuary with a sheet up to his shoulders. Seeing the picture of my dead father bothered me for the rest of the day. I just couldn't shake the image out of my mind.

Then I remembered a technique I teach my patients called "havening" (see sidebar). I recalled the image of my father at the mortuary, along with the upsetting feeling, and then put each of my hands on the opposite shoulders and gently stroked down to my elbows repeatedly for 30 seconds. I felt calmer, like I was washing away feeling upset.

Then I asked myself, *How do you feel?*

My response was quick: *I feel better.*

I did this havening technique five more times for 30 seconds each. By the time I finished, a picture that bothered me had turned into a photo I could appreciate because it was the last picture I had of my father, who was at peace.

This experience was another reminder that where I directed my mind mattered. I could use my brain to torture myself with questions—*Who was the idiot who placed that photo of my dead father in that stack of papers?*—or I could turn my grief into something positive, which I did.

In a world of negativity, it's good to have positivity bias training.

What Exactly Is Havening?

In the early 2000s, Dr. Ronald Ruden, an internist with a PhD in organic chemistry, developed havening, a healing technique using therapeutic touch to change pathways in the brain linked to emotional distress. Dr. Ruden theorized that certain touching techniques could help boost serotonin production in the brain, allowing us to relax and detach from an upsetting life experience. The practice of havening involves one or more of the following touch techniques:

- Rubbing the palms of your hands together, slowly, as if you're washing your hands.
- Giving yourself a hug. This technique involves placing the palms of your hands on your opposite shoulders and rubbing them down your arms to your elbows.
- "Washing your face" by placing your fingertips up high on your forehead, just below your hairline, and then letting your hands fall down your face to your chin.

From a neuroscience perspective, havening is a form of stimulating both sides of the brain (essential for healing) while you mentally bring up a stressful thought or past trauma.

Havening got a boost during the pandemic when singer Justin Bieber released a YouTube documentary video showing him using the touch technique. While Justin massages his temples in a hunched-over, sitting posture, his wife, Hailey, explains on-camera: "It's basically a self-soothing thing . . . when you're starting to feel really stressed out or just [want to] keep yourself calm. It's almost like when you're a kid, and your mom is rubbing your back to sleep, and it's the best feeling in the world. It's kind of like that, except you're doing it for yourself."[1]

Dr. Ruden reports that his research has shown that havening generates high amplitude neural oscillations known as delta waves, which we experience when asleep.[2] Delta waves calm regions of the brain involved in creating emotionally charged memories and trauma. One of these brain regions is the amygdala, which plays a significant role in recording the emotions of our experiences.

When it comes to traumatic experiences, the amygdala encodes the related emotions differently, becoming what neuroscientists call "potentiated." This means the trauma and emotions get hardwired into your brain and stick like superglue. Havening helps loosen the glue in your brain.

INTRODUCING THE POWER OF POSITIVITY

Saying, "Today is going to be a great day" and employing havening techniques are examples of positivity bias training exercises that can help eliminate or suck the energy out of bad moments and bad memories.

The "father of positivity psychology," Dr. Martin Seligman, influenced me in this area. When he was elected president of the American Psychological Association more than 25 years ago, he gathered a dozen top psychologists and asked them to help him develop a plan to move the discipline of psychology away from treating mental illness and toward human flourishing. For many years, psychology worked within the disease model—treating those with mental problems and psychopathological issues. In their rush to do something about repairing mental health damage, it had never occurred to psychologists to develop positive interventions that made people happier. That was the impetus for Dr. Seligman to work with Dr. Mihaly Csikszentmihalyi and other top psychologists on a strategy they called "positive psychology," which shifted the focus of interventions from problems to solutions.

They determined that positive psychology had five key aspects:

1. Positive psychology helps us look at life with optimism.
2. Positive psychology allows us to appreciate the present.

3. Positive psychology lets us accept and make peace with the past.
4. Positive psychology helps us to be more grateful and forgiving.
5. Positive psychology helps us to look beyond the momentary pleasures and pains of life.[3]

Dr. Seligman introduced the concept of positive psychology at the annual American Psychological Association convention in 1998. His message: The field of psychology needed to expand its myopic focus on treating mental illness to include mental health. Then Dr. Seligman exuded transparency when he told this story before a room filled with his colleagues:

I was out weeding in my garden last summer with my daughter, Nicki, who had turned five, some 11 months earlier. Now, you should know that I'm a very serious gardener, and this particular afternoon, I'm very focused on what I'm doing—which is weeding. Nicki, on the other hand, is having fun. Weeds are flying up in the air, and dirt is spraying everywhere.

Now, I should mention here, that despite all my work on optimism, I've always been somewhat of a nimbus cloud around my house. And despite all my work with children, and despite having five children of my own, ages five to 29, I'm really not that good with kids. And so, kneeling that afternoon in my garden, I yelled at Nicki.

Nicki got a stern look on her face, and she walked right over to me. "Daddy," she said, "I want to talk with you." And this is just what she said. "From the time I was three until I was five, I whined a lot. But I decided the day I turned five to stop whining. And I haven't whined once since the day I turned five."

Then Nicki looked me right in the eye and said, "Daddy, if I could stop whining, you can stop being such a grouch."[4]

The room erupted with laughter. Out of the mouths of babes, right?

With Dr. Seligman leading the charge, positive psychology started to change the landscape of psychology during the 2000s. In the past, scientists and psychologists have said that happiness is too subjective, too broad, and too culturally relative to explore seriously, but as discussed earlier in this book, neuroscientists have found that about 40 percent of a person's sense of positivity is due to their genetic makeup. The rest is all highly dependent on an individual's experiences, emotions, and thoughts.

Their studies also suggested that happiness could be achieved through various channels, such as:

- Social awareness (being aware of the physical senses of touch, smell, taste, hearing, and sight)
- Social communication (verbal and nonverbal forms of social interaction)
- Gratitude practices (expressing and showing heartfelt appreciation)
- Cognitive reformations (changing the way you think)

Taken together, these factors are clustered in practical techniques called positive psychology interventions, or PPIs.[5] These scientific tools and strategies are designed to boost happiness, well-being, and emotions.

POSITIVITY BIAS TRAINING EXERCISES: NINE STEPS TO RAISE YOUR HAPPINESS

Drs. Seligman and Csikszentmihalyi found that positive psychology interventions enhance one's life, regardless of one's mental state or circumstances. Now let's turn these into nine actionable steps I teach my patients to help them be happier and overcome negative feelings.

1. **Start each morning by saying, "Today is going to be a great day."** As I've said, where you bring your attention determines how you feel. If you want to feel happier, start the day by directing your attention to what you are excited about, what you like, what you want, what you hope for, and what makes you happy, rather than the negative. I recommend families do it together as they are waking up their kids or at the breakfast table in the morning. I love this exercise so much that it's at the top of my to-do list that I look at every day, just in case I miss saying it.

Now, I understand that saying, "Today is going to be a great day" may sound a bit, shall I say, Pollyannish, especially during a pandemic when thousands were dying from COVID-19 or restaurant owners were forced to close their businesses. My heart grieves for those families personally hit with the coronavirus (mine included), yet being negative won't help anyone. We had a lot to do at Amen Clinics helping the thousands of people with mounting anxiety, depression, and suicidal thoughts.

By saying, "Today is going to be a great day," I was protecting and focusing my mind to see what was right, not just what was wrong, which was so easy to find. This helped me do hundreds of live chats on social media during the pandemic, encouraging our patients and followers.

Another reason I recommend this practice is because it plants seeds of optimism into the soil of everyday life. Happy individuals look for the good that can come out of a situation, not what can go wrong. One of my favorite sayings is: "A pessimist sees the difficulty in every opportunity; an optimist sees the opportunity in every difficulty."

Optimists and pessimists approach problems differently. Optimists generally proceed with a positive outlook, while pessimists expect the sky to fall. Optimists know that things don't always go their way, so when life knocks them down, they get back up and try again. A sense of optimism lifts the immune system, helps prevent chronic disease, and gives you a better chance of coping with bad news, such as when my father passed away.

HAPPINESS TRANSFORMATION IN 30 DAYS

Thank you so much for this 30-day challenge. There are so many insights and tips to change my thinking. Just saying, "Today is going to be a great day!" has changed my outlook, and I say it every day.
—SD

☺ **2. Record your micro-moments of happiness for later viewing.** As I have shared in earlier chapters, happiness doesn't have to be something "big" or "off the charts." Happiness stemming from small moments can actually be more valuable than significant milestones like your birthday, a graduation ceremony, or a party.

By getting into the habit of looking for and finding the teeny-tiny, itty-bitty, micro-moments of happiness throughout your day, you train your brain to have a positivity bias. Keep a written journal or use the notes section of your phone to record these moments throughout your day. Then, refer to them at the end of your day to make sure you don't miss out on the little things that help you feel happy. When you really pay attention to these micro-moments, they can have a big impact on your chemicals of happiness and overall positivity. "Seek and you will find" (Matthew 7:7, NIV).

Here are some examples of micro-moments my patients have shared with me in each of the Four Circles of Happiness:

☺

Micro-Moments in the Four Circles of Happiness

Biological

Waking up and actually feeling rested
Seeing my baby smile
Noticing the leaves changing color
Hearing the first note of my favorite song come on the radio
The moment I splash under the water at the pool
The smells when I start cooking
The sound of live music at the start of a concert
Walking down the jetway at the start of a vacation
Holding an umbrella during a rainstorm
Savoring the taste of the first bite of a healthy dessert

Psychological

Finishing a puzzle
Tuning into my favorite TV series
Writing my thoughts in a journal and instantly feeling better
Playing my favorite instrumental music
Doing an ancestry search
Reading a book to my young child
Listening to a worthwhile podcast
Listening to a great audiobook
Trying out a new software program

Social

Hitting the "buy" button for airline tickets for my next vacation
When I pet my dog, and he looks at me with those eyes
Spotting the owl that visits my yard
When my spouse reaches out to hold my hand
Hearing someone else laugh
Receiving a "good job" from my boss
Getting an unexpected message from an old friend
Seeing my friends when I arrive at the tennis court
Sitting down for a dinner party
Driving to a scenic point and watching the sun go down

Spiritual

When I pray and feel connected to God

Attending religious services at church with people I care about

Caring for the planet (recycling)

Losing a sense of time when I meditate

Doing work that matters

Helping a friend get through a loss

Attending a men's or women's conference

Looking for inspiration

---

3. Express gratitude and appreciation as often as possible. Behavioral scientist Steve Maraboli, the author of *Unapologetically You*, published a gratitude journal in 2020 called *If You Want to Find Happiness, Find Gratitude.*[6] And why not? When we express gratitude, we feel more positive, as does the person we're recognizing.

Focusing on gratitude boosts your happiness, health, appearance, and relationships. Appreciation brings gratitude to a new level because it builds bridges between people. Write down three things you are grateful for each day and try to find one person to appreciate. This simple exercise can make a significant difference in your level of happiness in just a few short weeks.

Dr. Seligman came up with a practice to enhance people's happiness called "The Gratitude Visit." This is how he described it:

Close your eyes. Call up the face of someone still alive who years ago did something or said something that changed your life for the better. Someone who you never properly thanked; someone you could meet face-to-face next week. Got a face?

Gratitude can make your life happier and more satisfying. When we feel gratitude, we benefit from the pleasant memory of a positive event in our life. Also, when we express our gratitude to others, we strengthen our relationship with them. But sometimes our thank you is said so casually or quickly that it is nearly meaningless. In this exercise . . . you will have the opportunity to experience what it is like to express your gratitude in a thoughtful, purposeful manner.

Your task is to write a letter of gratitude to this individual and deliver it in person. The letter should be concrete and about 300 words: be specific about what she did for you and how it affected your life. Let her know what you are doing now, and mention how you often remember what she did. Make it sing! Once you have written the testimonial, call the person and tell her you'd like to visit her, but be vague about the purpose of the meeting; this exercise is much more fun when it is a surprise. When you meet her, take your time reading your letter.[7]

Dr. Seligman says that if you're able to read this testimonial in person, be prepared: You'll set off some waterworks. Everyone weeps when a gratitude letter is read. When Dr. Seligman tested those who participated in a gratitude letter one week, one month, and three months later, they were both happier and less depressed.

4. Show empathy and kindness to others. When we seek to understand another person's perspective, we better understand his or her feelings as well. Self-love meditations and mindfulness practices are two exercises that promote empathy and positive feelings toward ourselves and others. Effective communication and more informed perceptions help us create meaningful connections.

A lot of people have or are going through tough times these days. Is there someone you could call or video chat with to ask how he or she is doing? Is there someone you know who needs someone to talk to?

Research shows that kindness leads to happiness. We've all heard the term "random acts of kindness," those selfless actions performed by people to help or encourage a stranger for no other reason than to put a smile on someone's face. There are dozens of ways to show kindness, but here are a few ideas:

- Smile when you see someone walking toward you.
- Hold the door open for someone and be less in a hurry.
- Be a good listener.
- Ask the person who is serving you how his or her day is going and listen.
- Send flowers to a friend.
- Send a funny cartoon or joke to a friend.
- Spend time playing with your pet.

Gestures of altruism have been shown to increase both the giver's and receiver's well-being. However, research led by Timothy D. Windsor, PhD, at the Centre for Mental Health Research at Australian National University, showed that individuals who spent *too little* or *too much* time volunteering reported similarly low levels of well-being. Those who spent a moderate amount of time volunteering reported the highest levels of life satisfaction.[8]

Along those lines, I use an acronym for those I hire at Amen Clinics and BrainMD, and it comes from one of my favorite Los Angeles Lakers players, Kentavious Caldwell-Pope, who plays with such infectious energy and enthusiasm. On the way home from attending a Lakers game where Kentavious played well and seemed to be having so much fun, I thought I wanted team members who were just like him—KCP: Kind, Competent, and Passionate. That has truly helped the culture of our teams at Amen Clinics. We focus on kindness, competence, and being passionate about brain health.

5. **Focus on your strengths and accomplishments.** An essential virtue of positive psychological interventions is focusing on what's right rather than what is wrong. I once saw a recording artist who had sold more than 400 million records. She was going through a period of depression and was focused on all the things that were wrong in her life, including an article from 40 years prior in a rock 'n' roll publication that was critical of her musical style. Despite all of her money and fame, she had no ability to manage her mind. Her homework was to go home and write out a list of her accomplishments and strengths. The list made us both smile and was part of helping her heal.

Focusing on your strengths rather than your weaknesses is essential. Dr. Seligman participated in a 2005 study demonstrating that strength-based interventions boost happiness and reduce depressive symptoms after just a month. However, it's critical that a person actually *use* the identified strengths. Simply talking about them doesn't yield the same benefits.[9]

What are five things you're good at? If you aren't sure, what are five things your friends say you do well?

When you have written something down, think of ways to use those attributes in your everyday life. For instance, you may have grown up in a bilingual home and have a proficiency in another language. Could you be putting that skill to better use in your career? The same goes for computer expertise, an ability to cook, or an ability to lead teams. Your personal skills can become your signature strengths.

A key to focusing on your strengths is having the right expectations and aspirations. It's interesting how, from a young age, we hear the myth that we can become anything we want to be, even the president of the United States. We move into the adult years with lofty expectations and hopes for a bright future, but if we learned anything from the pandemic, it's that we can't expect *anything* these days.

You will increase your happiness if you scrap or reduce any unrealistic expectations. Chances are you're not going to have the perfect career, the perfect spouse, or the perfect kids. In fact, seeking perfection is a recipe for unhappiness because you will always be disappointed. Set expectations that make sense to the current situation you find yourself in. And match those expectations with what you've learned about yourself through a strengths-based assessment.

Likewise, focus on your accomplishments. What have you achieved? When I asked one of my patients this question, he answered with "I can't keep a relationship." He had been married 11 times. Using positivity bias training, we reframed the situation to show him that he was very good at starting relationships and getting women to fall in love with him. We were going to work on how the relationships could last. We noticed what was right and then focused on what could be improved.

What have you accomplished? Write it down. Look at it. I keep a file on my phone of cool events I've participated in or hosted, and I look at it whenever I feel down.

6. Train yourself to live in the present moment. We've all heard stock phrases like "Live in the here and now" or "Make the most of each day," but research shows that happy people live more fully in the moment than those who are unhappy. A pair of Harvard researchers put this concept to the test when they created an app to analyze people's minute-by-minute thoughts, feelings, and actions.[10] What they discovered is that people tend to think about what is *not* happening as much as they think about what *is* happening in the current moment—and this typically makes them unhappy. Conversely, happy people who focus on the present are not preoccupied with past hurts, stressed by regret, or wrapped up in what might happen in the future. Instead, their attention is focused on the present moment, meaning they are aware and mindful of what is happening right now.

Being present-minded is critical to health and happiness. It will ground you and ensure you remain connected to the world around you. This doesn't mean you empty your mind of all thoughts, but your attention is focused on what you're doing, who you're with, and what you're experiencing.

I happened to read the book *The Power of Now*, written by Eckhart Tolle, after I had lost someone important to me and I was grieving. The pain caused me to hunt through past memories, which filled me with regret, anxiety, and chest pain. My gut was not cooperating, and I was miserable. The most important concept I took from *The Power of Now* was that my thoughts were causing me to suffer as I allowed repetitive thoughts to steal my vital energy. If I wasn't mentally preparing myself for something that would happen in the future, then I was getting lost in the past. But the more I lived in the present moment, the more I felt free from the emotional pain of the past and the worries about the future.

Present moment thinking is important even during hard times. While we want to get away from or escape pain, we must go *into* the pain. In my book *Your Brain Is Always Listening*, I wrote about the importance of allowing grief to wash over you and to let your tears flow in times of loss.[11] When we acknowledge and go into our pain, it starts to dissipate. By being present and mindful of where we are, we are more apt to feel happy and secure, better handle pain, reduce the impact of stress on our health, and better cope with challenging emotions.[12]

Here's one thing I've done to focus my mind on the present moment. On several consecutive occasions, each time I sat down in my car, I'd feel the steering wheel before I turned on the engine. I would grip the wheel, noting my hand position and the molded material around the rim. Spending a good 20 or 30 seconds on this before driving off was a slowing-life-down exercise that allowed me to "anchor" myself to the present moment. By observing my hands and observing my breathing, I connected my body and mind in the here and now.

Who doesn't need a reminder to grip a steering wheel or smell the roses as we rush through life? When we choose to savor the world around us—from breathing in the comforting smell of fresh laundry coming out of the dryer or slowly enjoying the intricate tastes of food—we refresh our sensory experiences.

Part of living in the present means not worrying about the future, which will kill your happiness every day of the week and twice on Sunday. Worrying may be second nature to many, but most of us are not aware of how much we dwell on fearful thoughts. Research shows that happy people worry far less often than unhappy people do.[13] This insight isn't new, however. In fact, there's a wonderful passage on this concept in the Bible:

> Therefore I tell you, do not worry about your life, what you will eat or drink; or about your body, what you will wear. Is not life more than food, and the body more than clothes? Look at the birds of the air; they do not sow or reap or store away in barns, and yet your heavenly Father feeds them. Are you not much more valuable than they? Can any one of you by worrying add a single hour to your life?
>
> MATTHEW 6:25-27, NIV

7. Be positive by eliminating the negative. As much we want to think positively, our brains love to camp out in negative territories—what I call the Badlands. Early in my practice, I treated so many patients complaining about deep, dark, negative thoughts that it was like they were on autopilot, sharing their negative thoughts reflexively.

I recalled these automatic negative thoughts when I came home to an ant infestation throughout the kitchen. The little critters were everywhere, coming out of a light socket and spaces between the flooring and the walls. I found ants in the pantry, where they were crawling into cereal boxes. Word had gotten out to a sizable ant colony that the pickings were good in the Amen home.

I had relied on a concept called mnemonics to get me through medical school. This memory device was a way to retain and retrieve specific facts or large amounts of information in the brain. A mnemonic can range from a simple phrase—*In fourteen hundred ninety-two Columbus sailed the ocean blue*—to an acronym that takes the first letter from each word you want to remember and makes a new word from all those letters. So I mentally played around with the phrase "automatic negative thoughts" . . . and found the perfect acronym. They were ANTs! Not only did this make a ton of sense on a day when I came home to an ant infestation, but I knew my patients were infested with negative thoughts ruining their minds.

After giving this some thought, I identified nine types of negative thoughts that love to infest your mind, like ants at a Fourth of July picnic. (I've written about these extensively in some of my other books):

- **The all-or-nothing ANTs.** These are the ANTs crawling around in your brain, ready to pounce when you think everything is peachy keen or everything has gone to pot. There's no in-between for all-or-nothing ANTs, no gray area. Things are either all good or all bad—and usually bad. They rely on adverbs of frequency like *always* and *never*: *I always mess up . . . I'll never lose weight . . . I can't discipline myself . . . I could never stop eating chocolate.* I had a lot of patients with all-or-nothing ANTs during the pandemic. They were 100 percent sure we were all going to get the virus and die.

The most common brain types for all-or-nothing ANTs: Spontaneous and Persistent

- **The less-than ANTs.** These are the ANTs that continuously compare themselves to others and see themselves as coming up short. The less-than ANTs love to damage your self-esteem by reminding you that you don't measure up, and never have, which makes you feel less than your friends and acquaintances. People with a lot of less-than ANTs are sure they will never be good enough at what they do or who they are. They put unrealistic expectations and pressure on themselves, not realizing that their friends have the same issues and insecurities they do.

The most common brain types for less-than ANTs: Sensitive and Cautious

HAPPINESS TRANSFORMATION IN 30 DAYS

Because of my unhappiness, I tend to see the negatives before the positives. This past week I have tried to look at things from the opposite perspective. It is a challenge right now, but I hope that it will become second nature soon.

—AC

- **The just-the-bad ANTs.** These ANTs go out of their way to see the bad in every situation. Their eyes feast on mistakes and problems, saying you'll never find another job or never move out of your parents' basement. This kind of thinking leaves people feeling like they have no control over their actions or behaviors. For example, people filled with just-the-bad ANTs believe the pandemic torched their dreams and ambitions. They are the people who, when they learn about an unexpected inheritance, will complain about the taxes they have to pay.

The most common brain types for just-the-bad ANTs: Sensitive

- **The guilt-beating ANTs.** These types of ANTs are mired in the words *should, must, ought,* or *have to.* People with these ANTs have excessive guilt about never measuring up, never coming through in the clutch, or sowing their wild oats in their youth. They feel guilty about their past, readily recalling their miscues, bad decisions, and stupid stuff they said. They replay a litany of shortcomings they heard from parents and authority figures.

The most common brain types for guilt-beating ANTs: Sensitive and Cautious

- **The labeling ANTs.** When you call yourself a loser or when you tell your child that she's an undisciplined brat, you have a labeling ANT in your brain. The problem with labeling yourself or others with a negative term is that you lump them into a group and cannot see them as real people. Plus, labels can become self-fulfilling prophecies.

The most common brain types for labeling ANTs: All brain types

- **The fortune-telling ANTs.** This is one of the "red" ANTs, the worst of the bunch. These ANTs predict the worst in any situation and then make the situation worse still. These ANTs link and stack together to create Chicken Little on steroids. The fortune-telling ANT loves to make dire predictions when something unexpected happens: The mole on your chest is melanoma skin cancer, or the funny sound from the car engine means a total replacement.

The most common brain types for fortune-telling ANTs: Sensitive and Cautious

- **The mind-reading ANTs.** Those with these "red" ANTs are convinced they can see into someone else's mind and know *exactly* what that person is thinking about them—like how stupid they are. But just as you can't read other people's minds, other people can't read yours.

The most common brain types for mind-reading ANTs: All brain types

- **The if-only-and-I'll-be-happier ANTs.** These ANTs like to argue with the past and long for the future. They tend to wallow in regret, repeating "If only" as an excuse for why they don't have the life they want. *If only they had more money . . . if only they were skinnier . . . if only they'd never married the bum . . .* Living in the past is just that—spinning your wheels because you can't do anything to change what happened. And if you think you'll be happier when something "new" happens—*when you get that promotion, when you move into a bigger house, when you get married*—it just prevents you from finding ways to be happy now.

The most common brain types for the if-only-and-I'll-be-happier ANTs: All brain types

- **The blame ANTs.** A "victim mentality" has taken hold in recent years and has become a real phenomenon. Having a "victim mentality" means you blame challenges or setbacks on people or circumstances around you. Some people latch on to these ANTs because they like it when others feel sorry for them or receive attention for their victimhood status. Of all the ANTs, this one is the worst because blaming others often results in taking little to no responsibility for your life. Since you consider yourself to be a victim of others' negative actions, you feel powerless to change your behavior.

The most common brain types for the blame ANTs: All brain types

Most people don't know that positive and negative thoughts release different chemicals in the brain. Whenever you have a happy thought, a bright idea, or a loving feeling, your brain releases the chemicals of happiness, such as dopamine, serotonin, and endorphins that calm the body. Whenever you have a negative thought, the brain releases or decreases chemicals, leaving you angry, sad, or stressed out. The release of stress hormones, cortisol (the molecule of danger) and adrenaline, and the depletion of feel-good neurotransmitters, dopamine and serotonin, change your body's chemistry and brain's focus. This makes you unhappy.

It's hard to climb the ladder of happiness when negativity is pulling at your legs. Sure, life is filled with problems, heartbreaks, and disappointments. Bad things happen both personally and professionally. Relationships end, and friends and family members die. It's important to grieve losses, such as I did with my father, and grief can be better dealt with when you give yourself time and space to do so. Realize that it may be weeks or months before you return to roughly the same level of happiness that you had before.

What you *can* control is how you react to the negative things that happen to you. Challenge your thoughts to achieve a more positive outlook.

Stop Believing Every Thought You Have

Thoughts are powerful and cause physical, emotional, and chemical reactions in the body, but here's the truth: *You don't have to believe every thought you have, especially the negative ones.*

Through the years, I've often said this is a concept that we should teach every kid, which I do in my popular book *Captain Snout and the Super Power Questions.* Captain Snout encourages children to live a happier and healthier life with a more positive outlook. *Don't let ANTs steal your happiness!* That is what Captain Snout says loud and clear in this playful and encouraging book about living positively without the stress of negativity. Captain Snout says we can use his super power questions to overcome the tough stuff and be heroic, too! Captain Snout teaches children how to:

- Eliminate negative thinking by questioning their thoughts
- Adopt a positive outlook and improve their overall well-being
- Overcome automatic negative thoughts

Here's another reason to take on the ANTs in your life, especially as you grow older: If you wallow in negative thoughts, your memory goes to seed. That's one conclusion I drew from a 2020 University College London study showing a link between "repetitive negative thinking" and cognitive decline. Researchers found that people who exhibited higher repetitive negative thinking patterns experienced a more noticeable and measurable decline in cognitive abilities, including memory and thinking skills. "Our thoughts can have a biological impact on our physical health, which might be positive or negative," said Dr. Gael Chételat, the coauthor of the study, echoing what I've been saying for many years. "Looking after your mental health is . . . not only important for people's health and well-being in the short term, but it could also impact your eventual risk of dementia."[14]

When dealing with ANTs and negative thinking, the best defense is a good offense. That's why developing a positivity bias in your mindset can counterbalance the mind's tendency to focus on the negative.

Whenever you feel sad, mad, nervous, or out of control, write down what you are thinking and ask yourself if it is true. To kill the ANTs, write down your negative thoughts, identify which ANT species they are, and challenge them by asking yourself five questions that I learned from my friend, author Byron Katie.[15]

1. Is it true?
2. Is it absolutely true with 100 percent certainty?
3. How do you feel when you believe that thought?
4. How would you feel if you didn't have that thought?
5. Turn the thought around to its opposite and ask if the opposite is true. Is there any evidence that it is true?

Then meditate on this new thought. Here's an example.

ANT: Nobody likes me.

ANT species: All-or-nothing

1. **Is it true?** Yes.

2. **Is it absolutely true with 100 percent certainty?** Well, maybe my mom likes me.

3. **How do you feel when you believe that thought?** Sad and afraid that I will spend the rest of my life alone without friends or a significant other.

4. **How would you feel if you didn't have that thought?** Happier and more open to meeting people and connecting with others. I would be more confident and feel better about myself.

5. **Turn the thought around to its opposite and ask if the opposite is true.** Some people like me. Any evidence this is true? My coworkers invite me to eat lunch with them. They wouldn't do that if they didn't want me around. My neighbor stops to talk to me when I'm walking my dog. He could just pass by me without saying hi, but he initiates the conversation. People at church asked me to join their Zoom Bible study group.

Meditate on this new thought: Some people like me.

In an exchange with one of my patients, she said, "You know we talk about killing the ANTs and retraining our minds. Sometimes I ask myself, *Wait. How do I know that little voice isn't my instinct telling me that I'm supposed to listen to it?* You know that whole 'listen to your gut' theory?"

My response to her: "That's a great question about when to listen to your mind. Ask yourself if your thoughts are helping or hurting you. Do they serve your goals as a mother, partner, friend, businesswoman, or are they hurting you? Do your thoughts bring you joy, peace, and safety, or are they bringing you sadness, regret, and frustration? Keep the ones that serve you and question the ones that drag you down."

8. Find fun and laughter in your life. Want to inject a little positivity into your life? Laugh more. Every time you let out a chuckle, your brain releases the chemicals of happiness—dopamine, oxytocin, and endorphins—while lowering the stress hormone cortisol. A hearty laugh is like a drug, changing your brain chemistry to make you feel happier, and making it happen almost instantly.

However, laughter is in short supply these days, especially the older we become. "The collective loss of our sense of humor is a serious problem afflicting people and organizations globally," contend Jennifer Aaker and Naomi Bagdonas, authors of *Humor, Seriously*. They point to a Gallup Poll involving 1.4 million people in 166 countries showing that the frequency with which we laugh or smile each day starts to plummet around age 23.[16] This explains why adults laugh an average of 4.2 times a day, which is a fraction of the giggles, chuckles, and bursts of laughter from children. They laugh an average of 300 times a day.

So what is laughter, and how does it happen? Laughter shows emotion, such as mirth, joy, or scorn with a chuckle or explosive vocal sound.

What this definition lacks is where laughter *starts*, and that's the brain. We know that the left side of the brain is responsible for interpreting words, including jokes. The brain's right side is responsible for identifying what makes the joke, observation, or situation funny. The brain's PFC is responsible for emotional responses, but don't forget that the basal ganglia—the area of the brain that integrates movement and emotion—becomes active when we're watching a funny movie or sitcom on TV. These areas produce the physical actions of laughing.

The best thing about laughter is how good it is for you. A Loma Linda University study on the effect of laughter showed that hilarity and mirth release endorphins—the body's painkillers—and lower blood pressure.[17] As the old proverb goes, laughter is the best medicine, and "humor is mankind's greatest blessing"—a famous saying attributed to Mark Twain.

So how can you laugh more? Well, laughter is contagious, so if you and your friends are able to take in a comedy at the movies, visit a local comedy club, or watch a live production of a farce-type play, do it. If everyone is laughing together, a bond is created that makes you more likely to express your true feelings, which also has a positive effect on your life.

In *Humor, Seriously*, Aaker and Bagdonas write that using humor to make other people laugh can be just as beneficial, helping us appear more intelligent, deepening bonds, enhancing creativity, and strengthening resilience. So how can you make others laugh if you weren't born with a natural funny bone? With practice, even you can find your wittiness by using two common elements of humor:

- A foundation in the truth
- The unexpected

I often use these two principles of humor in my clinical practice as well as in my books and public television shows. It allows me to deliver complex information in a way that helps people understand it and remember it more easily. For example, here is something I said in my public television show *Change Your Brain, Heal Your Mind*.

I was telling the audience that it was my 14th public television show about the brain and that everywhere I go across the country people tell me how my programs have changed their lives. So I gave them the following few examples:

I was walking recently when I saw a couple running toward me. The wife recognized me and said, "Hey, you're the brain doctor. We are out here running because of you. My husband wouldn't listen to *me*, but he listens to *you*!"

I also met a flight attendant who told me that she lost 30 pounds and stopped feeling depressed since watching my shows because she completely changed her diet and was getting her husband and her children to walk with her.

And I met a Stanford professor who told me he completely stopped drinking because of my programs and now wakes up feeling 100 percent every day.

Then I threw in a zinger:

> But my favorite story is of the 87-year-old woman who told me that
> she started dating again after she watched my shows because she
> realized that being alone was not good for her brain. With a smile
> she told me that she had recently met a wonderful 80-year-old man
> online and they were having the time of their lives. I wondered if
> that qualified her as being a grandmother cougar.

As soon as I said "grandmother cougar," the audience burst
out into laughter. What I said was all rooted in truth, but I threw
in something unexpected that made the audience's brains do a
double take. And by making them laugh, my own brain released a
cocktail of feel-good neurochemicals that made me feel happy at the
same time.

9. End your day by asking yourself, *What went well today?* I've already
described how I've been using this example of positivity bias training in my
own life, especially the day I lost my father. You don't have to wait until your
head hits the pillow to ask yourself what went well. This is an excellent exercise that any family can do around the dinner table and something we do in
the Amen home.

A couple of years ago, two of my nieces came to live with us because their
parents were caught up in addictions, and Tana and I wanted to provide them
with a healthier home environment. They're now 17 and 12. At breakfast,
we ask them, "So why is today going to be a great day?" And at dinner, we
talk about what went well. That's how I recommend families do it. Find a
consistent time every day to point the day in a positive direction and wrap
up the day by reviewing what went well.

I can always find something that went well each day, and so can you,
even during tough times. Looking for the good things that happened during
your waking hours will train your brain to search for ESPN-like "Plays of
the Day." It doesn't matter if those plays are spectacular, good, average, or
routine—they are yours. Thinking about the good things that happened to
you sets up your dreams to be more positive, which will help you sleep better,
enhance your mood, boost your energy levels, and put a smile on your face.
When you fall asleep happier, you wake up happier, ready to embrace the day
with a positive bias.

A Little TLC Always Helps

How can you be happy while the world is falling apart? How come some people can survive the most horrific situations while others struggle? I can't tell you the number of patients who've sat in my office or over a video chat and described how desperate they feel. Researchers have found that in high-stress cases, people who can't weather the storm typically believe three things:

- The situation is *permanent.*
- The situation is *global.*
- They have *no control* over the situation.

Besides using the positivity psychological interventions or havening, another technique to try whenever you feel stressed and anxious flips your thinking to feeling more hopeful about the future. The technique is called TLC:

- The situation is *temporary.*
- The situation as *local.*
- You have some *control* over the situation.

Here's how I used TLC to see the COVID-19 pandemic in a more positive light:

Temporary: The coronavirus pandemic will not last forever. Think about all the pandemics from the past—the Spanish Influenza, bubonic plague, and cholera, for example. They all eventually resolved. This will pass too. And every time our economy has dipped into a recession, it has rebounded.

Local: Although COVID-19 cases have been reported worldwide, the illness has not hit every street in every neighborhood in every city in every country of the world. While far too many died, the vast majority of those who contracted the virus survived. Even though my dad died not long after contracting the virus, my mom and a few other family members survived it, and the vast majority of my friends and colleagues never got it.

Control: What can I do to "control" the spread of the coronavirus? Practice good hygiene, wear a mask, and shore up my immune system with vitamins D and C and with zinc. I also received one of the available vaccines.

For managing the control aspect of TLC, I have often said the Serenity Prayer, attributed to American theologian Reinhold Niebuhr,[18] thousands of times during 2020 and 2021. It is the essence of mental health:

God, grant me the serenity to
accept the things I cannot change,
the courage to change the things I can,
and the wisdom to know the difference.

This is the happy person's way of life. Practicing TLC by walking yourself through what is temporary, local, and under your control will strengthen your resilience to get through any significant issue in your life.

MASTER YOUR MIND AND GAIN PSYCHOLOGICAL DISTANCE FROM THE NOISE IN YOUR HEAD

To anchor happiness in your brain:

- Play the Glad Game.
- Give your mind a name (psychological self-distancing).
- Interrupt unnecessary unhappy moments and purposefully focus on happy memories.
- Feel great anytime, anywhere by anchoring memories to rooms or objects in your home.

For positivity bias training:

- Direct your day by injecting a dose of positivity right from the start by saying, "Today is going to be a great day."
- Pay attention to the micro-moments of happiness in your life.
- Look for ways to express gratitude to others.
- Perform a random act of kindness and see things from another person's point of view today.
- Focus on your strengths, put them to use in your daily life, and routinely remind yourself of your accomplishments.
- Anchor yourself to present moments.
- Eliminate the negatives from your life and learn to question your thoughts.
- Laugh more on purpose.
- Review what went well today before you fall asleep.

PART 4

THE SOCIAL
CONNECTIONS OF
HAPPINESS

NOTICE WHAT YOU LIKE ABOUT OTHERS MORE THAN WHAT YOU DON'T

QUESTION 6

*Am I reinforcing the behaviors
I like or dislike in others today?*

CHAPTER 14

HAPPY CONNECTIONS

The Neuroscience of Relationship Bliss

It is a wise thing to be polite; consequently, it is a stupid thing to be rude. To make enemies by unnecessary and willful incivility, is just as insane a proceeding as to set your house on fire.

ARTHUR SCHOPENHAUER

In 2021, I got a call from Laura Clery, the comedian and social media influencer I introduced you to earlier, and her husband, Stephen Hilton, a music composer who is also her social media collaborator. They'd had an argument, or rather a "blowout, horrible fight" as Laura put it in a post on social media, and they wanted some marital counseling. I didn't realize it at the time, but the pair posted nearly the entirety of our conversation on Instagram and Facebook, where it attracted millions of views and thousands of comments. I'm happy they did. At Amen Clinics, since the pandemic forced millions of Americans into lockdown, we saw a dramatic rise in the number of people who were struggling in their relationships. I am sure there are millions more couples throughout the nation who needed some relationship therapy too, and I am glad they had the chance to listen and learn as I counseled Laura and Stephen.

So what was it that triggered their monumental squabble?

Stephen came bounding into the bedroom one night where Laura, who was seven months pregnant at the time, had already retired for the evening, and he excitedly asked her about something work related.

It sounds fairly innocuous, doesn't it? But sometimes, timing is everything. That was the case in this instance. You see, Laura's a lark (a morning person), and Stephen's a night owl. She goes to bed early to relax, but that's right when he feels the most energized and creative and is just getting into the zone with his work.

"That's awesome," Laura said during our therapy session. "But then you'll come up to bed at 9:30 and be like, 'How are we going to do this?' You'll be on fire with work stuff . . . I feel badly because I want to be as excited. And then we got into some stupid argument."

For Stephen, the notion that his nighttime enthusiasm was an issue came as a surprise. "I didn't even know I was doing that until you just said it," he said.

Basically, it was a case of mismatched circadian rhythms (the natural sleep-wake cycle), which I see in so many of the couples I treat. What I recommend to my patients, and what I suggested to Laura and Stephen, is to set up meetings to talk about work and other important topics. They need to choose a time when they're both feeling productive and creative to go over those conversations.

"That's a great idea," Laura said, "because it stresses me out at night and then I can't sleep as well."

By honoring their individual circadian rhythms, Stephen won't get frustrated by his wife's seeming lack of interest in his late-night brainstorms, and Laura will be able to sleep better, which will make both of them happier as individuals and as a couple.

As their exchange illustrates, relationships can bring out the best in us, or they can make us feel miserable. Positive connections make us feel loved, secure, and content, while troubled relationships drive anxiety, stress, and unhappiness. How critical are social connections to your overall sense of satisfaction and well-being? A wealth of research points to healthy relationships as the greatest predictor of a happy life. Brain imaging studies show that strengthening relationships can actually improve brain function in people with depression.[1] By enhancing your relationships, you can optimize your brain and increase your happiness.

I will give you a brain-based blueprint to more blissful connections with the important people in your life. These clinically proven strategies are rooted in interpersonal psychotherapy, a field that has been shown to decrease depression, anxiety, and stress while elevating marital satisfaction. A 2016 meta-analysis in the *American Journal of Psychiatry* reviewed 90 studies on interpersonal psychotherapy involving 11,434 participants and found it to be effective in preventing new onset of depression and relapses of depressive disorder in addition to easing anxiety disorders and eating disorders.[2] It has also shown promise for other mental health issues that steal your happiness.

To help my patients remember these foundational relationship habits, I use the acronym RELATING, which I briefly mentioned in chapter 4 on the Balanced Brain Type:

Responsibility
Empathy
Listening (and good communication skills)
Assertiveness (appropriate)
Time
Inquiry (and correcting negative thoughts)
Noticing what you like more than what you don't
Grace and forgiveness

I wrote about these strategies in my book *Feel Better Fast and Make It Last*,[3] but here I will give you specifics on how your brain type and the brain types of others play into the picture. After scanning thousands of couples in marital therapy, it has become crystal clear that brain types are one of the most overlooked reasons why relationships either work well or fall apart. For example, people with the Balanced Brain Type are typically well-equipped to follow through with these strategies. Other brain types may have more challenges with some of the tactics. Understanding your brain type and the brain types of the people you love can help you navigate your way to a happier relationship. And it is critical in a couple's ability to succeed in marital therapy and implement the RELATING strategies.

R IS FOR RESPONSIBILITY

In a video by Dennis Prager titled "Why Be Happy?,"[4] he suggests that it is our responsibility to be happy because it enhances our relationships and the lives of our loved ones:

> No matter how unhappy you may feel at any given moment, you can—and have to—make a decision on how to act. We may not be free to control whether we feel sad or happy, but we are free to control whether or not we present a happy countenance to others. . . .
>
> We all have the capacity to control how we express ourselves, no matter how we feel. I can prove it. Imagine someone who is just acting miserably to his or her spouse when somebody comes to the door. Have you ever noticed how nicely such a person will treat the stranger? How were they able—in a split second—to go from inflicting their awful mood on their spouse to acting beautifully toward the stranger who's at the door? Obviously, we can control our moods.

As I told Laura and Stephen, when you accept that it is your moral obligation to be happy for the others in your life, then you are more motivated to work on your relationships to make them stronger. Taking responsibility in your relationships is not about taking the blame for everything or pretending everything is wonderful. It is your ability to respond to whatever is happening in your relationships and taking ownership for finding positive solutions for any existing issues. This is what taking responsibility looks like:

I want to help find a solution to this issue we're having so we don't fall into a negative pattern.

I can learn better ways to have disagreements without letting them escalate into hurtful fights.

I am responsible for addressing issues in a healthy way before they become big problems.

My moods and attitudes are my responsibility, not my spouse's.

Taking responsibility for your relationships helps you avoid the blame game, which is something I see in so many of the couples I counsel. They play the helpless victim, which takes away all their power to influence the love in their lives. For instance, when a spouse puts their own happiness in their partner's control, it fuels distress, anxiety, depression, resentment, helplessness, and hopelessness. Blame is so detrimental to relationships, it belongs with the other most damaging traits that predict divorce, including contempt, criticism, defensiveness, and stonewalling, according to marital therapy researcher Dr. John Gottman.[5]

To put this concept into action, take a sheet of paper and answer the following three questions so you can start taking more responsibility in your closest relationships.

1. What is the smallest thing I can do today to improve my relationship?

2. When is the last time I blamed my partner, family member, or friend for something, and how did I contribute to the problem? How could I have handled the situation differently?

3. What can I do today to enhance my mood to have a more positive influence on the other person?

E IS FOR EMPATHY

When I advised Laura and Stephen to respect their differing circadian rhythms, it was an example of nurturing empathy, the human ability to feel what others feel. If Stephen can get inside Laura's head at night and understand that she's tired and needs to relax, he'll be less likely to expect exciting ideas from her at that time of day.

This concept is based on mirror neurons in the brain, which were discovered by a trio of Italian neuroscientists in the late nineties. These neurons help us "read" other people's minds and tend to mimic certain actions—like yawning when we see someone else yawn or laughing when someone else starts chuckling.

Empathy is one of the secrets to a happy relationship. People with the Sensitive Brain Type are especially adept at empathy and putting themselves in someone else's shoes. Empathy becomes even more important when you are in a relationship with someone who has a different brain type. For example, let's say you have the Spontaneous Brain Type and love going on spur-of-the-moment adventures, but you're in a relationship with someone who has the Persistent Brain Type and loves routine. When you suggest a last-minute weekend trip, it may cause distress for your loved one. And if they shut you down every time you hint at doing something on the fly, it can leave you feeling frustrated. Developing empathy can help you work through these differences.

How can you fire up those mirror neurons and have more empathy for a loved one?

- **Know your loved one's brain type.** Encourage your loved ones to take the brain type quiz (brainhealthassessment.com) so you can develop a better understanding of how their brain works.

- **Write down what makes your loved one happy.** Do they love spontaneity, going out with friends, routine, or romantic dinners at home? Look at your list often to remind yourself of what makes them happy.

- **Write down what makes your loved one unhappy.** What are the things that make them irritated, nervous, sad, or stressed? When you are aware of what triggers them, you are less likely to push those buttons.

- **Make an effort to look at things from your partner's point of view.** Before you say or do something, filter it through their lens. And if you're having an argument, listen to their side and take a moment before responding to really try to understand where they're coming from. (See the next section about listening.)

- **Mirror your partner.** Watch their body language, and adopt a similar stance. Are they leaning forward, gazing into your eyes, or snuggling you? When you mirror their actions, you create a bond.

L IS FOR LISTENING (AND GOOD COMMUNICATION SKILLS)

Good communication is essential for happy relationships. On the flip side, poor communication can sabotage relationships, even when two people love each other. As a psychiatrist, I have witnessed some really bad listening habits, including:

- Focusing on what you want to say next rather than listening
- Interrupting
- Lack of feedback (verbal or nonverbal)
- Getting distracted
- Lack of eye contact
- Daydreaming
- Rushing the person who is talking
- Finishing the speaker's thoughts

Whenever I notice these traits in the couples I counsel, I encourage them to engage in active listening, which is a technique that marriage counselors are taught to enhance communication. Active listening helps couples build trust, strengthen connections, feel seen and heard, and truly understand each other.

Here are seven strategies to put active listening into practice:

1. **Give feedback to show you are listening:** Smile, nod silently, lean in, or say, "I see," "I understand," "Uh-huh," or "Hmmm."
2. **Allow for periods of silence:** Rather than filling up every second when the other person stops talking, be patient and let them take their time.
3. **Repeat back what has been said:** For example, say, "To make sure I understand, you said . . ." or "So are you saying that . . . ?"
4. **Be neutral and nonjudgmental:** Wait until they are done speaking before giving your opinion.

5. **Ask for clarification:** For example, "To clarify, is this what you mean?"
6. **Ask open-ended questions:** Allow the speaker to expand on their thoughts.
7. **Recap the conversation:** After you have finished, go over a summary of what was discussed.

Keep in mind that some of these active listening strategies may be more challenging for certain brain types. People with the Spontaneous Brain Type are more easily distracted, so they may tune out during a conversation. The Persistent Brain Types are more likely to be judgmental or to be oppositional rather than allowing the speaker to finish their thoughts. Those who are Cautious may be people pleasers, perfectionists, or so sensitive to criticism that they shy away from asking for clarification because they don't want to seem like they didn't understand something. And those in the Sensitive camp may withdraw, so they may not give the verbal and nonverbal feedback that helps you connect. Whatever brain type you have, work to improve your shortcomings in the listening department. Your relationship will thank you for it.

A IS FOR ASSERTIVENESS

Being assertive means expressing your thoughts and feelings in a firm yet reasonable way, not allowing others to emotionally run over you, and not saying yes when that's not what you mean.

Here are five simple rules to help you assert yourself in a healthy manner and the brain types that can benefit most from them:

1. *Do not give in to the anger of others just because it makes you uncomfortable.* This is especially important for people with the Cautious Brain Type. People who experience anxiousness or nervousness are more likely to agree with someone simply to avoid conflict. This strategy often backfires because it teaches the other person that they can bully you to get their way. When someone's anger makes you uncomfortable, take a time-out before responding to their requests or demands. Ideally, wait until they have calmed down—and your anxiety has subsided—before asserting yourself.

2. *Say what you mean, and stick up for what you believe is right.* People with the Persistent Brain Type are naturals in this arena. They have

fierce opinions and are strong-willed. For other brain types who may be hesitant to speak up because they fear they may offend others or their ideas won't be well-received, practice speaking up and sharing your opinions. You may be surprised to find that others respond more positively to you when you say what's on your mind.

3. *Maintain self-control.* Being angry, mean, or rude is not being assertive. People with the Spontaneous Brain Type who struggle with impulse control may inadvertently blurt out something in anger when they are actually trying to be assertive. If this sounds like you, practice being assertive in a more measured way. When you feel compelled to verbally let loose on someone, picture a big STOP sign in your mind, then take a couple of deep breaths, counting to three or four on the inhale and six to eight on the exhale. Pay attention to the tips under "*N* Is for Noticing."

4. *Be firm and kind, if possible.* Being firm is an essential part of assertiveness, but kindness also comes into play. People with the Sensitive Brain Type excel at the kindness part of this equation but may struggle with the firmness. Cautious Types may also have trouble being firm because they want to avoid conflict. When you take a firm stance, it teaches others how to treat you with respect and helps you respect yourself.

5. *Be assertive only when it is necessary.* Most everyday interactions don't require assertiveness. Persistent people can have a tendency to routinely assert themselves for unimportant things, which makes them appear controlling or oppositional. If you have a Persistent Brain Type, practice letting go of the little things that aren't that important. On the opposite end of the spectrum are those with the Cautious Brain Type, who struggle to assert themselves out of fear that it may make them unlikable or because they hate confrontation. Stand up for yourself in times when it is necessary, such as when someone is trying to take advantage of you, when asking for a deserved promotion at work, or when you need to set boundaries with family members.

T IS FOR TIME

During the counseling session with Laura and Stephen, they shared a situation that led to an argument. Laura said she wanted to take a few days off from posting to social media and Stephen countered by saying, "Successful people don't take days off."

On our call, Laura said, "I just wanted to not be on social media and not be working and just be with the family. And we got into a big argument about that." Stephen's reaction to her request made her "feel like I'm a failure for wanting to take Christmas, Christmas Eve, and New Year's off."

It was fascinating to hear the couple dissect this exchange for their audience:

> *Stephen: Well, I don't think I said that. I didn't even intimate that. You just took it as that.*

> *Laura: You did; you were so upset that I wouldn't post. I didn't want to post. I just wanted to take a break.*

This is where I stepped in to help them navigate. First, I had to let Stephen know that the idea that "successful people don't take days off" is a toxic thought, an all-or-nothing ANT. People who are successful absolutely take time off, and in fact, it's critical. I reminded him that in order to have a happy relationship and a happy home life, he needs to dedicate time to it. We can't devote all our energy to work because that means we're neglecting important relationships.

I saw this with my own father. He was successful in business and worked nonstop. But that meant he didn't have time for me. So we didn't have a great relationship while I was growing up. It was only in the last few years of his life that he finally started spending time with me, and we became best friends.

Laura explained that Stephen eventually came around and agreed that they should take a few days off from work and enjoy family time. For Laura, it was just what she needed. "Just from those couple of days," she said, "I felt invigorated again and energized and so happy." And when your partner is happy, it makes you happier.

For healthy relationships, you have to invest in what I call special time. During the pandemic, people were spending more time together at home, but it wasn't necessarily quality time. You may have both been working at home together, helping the kids with online learning, or bingeing Netflix but not really connecting on a deep level. What you need to do is carve out time when you can focus on each other. Here are some tips to help you make the most of special time with a loved one:

HAPPINESS TRANSFORMATION IN 30 DAYS

It's amazing how giving or sharing time with someone makes me feel better about myself. It can be the littlest thing you do that can benefit others and in turn give you joy! Share the happiness!!!

—A.M.

- **Make a date.** Just like you schedule meeting time at work, put your dates in your calendar. Not only does this help you remember to take this time, but it also enhances its importance in your mind.

- **Go outside.** Getting out of the house where there are so many distractions—the laundry, the internet, the furniture that needs repairing—can help you focus on each other.

- **Be present.** Keep your mind in the moment rather than thinking about something that happened yesterday or worrying about what might happen in the future.

- **Turn off your cell phones.** To help you stay in tune with each other, take a break from your devices.

- **Do something you both enjoy.** Love hiking? Bowling? Playing ping-pong (my personal favorite)? Adding physical activity to your time together encourages the release of the chemicals of happiness that can strengthen your time together.

- **Make time to get romantic (for those in committed relationships).** Sexual intimacy is critical for couples and releases several neurochemicals that promote happiness and bonding. If you have hectic schedules, planning for romance can keep your relationship strong.

I IS FOR INQUIRY (AND CORRECTING NEGATIVE THOUGHTS)

In chapter 13, I showed you how important it is to question your thoughts and kill the ANTs that infest your mind and steal your happiness. In my practice, I meet with a lot of couples who are filled with ANTs, such as:

> *All-or-nothing ANTs: He never listens to me.*
> *Mind-reading ANTs: She must be mad at me, because she didn't kiss me goodbye.*
> *Fortune-telling ANTs: He's going to leave me because we had an argument.*

These people are often so wrapped up in their negative thinking patterns that they sabotage their relationships without realizing it. Whenever you have a distressing thought about your relationship, write it down and ask yourself if it is true. Equally important is asking your loved one to explain what they really mean whenever they say something that you interpret in a negative way. Chances are they didn't mean it that way at all. The next time you have unhappy thoughts about your relationship or you are hurt or angered by something your significant other said, start inquiring.

- Write down your negative thought.
- Ask yourself if it is true.
- Ask your significant other what they meant by what they said. (Use active listening to help you avoid miscommunications.)
- Let them know how you initially interpreted their comment.
- Work together to find a solution to help avoid those miscues in the future.

N IS FOR NOTICING WHAT YOU LIKE MORE THAN WHAT YOU DON'T

Have you ever gone out with one of those cringe-worthy couples who bicker incessantly? Throughout a single dinner, they'll needle each other over nearly everything—criticizing their partner's choice of entrée, rolling their eyes when they share a story, and snapping when they "misremember" something. It can be painful to watch. And it is a sign of an unhappy relationship.

Laura and Stephen do *not* fall into this category, but like most couples, they occasionally criticize each other. Sometimes, it can lead to a full-fledged argument. In our therapy session, they told me about another incident that sparked a spat. Stephen was making a pasta dinner for their 20-month-old son, Alfie. Laura, who typically makes Alfie's dinner, noticed that Stephen didn't put as much sauce on it as she does, so she added a dollop.

When Stephen realized what she had done, he got irritated "because I wanted to make him dinner," Stephen explained. In retrospect, Laura could see that her action had upset her husband. "It made you feel like I didn't think you were capable of making him a good dinner," she admitted. "It wasn't that I didn't think you were competent . . ." But that's how Stephen interpreted it, and it hurt. Ultimately, pointing out what your loved one is doing wrong is a de-motivator that drives a wedge between you.

As I explained to Laura and Stephen, even if you do notice something you don't like about your significant other, family member, or close friend, *you don't have to say it!* We all have weird, crazy, stupid, sexual, violent thoughts that nobody should ever hear. Saying them out loud doesn't help anything. When you have unkind or critical thoughts, filter them through the question "Does it fit?" I must say that five times a week with my patients: There's no rule that you have to say everything you think. Process it, then ask yourself if it fits with your goals for your relationship. Does it get you what you want from your relationship? Assuming you want a kind, caring, loving, support-ive, passionate relationship, pointing out your loved one's flaws and short-comings does not help you achieve that.

What does help you achieve a more loving relationship? Researchers have been looking for the answer to that question for decades. Much of the sci-ence points to positive reinforcement as a gateway to a more blissful union. Look at foundational research on happy couples and unhappy couples: The scientists found that distressed married couples were more likely to forego rewarding their partner's loving behaviors in favor of punishing their spouse for bad behavior—criticizing them, interrupting them, complaining, or turn-ing away from them.[6] This pattern of ignoring the good and punishing the bad fueled discord and created an unhappy marriage—it can do the same in any close relationship.

A wealth of research reveals that noticing loving behaviors and rewarding them leads to even more positive behavior.[7] This is called positive reinforce-ment, and decades of science show it works. For example, married couples who give each other *five times* more positive comments than negative ones are *significantly less likely to get divorced.*[8] The same concept applies to business relationships, where workers who exchange five times more positive comments than negative ones are significantly more likely to be high performing.[9] In this study, the lowest-performing business teams had a higher rate of negativity. Be aware that you can have too much of a good thing. When the ratio of positive comments to negative ones rises beyond nine to one, the effect backfires.

To get started with this strategy, don't expect to be noticing grand gestures like a bouquet of roses, a surprise gift, or a romantic getaway. Look for the micro-moments of loving behavior, the little everyday things that say "I love you," such as:

☺ When they make dinner for the kids
When they get your favorite food from the grocery store
When they fill up your gas tank
When they compliment your new haircut
When they wear that shirt you gave them for their birthday
When they make your morning smoothie so you can sleep in a few minutes
When they organize a family fun night as a surprise for you

> **HAPPINESS TRANSFORMATION IN 30 DAYS**
>
> *I have gained new tools to use when the world threatens to crush my spirit. My life is filled with joy, happiness, and people I love who love me back. I am grateful for your instruction on how to keep happiness, positivity, and gratitude in plain sight.*
>
> —ML

G IS FOR GRACE AND FORGIVENESS

Do you hold grudges or keep reminding your significant other or a family member of past mistakes or transgressions? Do you keep having the same arguments over and over? This is a serious sign of trouble that can sabotage relationships and feed unhappiness. Scientists have found that a lack of forgiveness is associated with increased stress and negative impacts on mental health and physical well-being—all things that suck the happiness out of you.[10]

By contrast, learning to give grace and forgiveness plays an instrumental role in helping a relationship flourish, and it can be powerfully healing. In fact, findings in the *Journal of Happiness Studies* show that forgiveness can make you happier, both in the moment and on a deep-down level.[11] Other studies have linked forgiveness with decreases in depression, anxiety, and other mental health disorders, in addition to fewer physical health problems and reduced mortality rates.[12]

Whenever I talk to my patients about this important topic, I tell them about the REACH forgiveness method, which was developed by psychologist Everett Worthington of Virginia Commonwealth University.[13] REACH stands for:

- **R**ecall the hurt. Try to think about the hurt without feeling like a victim and without holding a grudge.

- **E**mpathize. Try to put yourself in the shoes of the person who hurt you and see the situation from their viewpoint. Can you empathize with what they may have been feeling?

- **A**ltruistic gift. Offer your forgiveness as a gift to the person who caused you pain. If you're having trouble with this step, think of someone who forgave you for something you did and remember how good it made you feel.

- **C**ommit to the forgiveness. Rather than simply thinking about forgiving someone, make it more concrete by writing it down or making a public statement about it.

- **H**old on to the forgiveness. If you come in contact with the person who hurt you, you may feel a visceral reaction—anxiousness, anger, or fear, for instance—and think this signals a retraction of your forgiveness. Not so. This is simply your body's way of giving you a warning.

To help you work through the REACH method, keep the following tips in mind:

1. **Know how your brain type influences your ability to forgive.** Some brain types have a much harder time forgiving. In particular, people with the Persistent Brain Type tend to hold on to past grudges. If that's you, acknowledge that it may take more time for you to forgive people who have hurt you. Allow yourself to go at your own pace.

2. **Think about the brain type and brain health of the person who hurt you.** Do they have abnormal brain function, mental health issues, or a past concussion that has negatively impacted their brain? Keep this in mind when making an effort to forgive.

3. **Forgiveness is a process.** Forgiveness does not always come easy, and it isn't a "one-and-done" event. You may take the necessary steps to forgive someone, but those resentful feelings may come creeping back in from time to time (I'm talking to you, Persistent people). Whenever you have one of these down times, analyze it. Think about what may have triggered those old emotions. Did you have a bad night's sleep? Did you drink alcohol? Did you skip lunch? Did you have a big deadline at work? All of life's ups and downs can impact your ability to maintain the grace you have given.

4. **Forgiveness does not mean you have to reconnect with the person who hurt you.** The act of forgiveness is for you. If someone was abusive to you, it is not in your best interest to keep them in your life or to re-invite them into your social circle. Tell them you forgive them but that you can't have them be a part of your life anymore.

5. **Grace and forgiveness are acts of strength, not weakness.** Grace and forgiveness do not mean rolling over and letting someone get away with unacceptable or hurtful behaviors. If you find yourself doing this, which is more common in the Cautious types, go back to the "A is for Assertive" section of this chapter.

Are "Mental" Dragons Ruining Your Relationship?

In my book *Your Brain Is Always Listening*, I introduced readers to the concept of the Dragons from the Past—the inner beasts that breathe fire on your emotional brain and steal your happiness.[14] Left untamed, these dragons can run wild and drive depression, anxiety, and other emotional health issues. We all have dragons—you have them, your significant other has them, and so do your boss, coworkers, friends, parents, siblings, and kids. Even I have them.

Your brain is always listening to your Dragons from the Past. But that's not all. Your brain is also listening to the words and actions of the other important people in your life, who are listening to their own dragons. That's why relationships can get so messy.

Over time, I have identified 13 Dragons from the Past:

Abandoned, Invisible, or Insignificant Dragons—feel alone, unseen, or unimportant

Inferior or Flawed Dragons—feel less than others

Anxious Dragons—feel fearful and overwhelmed

Wounded Dragons—bruised by past trauma

Should and Shaming Dragons—racked with guilt

Special, Spoiled, or Entitled Dragons—feel more special than others

Responsible Dragons—need to take care of others

Angry Dragons—harbor hurts and rage

Judgmental Dragons—hold harsh or critical opinions of others due to past injustices

Death Dragons—fear the future and lack of a meaningful life

Grief and Loss Dragons—feel loss and fear of loss

Hopeless and Helpless Dragons—have pervasive sense of despair and discouragement

Ancestral Dragons—affected by issues from past generations

Let's say you and your spouse are having an everyday discussion. Without either of you realizing it, something you say may trigger their inner dragons, and all of a sudden, their dragons roar to life and pick a fight with your dragons. Then your dragons roar back, and in the blink of an eye, you've both gone from talking calmly to having a shouting match. It's like a *Game of Thrones* battle inside your head. Unless you both tame your inner dragons, it can create an unhappy relationship, even when two people care deeply for each other.

Learning to recognize your dragons is the first step to taming them. Discover which dragons you have by taking my quiz at KnowYourDragons. com. You will also discover their origins, what triggers them, and how they make you react. Encourage your loved ones to take the quiz too, so you will be aware of their dragons and how they may be breathing fire on your dragons.

☺

NOTICE WHAT YOU LIKE ABOUT OTHERS MORE THAN WHAT YOU DON'T

Responsibility
Empathy
Listening (and good communication skills)
Assertiveness (appropriate)
Time
Inquiry (and correcting negative thoughts)
Noticing what you like more than what you don't
Grace and forgiveness

CHAPTER 15

HAPPINESS AROUND THE WORLD

What Different Cultures Teach Us about Happiness

The world is smaller than you think, and the people on it are more beautiful than you think.

BERTRAM VAN MUNSTER, *PRODUCER AND DIRECTOR*

Have you ever been on the ride "It's a Small World" at one of the Disney amusement parks?

"It's a Small World" is still among the most popular Disney attractions and one of my favorites. I had a great time sharing the boat ride with each of my kids when they were young, followed by the grandkids. The last time I went on "It's a Small World" was right before the pandemic hit, when I accompanied my granddaughter Haven, a busy, outgoing girl like her mother. Haven was amazed and gleeful during the entire 10-minute trip, looking around and pointing at the happy singing dolls.

I haven't forgotten my first time (I was 12) on this entertaining boat ride billed as the "Happiest Cruise That Ever Sailed." It lazily meanders past colorful audio-animatronic dolls dressed in native costumes representing various countries from around the world, who sing the same song in high-pitched children's voices.

By the end of the ride, they achieve universal harmony by chanting the catchy yet mind-numbing tune in different languages. You know what song I'm talking about—"It's a world of laughter, a world of tears. . . . It's a small world after all."

And now I can't get that song out of my head! Maybe you're gnashing your teeth as well because "It's a Small World" is now parked and playing in your brain. If so, you're not alone. "No song has gotten on people's nerves as consistently as that theme-park paean to global unity," wrote Jason Richards in the *Atlantic*, calling it "the most irritating song of all time."[1]

Why Do Songs Get Stuck in Our Brains?

If you're wondering why certain songs become embedded in your brain and get stuck there, it's because they're *earworms*, a term coined by the Germans a century ago (*ohrwurms* in their language). This explains why relentless tunes like "It's a Small World," "YMCA," and "Don't Stop Believin'" play in a continuous loop for up to 98 percent of people in the western world.[2]

Scientists have other names for this phenomenon: stuck tune syndrome and musical imagery repetition. Dartmouth College researchers discovered that when participants listened to a song, the left primary auditory cortex—the region of the brain associated with hearing and the processing of sounds—is activated. This brain region is also switched on when participants *think* of a song, which suggests that an earworm may be "fed" by the auditory cortex's memory mechanism.[3]

Treatment? There's not much you can do except ride it out. Researchers at the Department of Mental Health and Autism of Lentis Psychiatric Institute in Groningen, Netherlands, say that either singing the song aloud (engagement) or focusing on another activity (distraction) may stop the tune from replaying in your mind.[4]

In general, actively trying to block the annoying song in your head often doesn't work as well as simply passively accepting it.

Yet actor and Disney superfan John Stamos posted the lyrics to "It's a Small World" on his Instagram account as a way to cope during the COVID-19 pandemic. The song's words, Stamos wrote, assure us "that though we are divided by the mountains and oceans of geography, language, culture, and politics, the same moon and sun that shines on us here shines on Italy, Spain, and everywhere else in the world."[5]

Try as Disney might, happiness isn't the same everywhere. "Tell me how you define happiness, and I'll tell you who you are," declared British researchers Harry Walker and Iza Kavedžija,[6] stating that the way people define, measure, and pursue happiness tells us a lot about their lifestyles and values.

What makes people happy in other countries, and how can you incorporate their happiest customs into your own life at home? For some answers, let's board an imaginary boat that will lead us on a tour through nearly a dozen places around the world with a special word for happiness, contentment, and satisfaction with life. Keep an eye out for how the seven secrets to happiness show up.

DENMARK

I'll start with Denmark, which consistently ranks among the top two or three happiest countries in the world, according to the annual *World Happiness Report*. Are the Danes so happy because tuition for education and health care are free or because crime and political corruption in their country is relatively low? Or is it simply Danish *hygge*?[7]

Hygge (pronounced "hyoo-guh") can be loosely translated as "cozy contentment" and relates to a subtle but perceptive ambiance or quality of coziness. Appropriate to Denmark's dismal North Sea climate and 17 hours of daily darkness in winter, *hygge* is about hunkering down and getting snug, perhaps in your jammies, when it's dark and cold outside. Wintertime is when the Danes light candles, build wood fires, and bring out the warm blankets and fuzzy slippers. To show you how much *hygge* is part of the Danish mindset, it's the root of three everyday words:

- *Hyggekrog*, or reading nooks
- *Hyggebukser*, or comfortable pants
- *Hyggesokker*, or woolen socks

Danes like to plan "*hyggelig* evenings" that involve cooking together, gathering around the table for a hearty meal, and then clearing the plates and silverware and bringing out board games. While one can curl up by herself when rain is pelting the roof and binge-watch a TV series, *hygge* is heightened by gathering casually with friends, perhaps in a cozy cabin nestled in the woods, surrounded by snowdrifts.

Hygge helps people appreciate the things that matter most in life. The word originates from the 16th-century Norwegian term *hugga*, which means to comfort or console. It's where we get the word *hug*.

A *hygge* craze took root around 2016 here in the US, spawned by nearly two dozen books about getting in touch with your inner Dane and "taking pleasure in the presence of gentle, soothing things," like a cup of tea and a weighted blanket, said Helen Russell, a British journalist who wrote *The Year of Living Danishly*.[8]

The most well-known printed work is *The Little Book of Hygge* by Meik Wiking, which was released in the US in 2017 after being a big hit in England, where *Oxford Dictionaries* named *hygge* one of its top 10 new words for that year. Reviewers favorably compared the book to Marie Kondo's *The Life-Changing Magic of Tidying Up*. From Maine to Malta to Mauritius, *hygge* spurred a worldwide run on pillar candles and fuzzy blankets.

Wiking shared a typical story about *hygge* when he hung out in a woodsy cabin with friends on Christmas Day. After a long walk through the snow, everyone returned to the rustic hut, where they gathered around a roaring fireplace, wearing thick sweaters and woolen socks, enjoying mulled wine. At the same time, they watched the crackling fire and reminisced about Christmases past. One of Wiking's friends, caught up in the moment, said, "Could this be any more *hygge*?" Everyone nodded in agreement until one woman said: "Yes, if a storm were raging outside."[9]

This reminds me of a joke we have in Newport Beach about Christmas Day: "Let's turn on the air conditioning so we can light a fire." Fortunately, *hygge* is not reserved for Old Man Winter and 10-foot-high piles of snow. Experience *hygge* wherever you are anytime of the year.

Be happier with hygge:

- Light several candles in the house. Eating dinner by candlelight adds a layer of warm personality and different luminescence to your dining table. Try to use a good mixture of nontoxic scented and unscented candles.

- Drink warm, indulgent beverages, like my brain healthy hot chocolate (see page 181) or Tana's Pumpkin Spice-Up Cappuccino (available at tanaamen.com/recipes/pumpkin-spice-up-cappuccino/).

- Curl up on the couch with a good book and your shoes off. Put the electronic devices away.

- Take a walk in nature, away from crowds, through local mountains, along a lakeshore, or on the beach.

- Invite friends over for a nice dinner. Dinner parties were in rare supply during the pandemic. Get back in the habit of gathering with friends again. Share the cooking responsibilities and experience *hygge*!

THE NETHERLANDS

Our next stop borders Denmark—the Netherlands, the most densely populated country in the European Union (for countries with more than 1 million inhabitants) and the 12th most densely populated country globally. Known for their bulb fields, windmills, cheese markets, wooden shoes, countless canals, and old master paintings, the Dutch are among the happiest people in the world. Maybe it's because they're never stuck in traffic since they ride their bikes everywhere. Holland's 18 million residents have more than 22 million bikes,[10] many of them black three-speed *omafiets*, or "Grandma bicycles."

A Dutch word *gezelligheid* (pronounced "huh-ZELL-ick-hite") refers to a sense of well-being that encompasses feelings of comfort and ease as well as a sense of togetherness. Depending on its context, *gezelligheid* can be translated as a social and relaxed situation but also refers to coziness, conviviality, and fun.

The Dutch, who *love* saying this guttural-sounding word, will tell you that *gezelligheid* is untranslatable. They say that *gezelligheid* (the noun form) and *gezellig* (an adjective) are less about the word and more about a feeling. Often, *gezelligheid* is experienced in seemingly insignificant activities of daily life. Micro-moments!

"Things [get tricky] to comprehend because Dutch people tend to evaluate everything on its particular level of *gezelligheid*," wrote Colleen Geske, author of *Stuff Dutch People Like*. "A place can be *gezellig*, a room can be *gezellig*, a person can be *gezellig*, and an evening can be *gezellig*,"[11] she said, meaning cozy, quaint, or lovely, but also connoting time spent with loved ones, seeing friends after a long absence, or general togetherness. *Gezelligheid* has been called the Dutch secret to happiness.

So how could we incorporate more *gezellig* into our lives, short of riding past a windmill on a three-speed bike? Although *gezelligheid* possesses many similar characteristics to *hygge* and its reference to warm, fuzzy socks and a blazing fire, the Dutch word can apply to almost any situation. To be *gezellig* means doing something relaxing and fulfilling.

Be happier with **gezellighheid:**

- Take time out of your schedule to go on a bike ride or get on a boat. In Newport Harbor, near our home, we can rent electric boats—known as Duffy boats—that cruise at five miles per hour past amazing bayfront homes and mega yachts. Duffy boats hold around ten people, plenty of room for most families.

- Let the conversation flow. If you're with friends or family, don't be looking at your smartphone. The Dutch have a phrase for it: "*gezelligheid kent gee tijd*," which means, "coziness knows no time." Don't schedule things back to back. Allow for margin in your schedule.

- When you meet friends at a café, be intentional and present, which will make your time away from pressing matters more *gezellig*.

GERMANY

Germany, a country bordering Denmark and the Netherlands, embraces *gemütlichkeit* (pronounced "guh-myoot-lich-kite"), the German version of *hygge* but differing in that *gemütlichkeit* is not centered around the home. This mouthful of a word centers on the idea that having healthier relationships makes us happier.

You may have heard of *gemütlichkeit*, which has been adopted into English,[12] kind of like kindergarten, *angst* (fear), *schadenfreude* (taking pleasure in someone else's misfortune), and *über* (meaning above or beyond, not the ride-hailing company we use for trips to the airport). The word derives from the adjective *gemüt*, which means "heart, mind, temper, and feeling." *Gemütlichkeit* promotes a feeling of warmth, a relaxed sense of well-being, an open and welcoming attitude, and an awareness of profound comfort. It's a feeling of coziness and belonging that encourages people to celebrate each other's company.[13]

Gemütlichkeit is all about doing something active with others, like singing boisterously with tablemates at large Oktoberfest gatherings or chilling out with friends. That wasn't easy during the pandemic when millions of people were forced to defy their social instincts and stay inside their homes. In a moment of dark irony, our government leaders told us that the most social thing we could do was to be antisocial.

I witnessed lots of *gemütlichkeit* when I was stationed in Germany for nearly three years in my late teens and early twenties. Germans, when answering the door to friends they are expecting, will say, "Kommt rein. Mach's euch gemütlich" ("Come in. Make yourself *gemütlich*.").

So how can we incorporate *gemütlichkeit* into our lives, short of answering the door in German?

Be happier with **gemütlichkeit:**

- Be intentional about putting yourself out there in the social mix. Since our lives can be hectic, it's a constant struggle to schedule something fun to do with another couple or a group of friends. Take a spin class together, go dancing, or hang out at the local park.

- Head to a farmer's market to experience *gemütlichkeit* and take in the vibe while wandering the stalls, browsing fresh produce, checking out the homemade bath and beauty products like beeswax lip balm and bath salts, and touching handmade crafts like quilts and pottery.

- Have a *kaffeeklatsch* with friends you haven't seen in a while. While I don't recommend drinking more than one cup of regular coffee because of the caffeine (decaf is great), gathering at a friend's home and sipping herbal tea, kombucha, or some other healthy beverage can be a great way to catch up.

NORWAY

Another Scandinavian country, Norway, has its own twist on *hygge*. The Norwegians have a national expression called *friluftsliv* (pronounced "free-loofts-liv"), which means committing to celebrate time outdoors, no matter how bleak the weather forecast is. No huddling around a dazzling fire in jammies and slippers for the Norwegians, who believe that spending time outside, in the elements, can provide a powerful reset for their mental health. Where *hygge* is about finding comfort indoors, *friluftsliv* is about finding it outdoors.

Friluftsliv, coined in 1859 by Norwegian playwright Henrik Ibsen (his most famous work is *A Doll's House*), means "free air life" but is better translated as "open-air living." *Friluftsliv* suggests a complete understanding of nature's healing effects.

Norwegians will tell you that *friluftsliv* is badly needed because of our collective loss of access to nature. A 2015 study by Stanford researchers found quantifiable evidence that walking in nature yields measurable mental health benefits and may reduce the risk of depression. People who spent 90 minutes walking in a natural area showed decreased activity in the limbic regions of the brain as compared to those participants who strolled through congested urban areas.[14]

"These results suggest that accessible natural areas may be vital for mental health in our rapidly urbanizing world," said coauthor Gretchen Daily, a senior fellow at the Stanford Woods Institute for the Environment.[15] Presently, half of the world's population lives in an urban setting, which is forecast to rise to almost 70 percent by 2050.[16]

Friluftsliv became a deeper part of Norwegian culture during the pandemic when Norwegians looked to the country's love for the outdoors as a respite from enclosed spaces. You have to tip a woolen cap to the Norwegians because the Scandinavian country has some of the worst weather on the planet. A vale of gray clouds covers the country during the short days of winter, and drenching rains are commonplace in summer. But the Norwegians have a chin-up saying that rhymes in their language: *There's no bad weather, only bad clothing.*[17]

So how can we incorporate *friluftsliv*, the idea of reconnecting with nature and having an outdoor lifestyle?

Be happier with friluftsliv:

- Drive outside of town to a nature preserve and walk or hike on a trail that's new to you. Breathe in the fresh air and appreciate the simplicity of the outdoors.

- Go for a dip. Every January 1—except during the pandemic—thousands of people participate in Polar Plunges, where participants charge into freezing water that hits like a shot of adrenaline. I can't say I've done one because our local beaches don't have a formal "polar bear" event. But the idea of a bracing, short dip in chilly water would be one way to start the New Year off in a *friluftsliv* kind of way.

- Plan a cross-country ski trip. Even if you've never been on cross-country skis, there's not much of a learning curve. A cross-country ski trail can take you deep into the woods and to beautiful vistas you've never seen.

SWEDEN

Sweden is shoehorned between Norway and Denmark, so the Swedes know all about *hygge* and *friluftsliv* and have even informally adopted these words into their vocabularies. Swedes are all about getting cozy in winter and spending time outdoors, no matter what season it is.

What Sweden has that the other Scandinavian countries don't is a concept called *lagom* (pronounced "la-gum"), which comes from the phrase "lagom är bäst," which can be roughly translated as "just enough," "not too much or too little," or "just the right amount." A Swede asking a friend how she is might prompt "lagom" as a response.

"How's the weather?"

"Lagom."

"How tall is he?"

"Lagom."

Lagom plays to Swedish cultural norms and social ideals about having a balanced, sustainable, and equally enjoyable lifestyle. Here are some ideas to incorporate *lagom* into your life.

Be happier with lagom:

- Get rid of clutter. Decluttering your environment increases productivity and makes it easier for the brain to process information. Clutter has adverse effects on your mental and physical health as well. Studies show that people living in cluttered homes have higher levels of the stress hormone cortisol.[18]

- Keep life simple, which is easy to say and hard to do. But when you don't overcomplicate life, you will achieve far more at work and at home.

- Eat in moderation, just enough and not too much. Steffi Knowles-Dellner, author of *Lagom: The Swedish Art of Eating Harmoniously*, says the Swedish diet is varied, with a healthy mix of whole grains, lean protein (lots of fish and wild game), and a focus on vegetables, berries, and fermented dairy like kefir, a yogurt-like drink that dates back centuries.[19]

TURKEY

Heading southeast, the Turkish people have an expression that refers to taking a little time out during the day: *keyif* (pronounced "kay-eef"). The Turkish word, translated as "pleasure" or "joy" in English, is more about pursuing an idle moment of pleasure and stepping away from busyness.

Keyif is a reminder to savor the moment. For the Turks, this could mean sitting on a park bench by the Bosporus (the sea strait separating Europe from Asia) and watching the sunset, throwing bits of bread to seagulls from the back of a ferry, or listening to gypsy musicians busking on a street corner.

"In Istanbul, we have a pastime that westerners don't share," said Arzu

Tutuk, a city guide. "You could call it our secret—*keyif*. . . . Essentially, it's about sitting still and doing nothing. Most people, when they pause, they do something else, too—read a magazine, check their email, think about the future, or the past. But *keyif* is about stopping, and just enjoying now. . . . For me, it's about being somewhere that's not crowded."[20]

A certain sense of idleness comes with *keyif*, as seen in the way Turkish people like to sit for hours with a little company and a nice view. We may not have the time or the interest to let the day slide by, which is understandable. But the idea of seeking a quiet spot to replenish ourselves and recharge our batteries with a moment of relaxation and mindfulness before returning to the busy responsibilities of work and family life is worth pursuing. Here are some other ideas that fit with the concept of *keyif*.

***Be happier with* keyif:**

- Play a game of backgammon with a friend or partner in the middle of the day. If you're working at home, then have a jigsaw puzzle going. It's good for the brain to get out of your chair and put a few pieces together before returning to another influx of emails.

- In the Turkish bathhouse tradition, which is a relaxing and serene environment, luxuriate with a hot bath or take a far infrared sauna.

- Sit down at an outdoor café with friends and people watch.

NIGERIA

Moving to the African continent, Nigerians follow an ancient philosophy known as *ubuntu* (pronounced "oo-BOON-too"), coined from the Zulu phrase, "Umuntu ngumuntu ngabantu," which translates to "a person is a person through other people." In plain English, this phrase means that community is the building block of society.[21]

South African Archbishop Desmond Tutu, a Nobel Peace Prize winner who is the same age as my mother, said, "*Ubuntu* is the essence of being human. It speaks of the fact that my humanity is caught up and is inextricably bound up in yours. I am human because I belong. It speaks about communities."[22] Archbishop Tutu is credited with introducing the concept of *ubuntu* to the West.

The philosophy behind *ubuntu* did not originate with the South African prelate, however. *Ubuntu* is said to be 2,000 years old, and its collective meaning for life is found in every country south of the Sahara because of tribal migration. *Ubuntu* is a reminder that no one is an island, that every single thing we do, good or bad, has an effect on our families, our friends, and the community around us. It's also a reminder to think twice about the choices we make and our impact on others. *Ubuntu* puts the community's needs above the self through collective responsibility and showing respect and love for one another. Here are some ideas to incorporate *ubuntu* into your life.

Be happier with ubuntu:

- Participate in a "Community Serve Day" sponsored by a local service organization or church. Make appreciation gift bags for first responders, clean up a baseball field, or paint a single mom's house.

- Look for ways to celebrate the good things that happen in your friends' lives but often go unnoticed.

- Take this African proverb to heart: "If you want to go fast, go alone. If you want to go far, go together."[23]

INDONESIA

Can you imagine what it would be like to live among a population where joy is shared and pain is consoled? That concept may be hard to envision for Western readers, but for centuries, Javanese communities have lived by the principles of *guyub* (pronounced "guy-oob"), which has been called Indonesia's secret to happier, healthier communities.

Similar to the overall meaning of *ubuntu*, *guyub* refers to a connection and brotherly or sisterly bond between everyone in the community. *Guyub* is a way of mutually relating to one another and cultivating a strong sense of belonging, compassion, and sincere support for one another. You're happy for another's good fortune and confident that your own existence matters to other people. *Guyub* reflects many of the principles of RELATING from the previous chapter.

Be happier with guyub:

- Be an active listener. The brain is the most amazing organ in the universe, but it hasn't figured out how to use the tongue and the ears simultaneously. Holding your tongue will free up your ears to listen actively and allow you to learn more about people around you.

- Take the opportunity to say a kind and appropriately encouraging word. We can all dine for a long time on a compliment. Speaking of which: When's the last time you complimented the cook at home?

- Be careful about the noise you or your kids make. Can your neighbors hear your blaring TV? Are your kids running wild in the backyard? Sure, none of us want to squelch having fun, but if you know your neighbor goes to bed early while you like to stay up late on weekends, turn down the volume.

THE PHILIPPINES

The tongue-twisting Filipino compound noun *pakikipagkapwa-tao* (pronounced "pah-kee-kee-pagh-kap-wa-ta-oh") continues the theme of community happiness in which group harmony and unity are valued. The Filipino mindset is to get along rather than stand out. If progress is achieved, the entire group benefits and no one gets left behind, which increases everyone's happiness.

The spirit of *pakikisama-tao*, which means "getting along with others," is engrained in the Filipino psyche and value system. This is why families live in multigenerational households or different family homes near each other. Going to church also plays a vital role in the Philippines as a public space for communal bonding.[24]

During the pandemic, Christian relief organizations like SIM International distributed rice, eggs, instant noodles, and canned goods to poor communities, where they regularly conducted ministry. One SIM Philippines director (who preferred anonymity) observed a unique connection between these acts of kindness, the gospel, and Filipino culture. She said, "[We were] motivated by the Filipinos' primary core value *pakikipagkapwa-tao* from the word *kapwa*, which means 'shared identity' . . . and a sense of community, or *bayanihan*, from the word *bayani*, which means 'hero.' We became a hero for others."[25]

Here are some ideas on how to incorporate the spirit of *pakikipagkapwa-tao* and become a *bayani* in your community.

Be happier with pakikipagkapwa-tao:

- Become part of a food drive. Unemployment skyrocketed during the pandemic, and we all saw the dispiriting images of long lines of cars filled with hungry families.

- Sponsoring a child in a foreign land gives a disadvantaged boy or girl a hand up, not a handout. Two reputable ministries are World Vision and Compassion International.

- Check into how you can help out with international humanitarian organizations, such as Doctors Without Borders.

JAPAN

For a proud culture that's been around for thousands of years, Japan has a relatively new tradition known as *shinrin-yoku*, which can be translated as "forest-bath" or "taking in the forest atmosphere." The term emerged in the eighties as an antidote to city-life burnout and inspired the Japanese to reconnect with its vast forests. The simple practice involves taking slow walks in the woods to get in touch with nature through the five senses.

The concept is not new; it's similar to the Norwegian practice of *friluftsliv*. But forest-bathing has become a welcome way to reduce urban stress and boost mood among the Japanese. Tokyo salarymen, ingrained with an extreme work ethic, have found that walks through lush forests leave them happier. *Shinrin-yoku* has taken deep root in the Land of the Rising Sun; the country has 44 accredited *shinrin-yoku* forests with certified guides.

And why wouldn't a stroll through an enchanting, peaceful, and emerald-green scenery be beneficial? In fact, research undertaken in 24 Japanese forests revealed that spending time in the forest "could reduce concentrations of cortisol, lower pulse rate, lower blood pressure, increase parasympathetic (rest and digest) nerve activity, and lower sympathetic (fight or flight) nerve energy."[26]

If you're thinking you need to get out of the city and submerge yourself in a "bath" of verdant forest, here are some ideas.

Be happier with shinrin-yoku:

- Make your next vacation a place where you can forest-bathe. Ever been to the Adirondack Mountains in New York State? Larger than Yellowstone, Yosemite, and the Grand Canyon combined, Adirondack Park is home to more than 2,000 miles of hiking trails.

- Use your senses like never before. As you walk, stop now and then to take a look at the nature around you. Engage four of the five senses: sight, smell, hearing, and touch. If there's a leafy canopy, pay attention to the light coming through. Examine the patterns on leaves and tree bark. Listen for the chirping of birds. Smell the richness of loam and soil.

• If you don't have an actual forest nearby or you live in an arid climate, opt for a stroll in a park. Leave your phone as well as your problems at home.[27]

HAWAII

We're almost home from our trip around the world. Our last stop is Hawaii, an archipelago of eight major islands that was named the "Happiest State in America"[28] in 2020, according to the personal finance website WalletHub, which compared the 50 states across three key dimensions:

• Emotional and physical well-being
• Work environment
• Community and environment

Hawaii was my home for two years. It is where I did my child and adolescent psychiatry fellowship at Tripler Army Medical Center in Honolulu. It was one of the happiest times in my life, with incredible rainbows, weather, beaches, and memories. Whenever I go back, I get a flood of happy chemicals when the plane is about to land at the Honolulu International Airport.

The Aloha State was the big winner with its low numbers of depressed adults and low divorce rate, which was among 30 metrics that were studied. I'm figuring that Hawaii's beaches, warm trade winds, swaying palm trees, and majestic mountains tipped the scales in its favor as well.

The Hawaiian people are beautiful, too, in how they are continuing a tradition from their indigenous ancestors who inhabited Hawaii long before the arrival of Westerners. This custom is known as *ho'oponopono* (pronounced "hoe-oh-pono-pono") and comes from the Hawaiian words *ho'o* (to make) and *pono* (right or correct). Saying *pono* twice makes it emphatic, as in "doubly right," and it applies to yourself and others.

In a Hawaiian dictionary, *ho'oponopono* is defined in this manner: "mental cleansing: family conferences in which relationships are set right through prayer, discussion, confession, repentance, and mutual restitution and forgiveness."[29] Ancient islanders believed that errors, guilt, or anger caused physical illness. The cure, they decided, was forgiveness.

Be happier with ho'oponopono:

- Ask yourself if you need to ask someone for forgiveness or you need to forgive someone. If so, *ho'oponopono*-inspired forgiveness is based on four key phrases, which are called the *Ho'oponopono Prayer*:

  "I love you."
  "I'm sorry."
  "Please forgive me."
  "Thank you."

  Though short in length and simple to say, this prayer can be difficult to express face-to-face, but give it a try.

- Write the *Ho'oponopono Prayer* on a piece of paper and place it somewhere you will see it every day. Let it serve as a reminder to forgive yourself and others as a way to promote healing.

- A more straightforward form of *ho'oponopono* is having a family discussion known as a *pule 'ohana*. This is where the family gathers to review the day, precisely what we do in the Amen house when we gather for dinner and discuss what went well that day.

Some things are universal, aren't they?

COMING TO THE END OF THE RIDE

In my travels, I've also noticed the happiness of Italians, with the Greeks right behind them. I've long wondered if it's because of all the vitamin D they receive living in sun-splashed climates. Vitamin D, manufactured by the body from the sun's ultraviolet rays, is called the "happy hormone" because it plays an important role in mood, cognitive function, and digestion.

The Mediterranean countries also consume plenty of fish. Dr. Cyrus Raji was a lead researcher in a study about fish consumption. "If you eat fish just once a week, your hippocampus—the big memory and learning center—is 14 percent larger than in people who don't eat fish that frequently," he said in the *Atlantic*.[30]

Scandinavian people, among the world's happiest folks, not only eat lots of fish, but they also consume cod liver oil in copious amounts, especially during the winter when a lack of sunlight prevents vitamin D absorption.

When it comes to happy people, I want to mention one more country: Bhutan, which takes its citizens' happiness seriously. This remote, tiny, and mystical Buddhist kingdom nestled between India, Nepal, and China has prioritized national happiness over economic growth. Instead of focusing on Gross National Product, the Bhutanese enshrined a concept known as the "Gross National Happiness Index" into their constitution in 2008.

What that means in practice is that this Himalayan country cannot pass any laws unless they improve the citizens' well-being. During the national census, every Bhutanese person is asked, "Are you happy?" As word got out about what Bhutan was doing, countries like Canada, France, and Great Britain began reporting on citizen happiness in their official statistics.[31]

What the Bhutanese initiated prompted the United Nations (UN), in 2011, to call for a meeting in Bhutan's capital, Thimphu, where UN delegates invited national governments to "give more importance to happiness and well-being in determining how to achieve and measure social and economic developments."[32] The result was the release of the first *World Happiness Report* in 2012, conducted by the Gallup Organization for the United Nations. Six key variables measured a country's happiness:

1. GDP per capita
2. Healthy life expectancy
3. Social support
4. Freedom of choice
5. Generosity
6. Perceptions of corruption

In the last decade, four countries have held the top position: Denmark in 2012, 2013, and 2016; Switzerland in 2015; Norway in 2017; and Finland in 2018, 2019, and 2020. That *hygge* and *friluftsliv* must really be working.

The United States has never cracked the Top 10. After being ranked No. 11 in the first *World Happiness Report*, we've slipped to as low as No. 19. "The years since 2010 have not been good ones for happiness and well-being among Americans," stated the 2019 report.[33]

We can do better, which is one of the reasons I was inspired to write *You, Happier*.

HAPPINESS HIGHLIGHTS FROM AROUND THE WORLD

- Denmark: *Hygge*—cozy contentment inside
- The Netherlands: *Gezelligheid*—well-being that encompasses comfort, ease, and togetherness
- Germany: *Gemütlichkeit*—open, welcoming attitude about social gatherings
- Norway: *Friluftsliv*—reconnection with nature
- Sweden: *Lagom*—balanced, sustainable living, just right
- Turkey: *Keyif*—savoring moments of relaxation
- Nigeria: *Ubuntu*—community
- Indonesia: *Guyub*—mutual connection in community
- The Philippines: *Pakikipagkapwa-tao*—getting along with others
- Japan: *Shinrin-yoku*—forest bathing
- Hawaii: *Ho'oponopono*—doubly right relationships

PART 5

THE SPIRITUALITY
OF HAPPINESS

SECRET 7

LIVE EACH DAY BASED ON YOUR CLEARLY DEFINED VALUES, PURPOSE, AND GOALS

QUESTION 7

Does it fit? Does my behavior today fit the goals I have for my life?

CHAPTER 16

CLARITY

Core Values, Purpose, and Goals in the Four Circles

If we have our own "why" of life, we shall get along with almost any "how."
FRIEDRICH NIETZSCHE

You must know your "why" in order to do the
"what" of getting and staying healthy.
TANA AMEN

Happiness comes from moving your life forward toward your life goals with meaning and purpose, based on your values, despite whatever obstacles are in your way. A happy life doesn't focus on the past with regret or look to the future with fear. That's why I love the song by pop sensation Ariana Grande, "thank u, next." The lyrics are about learning from and being grateful for the past: "One taught me love, one taught me patience, and one taught me pain . . . thank u, next," while focusing on the future with clarity of purpose, which in her case was connection: "One day I'll walk down the aisle."

Just as every great organization has core values, a purpose statement, and clearly defined quarterly, yearly, and three-to-five-year goals, we should too. Yet, as I've found in my clinical practice, very few people are aware of their own core values, rarely get in touch with their deepest sense of meaning and purpose, and, more often than not, lack clearly defined goals for the short and long term.

Guiding my patients to discover their own core values, purpose, and goals in the Four Circles (biological, psychological, social, and spiritual), and then making decisions that fit these four areas, is the last piece in the happiness puzzle. That's what happened when I helped Laura Clery (the actress, comedian, and social media influencer I've mentioned before) pinpoint her overall purpose with great clarity: "to deliver a little dose of happiness to others every day."

I am going to guide you through the same series of exercises I did with Laura to help you find what satisfies your soul and directs your life. I'll show you how to identify your core values, refine your sense of purpose (your why), and develop biological, psychological, social, and spiritual goals through an exercise I call the One Page Miracle (OPM),[1] which will illuminate what you want to strive for in the Four Circles. The OPM is an excellent way to add clarity to your life and ensure you have a balanced life that will help you be happier. I will help you:

- Clarify your core values.

- Develop a clear sense of meaning and purpose.

- Create your goals in the Four Circles for the next three months, next year, and next three to five years and longer.

- Remind you to ask yourself every day this important question: "Does it fit? Do my thoughts and behaviors fit the goals I have for my life?"

As we go along I will have you complete the OPM forms, which can also be downloaded at amenuniversity.com/youhappier.

Psychiatry and Spirituality?

Albert Einstein, 20th-century theoretical physicist, said, "Everyone who is seriously involved in the pursuit of science becomes convinced that a spirit is manifest in the laws of the Universe—a spirit vastly superior to that of man, and one in the face of which we with our modest powers must feel humble."[2]

Spirituality involves the belief that there is something greater than ourselves; something more to being human than our immediate sensory experiences, and that our lives are, in part, divine in nature with ongoing or lasting value.

Even before I started medical school, I believed faith and spirituality were important for developing a sense of wholeness. I wanted to learn medicine in the context of my faith, which was why I was thrilled when I got accepted to Oral Roberts University in Tulsa, Oklahoma. At the time, ORU was one of the few Christian medical schools in the nation. We were taught not to see patients as their diseases but rather as whole people in body, mind, relationships, and spirit. Learning to pray with patients, for example, was incredibly powerful.

When I did my psychiatric internship and residency at Walter Reed Army Medical Center in Washington, DC, I taught a course on spirituality and psychiatry to the other residents and hospital staff. In most medical schools, spirituality is nowhere to be found in the psychiatric curriculum. Sigmund Freud, the founder of psychoanalysis, was an atheist who described religion as "a universal obsessional neurosis" and "science's really serious enemy . . . unworthy of belief."[3]

Yet, according to psychiatrist Harold Koenig, Director of the Center for Spirituality, Theology and Health at Duke University Medical Center, 89 percent of Americans believe in God, 90 percent pray on a regular basis, and 82 percent acknowledge the need for spiritual growth.[4] Psychiatrists should understand those beliefs, work within their context, and never diminish or dismiss them. They should explore supporting a person's deepest sense of meaning and purpose.

Science is beginning to catch up to the importance of spirituality in people's mental health and well-being. For example, research has shown that attending religious services on a regular basis and daily prayer are associated with many health benefits, including a decreased risk of stress, depression, addiction, hypertension, and heart disease, and an increase in forgiveness, self-control, longevity, happiness, and life satisfaction.[5]

Without faith in our lives, we would be like a four-legged stool that is missing one leg.

ONE PAGE MIRACLE
Does It Fit?

Core Values

Biological:_____

_____

Psychological:_____

_____

Social: _____

_____

Spiritual: _____

_____

Purpose

_____

_____

_____

_____

_____

_____

_____

Overall

Biological Goals *Brain and Body*	**Psychological Goals** *Mind*	**Social Goals** *Relationships, Work, Money*	**Spiritual Goals** *Meaning and Purpose*
_____ _____ _____	_____ _____ _____	_____ _____ _____	God _____ _____ _____
3 Brain and Health Strategies Brain Envy—test on a regular basis Avoid Bad—BRIGHT MINDS Risks Do Good—BRIGHT MINDS Strategies	**Eliminate ANTs with 5 Questions** Write down the negative belief. Ask: Is it true? Is it absolutely true? How do I feel with the thought? How do I feel without the thought? Is the opposite of the thought true or even truer than the original thought?	**Relationships** Partner _____ Family _____ Friends _____	Planet _____ _____ _____ **Connection to past generations**
BRIGHT MINDS **Blood flow**—exercise (walk like you are late for 10,000 steps a day) **Retirement/aging**—new learning **Inflammation**—eliminate processed foods, floss, take omega-3s and probiotics daily **Genetics**—know and prevent vulnerabilities **Head trauma**—protect your head **Toxins**—avoid and support four organs of detoxification		**RELATING** Responsibility Empathy Listening Assertiveness Time Inquire Notice what you like Grace/forgiveness	_____ _____ **Connection to future generations** _____ _____
Mental health—see Psychological goals **Immunity/infections**—optimize gut, vitamin D level **Neurohormones**—test and optimize regularly **Diabesity**—healthy weight and blood sugar **Sleep**—seven to eight hours a night		**Work/School** _____ _____ _____ **Money** _____ _____ _____	

CLARIFY YOUR CORE VALUES

What are core values, and why are they important for your happiness? Core values are the characteristics or traits you think are most important in the way you live. They help you make decisions when you are faced with challenging situations. For example, let's say you are training to run a marathon, but on the morning of one of your long training runs, your child gets a tummy ache. Do you forego your run to care for your child? What if you have a rehearsal dinner for your best friend's wedding, but your supervisor at work hands you a last-minute project that needs to be done *stat!* The decisions you make come from your core values. Knowing which core values are most important to you helps guide you to the decisions that fit with your life goals.

This is an important exercise for all the brain types, but it is especially critical for people with the Spontaneous Brain Type, like Laura Clery, because they tend to make impulsive decisions without considering their core values. Staying focused on your core values will help you make better decisions. And better decisions are essential to happiness.

Here's how to clarify your core values in just three steps.

Step 1: Choose one or two of the following characteristics or traits that are important to you in each of the Four Circles. Feel free to add your own.

BIOLOGICAL	PSYCHOLOGICAL	SOCIAL	SPIRITUAL
Athleticism	Authenticity	Caring	Acceptance
Beauty	Confidence	Connection	Appreciation
Brain/body love	Courage	Dependability	Awareness (Awe)
Brain health	Creativity	Empathy	Compassion
Energy	Flexibility	Encouragement	Generosity
Focus	Forthrightness	Family	Gratitude
Fitness	Fun	Friendships	Growth
Longevity	Happiness/Joy	Independence	Humility
Mental clarity	Hard work	Kindness	Inspiration
Physical health	Individuality	Love of others	Love/relationship w/God
Safety	Open-mindedness	Loyalty	Morality
Strength	Positivity	Outcome-driven/ service	Patience
Vitality	Resilience	Passion	Prayerful

BIOLOGICAL	PSYCHOLOGICAL	SOCIAL	SPIRITUAL
	Responsibility	Significance	Purposeful
	Science-based	Success	Religious community
	Security	Tradition	Surrender
	Self-control		Transcendence
	Self-love		Wonder

For example, at Amen Clinics, our core values help guide all our decisions. They are:

- **Brain health.** The brain is central to all health and success. When your brain works right, you work right, and when your brain is troubled for whatever reason, you are much more likely to have trouble in your life.
- **Authenticity.** We live the message of our lives, but without being authentic, others would not believe in what we are trying to do.
- **Science-based.** We live by the available evidence to help our patients live better lives.
- **Outcome-driven.** We are here to change lives. This is why we go to work every day. It is central to our purpose.
- **Responsibility.** What is it I can do today to make the organization better?
- **Compassion.** We are here for the people we serve and teach.
- **Growth.** We always strive to be better.

On a personal level, my values in the Four Circles include:

- **Biological**
  Brain/body love
  Vitality

- **Psychological**
  Authenticity—living the message of my life
  Happiness

- **Social**
  Significance
  Independence

- **Spiritual**
  Love/relationship with God
  Compassion

Step 2: Think of six to eight heroes (past and present) you admire most, and write down the values you think represent their lives. Your heroes can be people you know personally, public figures, or even entities (such as a fire department, sports team, or school)—anyone who has inspired you in some important way.

Here's how this looks when I do this step:

DR. AMEN'S HEROES

HERO	VALUES THEY REPRESENT
Grandfather	Kindness
Father	Hard work, success, forthrightness
Mother	Fun, connection
Tana	Responsibility (ability to respond)
Abraham Lincoln	Resilience, courage
US Army	Flexibility (because things never go as planned)
Medical training	Science-based

Step 3: Review your values. Over time, observe yourself and pay attention to the decisions you make and why. What values do they reflect and how do they impact your life? Write them down and post them where you can see them often. Make it a habit to review your values from time to time to see if they still resonate with you or if you should update them. Do they reflect the values you want? Note that this may be difficult for people with the Persistent Brain Type. These are the people who choose a set of values and then refuse to stray from them, even if those values no longer serve them. If this sounds like you, consider sharing your values with a trusted friend or family member to see if they can offer you an objective perspective about whether those values still fit in your life.

Step 4: Write your top 6–8 core values in the top left portion of the OPM form.

KNOW YOUR PURPOSE IN SIX QUESTIONS

Believing your life matters is essential to happiness. When you know your purpose, you feel more significant, happier, and more connected. A study in the *Archives of General Psychiatry* followed more than 900 people for up to 7 years to look at the effects of having a sense of purpose, which they defined as "the psychological tendency to derive meaning from life's experiences and to possess a sense of intentionality and goal directedness that guides behavior."[6] The researchers found that the people who were more purposeful at the start of the study had:

- Greater happiness
- Less depression
- More satisfaction
- Better mental health
- Personal growth, self-acceptance
- Better quality sleep
- Longevity

This is only one of many studies linking purpose with life satisfaction and lowered mortality rates. A 27-year study concluded that living with purpose and meaning is the key to happiness and longevity.[7] Another paper in a 2015 issue of the *Lancet* measured "eudemonic well-being," a type of well-being that relates to having a sense of purpose and meaning in life, and found that it was tied to longevity.[8] Scoring higher in "purpose in life" also reduces the chances that negative social media issues (such as not having as many followers as your peers, not getting the number of likes you want, or receiving negative comments about your posts) will affect your self-esteem.[9] This body of research points to purpose as a foundational element for a happy life.

Anytime I talk to my patients about purpose, I bring up Viktor Frankl, the famed psychiatrist, Holocaust survivor, and author of the remarkable book, *Man's Search for Meaning*. He said that "life is never made unbearable by circumstances, but only by lack of meaning and purpose" and explored three elements of purpose:

- Purposeful work or being productive. This involves asking yourself questions such as "Why is the world a better place because I am here?" or "What do I contribute?"
- Loving other people.

- Courage despite difficulty. Bearing whatever challenges you have and helping others with theirs.

To find your true purpose in life, you simply need to know where to look. To help you zero in on what gives your life meaning, write down your answers to the following questions.

1. **Look inward.** What do you love to do? Examples include writing, cooking, design, parenting, creating, speaking, teaching, and so on. What do you feel qualified to teach others about?

2. **Look outward.** Who do you do it for? How does your work connect you to others?

3. **Look back.** Are there hurts from your past that you can turn into help for others? Turn your pain into purpose.

4. **Look beyond yourself.** What do others want or need from you?

5. **Look for transformation.** How do others change as a result of what you do?

6. **Look to the end.** Psychiatrist Elisabeth Kübler-Ross, author of the well-known book *On Death and Dying*, said, "It is the denial of death that is partially responsible for people living empty, purposeless lives; for when you live as if you'll live forever, it becomes too easy to postpone the things you know that you must do."[10] Ask yourself, *Does this worry, problem, or moment have eternal value? When I die, how do I want to be remembered?*

Notice that only two of the six questions are about you; four of them are about others. A wise Chinese saying is: "If you want happiness for an hour, take a nap. If you want happiness for a day, go fishing. If you want happiness for a year, inherit a fortune. If you want happiness for a lifetime, help someone else."[11] Happiness is often found in helping others.

Dr. Amen's Purpose in Six Questions

1. What do you love to do? *I love working with patients, looking at brains, writing, teaching, inspiring, and creating a brain health revolution!*

2. Who do you do it for? *I do it for myself, my family, and those who come to our clinics, read our books, watch our shows, buy our products, and are a part of our community.*

3. Are there hurts from your past that you can turn into help for others? *Someone I loved tried to kill herself, which led me on a healing journey for those with mental health/brain health challenges.*

4. What do others want or need from you? *The people we help want to suffer less, feel better, be sharper, and have greater control over their lives.*

5. How do others change as a result of what you do? *People have better brains and better lives. They suffer less, become happier and healthier, and pass what they have learned on to others.*

6. Look to the end. *I want to be remembered as a husband, best friend, father, grandfather, teacher, someone who helped to change psychiatry by adding brain imaging and natural ways to heal the brain, and as a leader of the brain health revolution that helped millions feel better, have brighter minds, and live better lives.*

Here's how Laura Clery answered these questions:

1. What do you love to do? *Making content that connects (comedy) with large groups, how to get sober*

2. Who do you do it for? *Brings me joy, connects with audience*

3. Are there hurts from your past that you can turn into help for others? *Past addiction and growing up in an alcoholic home gives me great empathy and desire to help others.*

4. What do others want or need from you? *To feel better, less alone, more connected, and to feel good about themselves.*

5. How do others change as a result of what you do? *I give people a "daily dose of happiness" to improve their moods and their lives.*

6. Look to the end. *I want to be remembered as a great mother and wife and as a teacher with humor and happiness.*

When someone asks you, "What do you do?" answer by telling them the answer to question 5. For example, when people ask me this question, I say, "I help people have better brains and better lives, so they suffer less, become happier and healthier, and pass what they have learned on to others." And now, when people ask Laura what she does, she automatically says, "I give people a daily dose of happiness."

By answering this simple question about what you do, you get to share your life's purpose with the many people you know and meet, which increases dopamine and thus your happiness.

Place your answer to question 5 in the Purpose Section of the OPM.

THE SECRET TO STAYING FOCUSED ON YOUR MEANING, PURPOSE, AND GOALS

After I help my patients identify their values and purpose in life, I ask them to keep these things in mind as they pinpoint their goals in the Four Circles with the rest of the OPM exercise. I call it the One Page Miracle because I have seen this exercise quickly focus and change many people's lives. In three decades of working with patients, I have found that when you tell your brain what you want, your brain will help you make it happen. The OPM will help guide your thoughts, words, and behaviors. When you have your OPM, you can quickly determine if your words, deeds, and actions are helping you reach your goals or if they are hindering you from accomplishing what you want in life. The OPM is a powerful tool for all brain types. And like the Core Values exercise, the OPM can be especially beneficial for helping people with the Spontaneous Brain Type stay focused on their goals.

Completing the OPM gives you the opportunity to gain clarity about what you want in each of the important areas and stay true to your values and purpose. This

HAPPINESS TRANSFORMATION IN 30 DAYS

The last 30 days have been a joy! My brain is sharper, my decision-making is better, I laugh a ton more, I have a lightness and self-awareness that have brought me confidence. My focus is on my purpose and goals! I love being me!
—MD

exercise creates a personal vision of what a balanced, meaningful, and happier life will look like for you. To develop your own OPM, ask yourself what you truly want in the Four Circles, including how these areas reflect your values, meaning, and purpose. Here are questions, tips, and corresponding examples:

ONE PAGE MIRACLE
Does It Fit?

Core Values	Purpose
Biological: Love—brain/body; Vitality **Psychological:** Authenticity, Happiness **Social:** Significance, Independence **Spiritual:** Love/relationship with God, Compassion	For people to have better brains and better lives so they suffer less, become happier and healthier, and pass it on to others.

Overall

Biological Goals *Brain and Body*	Psychological Goals *Mind*	Social Goals *Relationships, Work, Money*	Spiritual Goals *Meaning and Purpose*
Ex: I want to be mentally sharp and physically strong for as long as possible. It is the foundation of my happiness, success, and independence.	*Ex: I want to be happy, authentic, and able to manage my mind with positivity, while having enough anxiety to keep me on track.*	**Relationships** **Partner** *Ex: I want a kind, caring, loving, supportive, passionate relationship with Tana.* **Family** **Friends**	**God** *Ex: Be attentive to God's will for my life with daily prayer.* **Planet** *Ex: Do my part to keep the planet healthy.*
3 Brain and Health Strategies Brain Envy—test on a regular basis Avoid Bad—BRIGHT MINDS Risks Do Good—BRIGHT MINDS Strategies	**Eliminate ANTs with 5 Questions** Write down the negative belief. Ask: Is it true? Is it absolutely true? How do I feel with the thought? How do I feel without the thought? Is the opposite of the thought true or even truer than the original thought?	**RELATING** Responsibility Empathy Listening Assertiveness Time Inquire Notice what you like Grace/forgiveness	**Connection to past generations** *Ex: Honor my ancestors by keeping the memory of my grandfather alive. Live in a way that would make him proud.*
BRIGHT MINDS **Blood flow**—exercise (walk like you are late for 10,000 steps a day) **Retirement/aging**—new learning **Inflammation**—eliminate processed foods, floss, take omega-3s and probiotics daily **Genetics**—know and prevent vulnerabilities **Head trauma**—protect your head **Toxins**—avoid and support four organs of detoxification		**Work/School** _____ _____ _____ **Money** _____ _____ _____	**Connection to future generations** *Ex: Nurture my grandchildren.*
Mental health—see Psychological goals **Immunity/infections**—optimize gut, vitamin D level **Neurohormones**—test and optimize regularly **Diabesity**—healthy weight and blood sugar **Sleep**—seven to eight hours a night			

ONE PAGE MIRACLE IN FOUR CIRCLES

Biological
What do I want for my brain and body?

Stay healthy by always being aware of the BRIGHT MINDS risk factors and strategies.

Write down your Biological Goals in the corresponding section of the OPM.

Psychological
What do I want for my mind?

Eliminate the ANTs. When a negative thought pops up, ask, "Is it true?"

Write down your Psychological Goals in the corresponding section of the OPM.

Social
What do I want for my relationships (partner, children, family, friends, coworkers), work/school, and money?

Remember the steps of RELATING.

What do I want in my work?

What do I want for my finances?

HAPPINESS TRANSFORMATION IN 30 DAYS

Before taking this happiness challenge, I was severely depressed and on medication that was not helping. I had lost my way and my purpose in life. I feel like I am looking at life with renewed hope. You have literally saved my life.

—DJ

Write down your Social Goals in the corresponding section of the OPM.

Spiritual
Spirituality can be defined as a sense of connection to a higher power, a deeper sense of meaning and purpose beyond yourself, or a sense of transcendence, which some find in religion and others find in contemplation or meditation. Spirituality can also be defined as discovering your own inner awareness of why you believe you are on this planet; why you have life; your connection with God, as you know Him; your connection to the planet; and to past generations (I think of my grandfather) and future generations (I think of my grandchildren).

What do I want spiritually? What do I want for my relationship with God, for the health of the planet, for my connection to past generations, and my connection to future generations?

Write down your Spiritual Goals in the corresponding section of the OPM.

Wondering what the OPM process looks like? You can watch Laura and Stephen as they lay out their life goals.[12] In the 11-minute video, they spend the last 5 minutes talking about what they want in their relationships, work, and spiritual life. They don't cover the biological circle in the video, but I can tell you that they have both become committed to better brain health.

Here's how their OPM took shape.

Relationships
Spouse: I want a loving, passionate, fun, considerate, exciting, trusting, funny, lifelong, creative, understanding marriage.

Parents: I want to see them regularly. Maybe call my dad more (Laura).

Children: I want a close, loving relationship and for them to always know I will love and accept them for exactly who they are. I just want to love them unconditionally. And I want them to know and feel that love, always feel safe, and to have fun. And support them in all their endeavors.

Family and friends: I'd love to see them regularly—really put in that effort to see them once a month.

Work
Continue to grow the business and grow our brands. Continue to write books. Continue to make millions of people laugh. Move into new things. Move into film. Move into TV.

Spiritual health
Daily prayer and meditation (Stephen prays; Laura does a daily prayer and meditates).

Now it's your turn. Spend some time creating your own OPM; be thoughtful in your answers. Always ask yourself this question: "Does this have eternal value?" Once you have completed the OPM, place it somewhere that you will see it every day. The OPM will serve as a powerful reminder to live each day based on your clearly defined core values, purpose, and goals in the Four Circles. When you live, love, and act with this in mind, you will consistently make decisions that will help you be happier.

It is also helpful to do a version of your OPM for the next three months, the next year, the next three-to-five years, and even for the rest of your life. For example, I love my four children and five grandchildren, but I never want to have to live with any of them. I never want to be a burden to anyone or end up living in a senior care facility. I want to be independent for as long as I live, which means at each stage of my life I need to be serious about my biological, psychological, social, and spiritual health.

Retaining independence throughout my entire life is part of happiness for me. How about you?

---------------- ☺ ----------------

HAPPINESS HIGHLIGHTS FOR SECRET 7:

LIVE EACH DAY BASED ON YOUR CLEARLY DEFINED VALUES, PURPOSE, AND GOALS

- Clarify your core values.
- Develop a clear sense of meaning and purpose.
- Create your goals within the Four Circles—biological, psychological, social, spiritual.
- Ask yourself, *Does it fit with the goals I have for my life?*

THE DAILY JOURNEY OF HAPPINESS

The best way to reduce stress is to stop screwing up.

ROY F. BAUMEISTER AND JOHN TIERNEY,
WILLPOWER: REDISCOVERING THE GREATEST HUMAN STRENGTH

Consistent happiness is about making the right decisions again and again over time, which builds the neural pathways of feeling good. It is a daily journey, just like maintaining good health. I've had patients who, after starting therapy, quit after one or two sessions. "This didn't work for me," they say. That's like someone who needs to lose 50 pounds because they made thousands of poor health decisions, then has a healthy salad for lunch on a Monday and expects to have lost 10 pounds by that Friday. Happiness, like health, takes time; it is built on the seven secrets of happiness and occurs within the Four Circles.

You have to work at it. That's what Laura Clery and Stephen Hilton are doing. When I followed up with these influencers in July 2021, they told me they were improving dramatically. Stephen said his depression was gone. Laura said she was coming out of the sadness, hormonal mood swings, and postpartum depression she had been experiencing since the birth of their second baby, Penelope, whom they call Poppy. "I started really taking the supplements seriously," she said. "The vegan omega-3s, Happy Saffron, my postnatals . . . and within three weeks, like you said, I started feeling so much better."

Their relationship is smoother and stronger too, which makes them both happier. Remember what sparked that blow-out argument between them that I wrote about earlier in this book? Laura was irritated with Stephen because he would often race into the bedroom at night to talk to her excitedly about something work-related. But that's when she's winding down after a busy day and needs to relax and calm her busy mind. That issue has been largely resolved. "It's been going amazingly," Laura said. "Stephen still sometimes goes into the bedroom with a thought he's dying to share, but now he stops himself, says, 'Never mind' and holds the thought until the next day." With practice and a daily commitment, they're getting happier together.

When you employ the seven secrets and consider the seven related questions each day, you boost the neural pathways of feeling good while shrinking those that make you feel bad. You can do this. None of what I have written is complicated or hard. It is about asking yourself the seven simple questions that promote the seven simple secrets to happiness and help you make the best decisions:

Secret 1: Know your brain type.
Question 1: Am I focused on what makes me uniquely happy?

Secret 2: Optimize the physical functioning of your brain.
Question 2: Is this good for my brain or bad for it?

Secret 3: Nourish your unique brain.
Question 3: Am I nourishing my unique brain?

Secret 4: Choose foods you love that love you back.
Question 4: Do I choose foods today I love that love me back?

Secret 5: Master your mind and gain psychological distance from the noise in your head.
Question 5: Is it true? What went well today?

Secret 6: Notice what you like about others more than what you don't.
Question 6: Am I reinforcing the behaviors I like or dislike in others today?

Secret 7: Live each day based on your clearly defined values, purpose, and goals.
Question 7: Does it fit? Does my behavior today fit the goals I have for my life?

Post these secrets and questions where you can see them every day. If your mood lags or unhappiness starts to creep in to your mind, ask yourself what you can do to make it better based on these secrets and questions.

Nothing is more important to your health and happiness than the quality of the decisions you make. And the quality of your decisions is a direct reflection of the physical health of your brain. Neuroscience teaches us that better decisions occur when you:

1. **Know what you want,** which is why knowing your values, purpose, and goals (One Page Miracle) is so important.

2. **Balance your blood sugar.** Low blood sugar is associated with low blood flow to the brain, especially the PFC, which leaves you susceptible to making bad decisions. Skipping meals, drinking alcohol, or eating a jelly doughnut (which causes an initial spike in blood sugar before you crash 30 minutes later) are examples of decisions that lead to a blood sugar imbalance.

3. **Manage your stress.** The hypothalamus is responsible for turning the stress switch on or off in the body. When the stress switch is turned on, people tend to fly off the handle, become a bundle of nerves, or shut down emotionally. Counteract stress by practicing your favorite stress-management techniques, such as prayer, meditation, medical hypnosis, focusing on your breathing, taking a walk, or doing something creative (cooking, painting, gardening).

4. **Exercise.** According to a study by researchers from the University of Western Australia, participants who engaged in 30 minutes of moderately intense aerobic exercise each morning showed improved cognitive function in relation to better decision-making all day.[1] The main problem is that we sit too much, and we're sitting more than ever. A nationwide study that tracked 51,896 Americans over 15 years found that living in the age of Netflix, streaming video games, social media posting, and watching binge-worthy series meant that adults over the age of 20 spent 6.4 hours per day sitting. Teens were even more sedentary: They sat for 8.2 hours per day. People in each age group were generally sitting one more hour than they were in 2007, the year the iPhone was released.[2] When you exercise, you also sleep better at night, have a sharper memory, and feel more positive about yourself.

5. **Protect your decisions.** Many drug treatment programs use the acronym HALT to decrease cravings and help their patients make better decisions. It's a reminder to never to get too Hungry, Angry, Lonely, or Tired. Hunger comes from low blood sugar, which results in inadequate blood flow to the PFC, where more bad decisions get made. Anger also lowers PFC function, while being lonely increases

feelings of disconnection to others. Being tired is the fourth factor that impairs decision-making skills and the brain's ability to control cravings. Sleep is essential to good decision-making.

BE CURIOUS, NOT FURIOUS

I'll tell you what I say to my patients right before they leave my office after our first evaluation session. I go to my white board and draw this diagram about how people change:

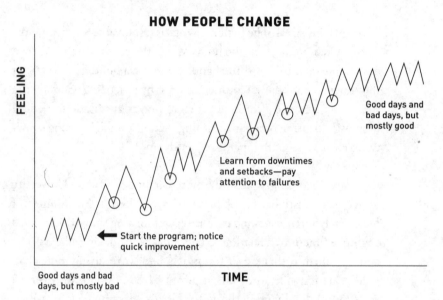

HOW PEOPLE CHANGE

FEELING

TIME

Good days and bad days, but mostly good

Learn from downtimes and setbacks—pay attention to failures

Start the program; notice quick improvement

Good days and bad days, but mostly bad

Then I say, "When people come to see me as a patient, they have good days and bad days, but usually their days are not very good. Then we work together to change things, and they get better. I love that. If you do what I ask, you are likely to get much better. But no one just gets better. It doesn't happen in a straight line. There are ups and downs. Don't let the downs discourage you. Let's learn from them, study them, and investigate what happened. If we do that, we can turn bad days into good data, and make the bad times less likely to happen in the future. Over time, if we learn from the down times—maybe our diet wasn't good, we believed the negative thoughts we had, or we had a disagreement with a loved one—we can develop strategies to prevent them. We will always be in a learn mode to reach toward our goal of more stability and more happiness."

Lasting happiness is a simple process that occurs in steps and in the decisions we make every day, and it is never too late to get started.

NANCY SHOWS US THE WAY TO LASTING HAPPINESS

Nancy came to our clinic from Oxford, England. When she was 80, she had bought a copy of *Change Your Brain, Change Your Life* in a used bookstore for about 50 cents. In her own words, "The book just laid around for a year or two, but when I picked it up I couldn't put it down. It was the most revealing, startling read I think I ever had. Up to that time I had been obese, prone to depression with long low periods, unmotivated, uninspired, and had arthritis. Then I began by thinking about what were the things I could change easily. Little by little I added some of the things recommended."[3]

First, she took the Brain Health Assessment (brainhealthassessment.com) and discovered she had the Sensitive Brain Type, which made her prone to depression. She found that the supplement saffron and the scent of lavender made her feel better.

Second, she started to drink more water once she learned that staying hydrated was important for brain health and energy. She started to ask herself if what she did throughout the day was good for her brain or bad for it. As her energy increased, she began to exercise more, including walking, dancing, and table tennis, which boosted her mood. For her brain, she also engaged in new learning. She started learning French (as well as two other languages) and the guitar.

Third, she added a multivitamin, omega-3 fatty acids, vitamin D (her level tested low), ginkgo biloba, acetyl-l-carnitine, and phosphatidylserine to her daily routine. "They made a big difference," she said. "I feel like I am nourishing my brain each day, like watering my plants."

Fourth, motivated by her progress, she changed how she ate, following a diet like the You, Happier Diet described in chapter 11. "I started by eating the good things first, so I lost my cravings for the things that were not good. There was less room for the trash [bad food] in my body." She often asked herself if the foods she loved actually loved her back.

Fifth, she stopped believing every thought she had. She wrote down her ANTs and found that with a healthier mind, she was able to quickly dismiss them. She also started every day with the phrase, "Today is going to be a great day," and ended every day with the treasure hunt of "What went well today?"

Sixth, she got her family onboard the brain health train by noticing what she liked about her loved ones more than what she didn't, which was a change for her. Nancy's transformation astonished them. When her children saw her lose weight and shed her depression, they started paying attention to what she was doing. In a positive way, she showed her family how to care for their own brains and happiness.

Finally, Nancy constantly asked herself if what she did and thought had eternal value based on her values, purpose, and goals. She told me, "The best thing I can do for my children is keep myself healthy for as long as I can. I never dreamt that I could be this happy and have so much fun at this time in my life. My life totally changed. My energy, mood, and memory are remarkably better and I am pain-free."

When I met Nancy, she had saved her money to travel to one of the Amen Clinics for a scan as her 83rd birthday present to herself. When I talked to her, I started to tear up. Nancy is the reason I do what I do. She was so kind, so thankful, and so humorous. She told me she had lost 5 stones.

"How much is that?" I asked.

"Seventy pounds—without counting calories, without depriving myself of anything I wanted," Nancy replied. "I used to be like this [she made a face like a blowfish], now I am not. I am off the couch and feeling better than I have in 40 years."

Below is a group of typical 80-to-90-year old brains. As we age, our brain gets less and less active.

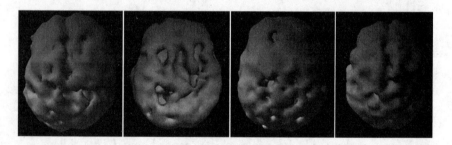

But Nancy's scan looked like someone in her forties! Her brain was healthy and strong. When she saw it, she cried because she was so happy, knowing it would not have looked this way just a year earlier. Nancy changed the trajectory of her happiness and the rest of her life. You can too. You are not stuck with the brain you have. You can make it better, no matter what age you start.

NANCY'S SURFACE SPECT SCAN

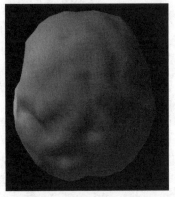

The main reason for Nancy's success was that she was serious, even relentless, about making better decisions. She never felt deprived or had the feeling that her new way of living was hard. Being a couch potato was hard. Being depressed was hard. Feeling isolated and alone was hard. So she developed the daily habits and routines that propelled her success and happiness forward.

NANCY AND DR. AMEN

Nancy shows us it's never too late to start taking responsibility for your own life. Now it's your turn to take responsibility for your own happiness. You have the secrets to help you do it.

Let me tell you why *responsibility* is one of my wife, Tana's, favorite words. It was the one word that changed everything for her. When she was in her twenties and recovering from cancer and depression, she went to a motivational seminar that her uncle Bob was teaching. He had been a heroin addict but was able to transform his life. At the seminar when Bob saw Tana's self-pity, he asked her, "How much responsibility are you willing to take?"

Stunned, Tana said, "I can't take responsibility for cancer."

"I didn't ask you to take the blame," he replied. "Responsibility is not blame. It is the ability to respond. Do you want 50 percent responsibility? Then you have a 50 percent chance to change the outcome. Or do you want 100 percent responsibility? Otherwise someone or something other than you is in control."

Tana answered, "I want 100 percent ability to respond." It was a light-bulb moment for her. It caused her to immediately start taking responsibility for her decisions. You have the same choice before you now. Do you want 50 percent responsibility for your happiness or 100 percent? How much power and control over the outcome do you want?

When you take responsibility and start changing your happiness *today*, it can change your future and the future of those you love.

Gratitude and Appreciation

So many people have been involved in creating *You, Happier: The 7 Neuroscience Secrets of Feeling Good Based on Your Brain Type*. I am grateful to them all, especially the tens of thousands of patients and families who have come to Amen Clinics and allowed us to help them on their healing journey, with special thanks to the patients who allowed me to tell part of their stories in this book, including Laura Clery and Stephen Hilton.

I am grateful to the amazing staff at Amen Clinics who work hard every day serving our patients. Special appreciation to Frances Sharpe, Mike Yorkey, and Jenny Faherty, who helped me craft the book to make it accessible to our readers. Also to my friends and colleagues Dr. Rob Johnson, Kim Schneider, Christine Perkins, Rob Patterson, Jim Springer, Natalie Buchoz, Al Madi, Kevin Richards, Mark Silvestro, Stephanie Villafuerte, Jeff Feuerhaken, and James Gilbert for their input, love, and support. I am also grateful to Jan Long Harris and the team at Tyndale for their belief in the book and help in getting it out into the world, and my editor, Andrea Vinley Converse, who helped make this book the best it can be.

I am grateful to my amazing wife, Tana, who is my partner in all I do, and to my family, who have tolerated my obsession with making brains better. I love you all. You make me happier every day.

About Daniel G. Amen, MD

Daniel G. Amen, MD, believes that brain health is central to all health and success. When your brain works right, he says, you work right, and when your brain is troubled, you are much more likely to have trouble in your life. His work is dedicated to helping people have better brains and better lives.

Sharecare named him the web's #1 most influential expert and advocate on mental health, and the *Washington Post* called him the most popular psychiatrist in America. His online videos have been viewed more than 150 million times.

Dr. Amen is a physician, board-certified child and adult psychiatrist, award-winning researcher, and 12-time *New York Times* bestselling author. He is the Founder and CEO of Amen Clinics in Costa Mesa, Walnut Creek, and Encino, California; Bellevue, Washington; Washington, DC; Atlanta, GA; Chicago, IL; Dallas, TX; New York, NY; and Hollywood, FL.

Amen Clinics has the world's largest database of functional brain scans relating to behavior, with more than 200,000 SPECT scans and more than 10,000 QEEGs on patients from over 155 countries.

Dr. Amen is the lead researcher on the world's largest brain imaging and rehabilitation study on professional football players. His research has not only demonstrated high levels of brain damage in players but also the possibility of significant recovery for many with the principles that underlie his work.

Together with Pastor Rick Warren and Dr. Mark Hyman, Dr. Amen is also one of the chief architects of The Daniel Plan, a program to get the world healthy through religious organizations, which has been done in thousands of churches, mosques, and synagogues.

Dr. Amen is the author or coauthor of more than 80 professional articles, 9 book chapters, and over 40 books, including 17 national bestsellers and 12 *New York Times* bestsellers, including the #1 *New York Times* bestsellers *The Daniel Plan* and the over-one-million-copies-sold, 40-week bestseller *Change Your Brain, Change Your Life*; as well as *The End of Mental Illness*; *Healing ADD*; *Change Your Brain, Change Your Body*; *The Brain Warrior's Way*; *Memory Rescue*; and *Your Brain Is Always Listening*.

Dr. Amen's published scientific articles have appeared in the prestigious journals of *Journal of Alzheimer's Disease*, Nature's *Molecular*

Psychiatry, PLOS ONE, Nature's *Translational Psychiatry,* Nature's *Obesity, Journal of Neuropsychiatry and Clinical Neuroscience, Minerva Psichiatrica, Journal of Neurotrauma, American Journal of Psychiatry, Nuclear Medicine Communications, Neurological Research, Journal of the American Academy of Child and Adolescent Psychiatry, Primary Psychiatry, Military Medicine,* and *General Hospital Psychiatry.*

In January 2016, his team's research on distinguishing PTSD from TBI on over 21,000 SPECT scans was featured as one of the top 100 stories in science by *Discover* magazine. In 2017, his team published a study on over 46,000 scans, showing the difference between male and female brains; and in 2018, his team published a study on how the brain ages based on 62,454 SPECT scans.

Dr. Amen has written, produced, and hosted 16 national public television programs about brain health, which have aired more than 130,000 times across North America. As of March 2022, his latest show is *You, Happier: The Neuroscience of Feeling Good.*

Together with his wife, Tana, he has hosted *The Brain Warrior's Way Podcast* since 2015, with over 1,000 episodes and 14 million downloads. It has been listed as one of the top 20 all-time podcasts in Mental Health on Apple.

Dr. Amen has appeared in movies, including *Quiet Explosions, After the Last Round,* and *The Crash Reel* and was a consultant for *Concussion,* starring Will Smith. He appeared in the docuseries *Justin Bieber: Seasons* and has appeared regularly on *The Dr. Oz Show, Dr. Phil,* and *The Doctors.*

He has also spoken for the National Security Agency (NSA), the National Science Foundation (NSF), Harvard's Learning and the Brain Conference, the Department of the Interior, the National Council of Juvenile and Family Court Judges, the Supreme Courts of Ohio, Delaware, and Wyoming, the Canadian and Brazilian Societies of Nuclear Medicine, and large corporations, such as Merrill Lynch, Hitachi, Bayer Pharmaceuticals, GNC, and many others. In 2016, Dr. Amen gave one of the prestigious Talks at Google.

Dr. Amen's work has been featured in *Newsweek, Time, Huffington Post, ABC World News, 20/20,* the BBC, *London Telegraph, Parade* magazine, the *New York Times,* the *New York Times Magazine,* the *Washington Post, MIT Technology, World Economic Forum,* the *Los Angeles Times, Men's Health, Bottom Line, Vogue, Cosmopolitan,* and many others.

In 2010, Dr. Amen founded BrainMD, a fast-growing nutraceutical company dedicated to natural ways to support mental health and brain health.

Dr. Amen is married to Tana and is the father of four children and grandfather to Elias, Emmy, Liam, Louie, and Haven. He is an avid table tennis player.

Resources

AMEN CLINICS, INC.

amenclinics.com

Amen Clinics, Inc. (ACI), was established in 1989 by Daniel G. Amen, MD. ACI specializes in innovative diagnosis and treatment planning for a wide variety of behavioral, learning, emotional, cognitive, and weight issues for children, teenagers, and adults. Brain SPECT imaging is one of the primary diagnostic tools used in our clinics. ACI has the world's largest database of brain scans for emotional, cognitive, and behavioral problems. It has an international reputation for evaluating brain-behavior problems, such as ADD/ADHD, depression, anxiety, school failure, traumatic brain injury and concussions, obsessive-compulsive disorders, aggressiveness, marital conflict, cognitive decline, brain toxicity from drugs or alcohol, and obesity, among others. In addition, we work with people to optimize brain function and decrease the risk for Alzheimer's disease and other age-related issues.

ACI welcomes referrals from physicians, psychologists, social workers, marriage and family therapists, drug and alcohol counselors, and individual patients and families.

Our toll-free number is (888) 288-9834.

Amen Clinics Orange County, California
3150 Bristol St., Suite 400
Costa Mesa, CA 92626

Amen Clinics Northern California
350 N Wiget Ln., Suite 105
Walnut Creek, CA 94598

Amen Clinics Northwest
616 120th Ave. NE, Suite C100
Bellevue, WA 98005

Amen Clinics Los Angeles
5363 Balboa Blvd., Suite 100
Encino, CA 91316

Amen Clinics Washington, D.C.
1875 Campus Commons Dr.
Reston, VA 20191

Amen Clinics New York
16 East 40th St., 9th Floor
New York, NY 10016

Amen Clinics Atlanta
5901-C Peachtree Dunwoody Rd.,
N.E., Suite 65
Atlanta, GA 30328

Amen Clinics Chicago
2333 Waukegan Rd., Suite 100
Bannockburn, IL 60015

Amen Clinics Dallas
7301 N. State Hwy 161, Suite 170
Irving, TX 75039

Amen Clinics Miami
200 South Park Rd., Suite 140
Hollywood, FL 33021

BRAINMD

brainmd.com
For the highest-quality brain health supplements, courses, books and information products

AMEN UNIVERSITY

amenuniversity.com
In 2014, Dr. Amen formed Amen University with courses on practical neuroscience, including:

- Amen Clinics Professional Brain Health Certification Course (with coaches in 56 countries)
- Brain Health Licensed Trainer Course
- Brain Thrive by 25, which has been shown to decrease drug, alcohol, and tobacco use, decrease depression, and improve self-esteem in teens and young adults
- Change Your Brain Master's Course
- Memory Rescue
- Concussion Rescue
- Healing ADD
- 6 Weeks to Overcome Anxiety, Depression, Trauma & Grief
- Autism: A New Way Forward
- The Brain Warrior's Way
- Brain Fit for Work and Life
- Overcoming Insomnia

Notes

INTRODUCTION

1. Tamara Lush, "'It's Been One Thing After Another': Americans Are Unhappiest They've Been in 50 Years, Poll Shows," *USA Today*, June 16, 2020, https://www.usatoday.com/story/news/nation/2020/06/16/amid-bad-news-2020-americans-unhappier-more-lonely-poll-shows/3197440001/.

2. Express Scripts, "America's State of Mind Report," April 16, 2020, https://www.express-scripts.com/corporate/americas-state-of-mind-report.

3. Catherine K. Ettman et al., "Prevalence of Depression Symptoms in US Adults before and during the COVID-19 Pandemic," *JAMA Network Open* 3, no. 9 (September 2, 2020): e2019686, https://jamanetwork.com/journals/jamanetworkopen/fullarticle/2770146.

4. Michael Argyle, Peter Hills, and Stephen Wright, "Take the Oxford Happiness Questionnaire," *Guardian*, November 3, 2014, https://www.theguardian.com/lifeandstyle/2014/nov/03/take-the-oxford-happiness-questionnaire.

CHAPTER 1: THE SEVEN SECRETS TO HAPPINESS NO ONE IS TALKING ABOUT

1. Katherine Nelson-Coffey, "The Science of Happiness in Positive Psychology 101," *Happiness & SWB* (blog), PositivePsychology.com, last updated June 5, 2021, https://positivepsychology.com/happiness/.

2. Dennis Prager, "Why Be Happy?" PragerU, January 20, 2014, video, 5:05, https://www.youtube.com/watch?v=_Zxnw0l499g.

3. Howard S. Friedman and Leslie R. Martin, *The Longevity Project: Surprising Discoveries for Health and Long Life from the Landmark Eight-Decade Study* (New York: Plume, 2012).

4. Joel Fuhrman, "The Hidden Dangers of Fast and Processed Food," *American Journal of Lifestyle Medicine* 12, no. 5 (September–October 2018): 375–81, https://www.ncbi.nlm.nih.gov/pmc/articles/PMC6146358/.

   Joel Fuhrman, "An Interview with Dr. Joel Fuhrman on the Importance of Diet," interview by Oliver M. Glass, *American Journal of Psychiatry Residents' Journal* 14, no. 3 (March 8, 2019): 6–7.

5. Justin B. Echouffo-Tcheugui et al., "Circulating Cortisol and Cognitive and Structural Brain Measures: The Framingham Heart Study," *Neurology* 91, no. 21 (November 2018): e1961–e1970, doi:10.1212/WNL.0000000000006549.

6. Deyan Georgiev, "How Much Time Do People Spend on Social Media? [63+ Facts to Like, Share and Comment]," Review 42, last updated May 29, 2021, https://review42.com/resources/how-much-time-do-people-spend-on-social-media/.

7. Ian Bogost, "The Cigarette of This Century," *Atlantic*, June 6, 2012, https://www.theatlantic.com/technology/archive/2012/06/the-cigarette-of-this-century/258092/.

8. World Health Organization, "Addictive Behaviours: Gaming Disorder," September 14, 2018, https://www.who.int/news-room/q-a-detail/gaming-disorder.

9. Shawn Achor and Michelle Gielan, "Consuming Negative News Can Make You Less Effective at Work," *Harvard Business Review*, September 14, 2015, https://hbr.org/2015/09/consuming-negative-news-can-make-you-less-effective-at-work.

10. Daniel G. Amen et al., "Discriminative Properties of Hippocampal Hypoperfusion in Marijuana Users Compared to Healthy Controls: Implications for Marijuana Administration in Alzheimer's Dementia," *Journal of Alzheimer's Disease* 56, no. 1 (January 12, 2017): 261–73, https://pubmed.ncbi.nlm.nih.gov/27886010/.

11. Daniel T. Malone, Matthew N. Hill, and Tiziana Rubino, "Adolescent Cannabis Use and Psychosis: Epidemiology and Neurodevelopmental Models," *British Journal of Pharmacology* 160, no. 3 (June 2010): 511–22, https://pubmed.ncbi.nlm.nih .gov/20590561/.

12. Gabriella Gobbi et al., "Association of Cannabis Use in Adolescence and Risk of Depression, Anxiety, and Suicidality in Young Adulthood," *JAMA Psychiatry* 76, no. 4 (February 13, 2019): 426–34, doi:10.1001/jamapsychiatry.2018.4500.

13. Joe Leech, "13 Ways That Sugary Soda Is Bad for Your Health," Healthline, February 8, 2019, https://www.healthline.com/nutrition/13-ways-sugary-soda-is-bad-for-you.

14. Grant Edward Donnelly et al., "The Amount and Source of Millionaires' Wealth (Moderately) Predicts Their Happiness," *Personality and Social Psychology Bulletin* 44, no. 5 (May 2018): 684–99, https://www.hbs.edu/faculty/Pages/item.aspx?num=53540.

15. Sara Miñarro et al., "Happy without Money: Minimally Monetized Societies Can Exhibit High Subjective Well-Being," *PLOS ONE* 16, no. 1 (January 13, 2021): e0244569, https://journals.plos.org/plosone/article?id=10.1371/journal.pone.0244569.

16. Amit Kumar, Matthew A. Killingsworth, and Thomas Gilovich, "Spending on Doing Promotes More Moment-to-Moment Happiness Than Spending on Having," *Journal of Experimental Social Psychology* 88 (May 2020): 103971, https://www.sciencedirect .com/science/article/abs/pii/S0022103119305256?via%3Dihub.

17. National Library of Medicine, "Omega 3 and Mood" PubMed search results, accessed June 13, 2021, https://pubmed.ncbi.nlm.nih.gov/?term=omega+3+and+mood.

18. National Library of Medicine, "Vitamin D and Mood" PubMed search results, accessed June 13, 2021, https://pubmed.ncbi.nlm.nih.gov/?term=vitamin+d+and+mood.

19. National Library of Medicine, "St. John's Wort" PubMed search results, accessed June 13, 2021, https://pubmed.ncbi.nlm.nih.gov/?term=st.+john%27s+wort.

20. Majid Fotuhi, "Can You Grow Your Hippocampus? Yes. Here's How, and Why It Matters," SharpBrains, November 4, 2015, http://sharpbrains.com/blog/2015/11/04/can-you-grow -your-hippocampus-yes-heres-how-and-why-it-matters/.

21. Felice N. Jacka et al., "A Randomized Controlled Trial of Dietary Improvement for Adults with Major Depression (the 'SMILES' Trial)," *BMC Medicine* 15, no. 23 (January 30, 2017), https://bmcmedicine.biomedcentral.com/articles/10.1186/s12916-017-0791-y.

22. James Cook University, "Study Firms up Diet and Depression Link," ScienceDaily, October 10, 2018, http://www.sciencedaily.com/releases/2018/10/181010093645.htm.

23. Daniel G. Amen, *Healing ADD from the Inside Out*, rev. ed. (New York: Berkley Books, 2013), chapter 23.

CHAPTER 2: FINDING HAPPINESS IN THE BRAIN

1. I've told the story of my mother's first SPECT scan many times, including in my book *Change Your Brain, Change Your Life*, rev. ed. (New York: Harmony Books, 2015), 58–59.

2. In most of my books, I like to start with a brief lesson on brain biology and how its regions play a role in certain mental health and physical health issues. The better you understand your brain, the more likely you are to care for it.

3. Daniel Kahneman, introduction to *Thinking, Fast and Slow* (New York: Farrar, Straus and Giroux, 2011).

4. Michael Argyle, Peter Hills, and Stephen Wright, "Take the Oxford Happiness Questionnaire," *Guardian*, November 3, 2014, https://www.theguardian.com/lifeandstyle/2014/nov/03/take -the-oxford-happiness-questionnaire.

5. Silvia H. Cardoso, "Hardwired for Happiness," *Cerebrum*, Dana Foundation, December 15, 2006, https://dana.org/article/hardwired-for-happiness.

CHAPTER 3: AN INTRODUCTION TO BRAIN TYPING

1. I've written about the five main brain types in light of several mental health issues, starting in Daniel G. Amen and Tana Amen, *The Brain Warrior's Way* (New York: New American Library, 2016), 65–69.

2. I've written about brain types in *The Brain Warrior's Way* (New York: New American Library, 2016); *Change Your Brain, Change Your Grades* (Dallas: BenBella Books, 2019); and *Your Brain Is Always Listening* (Carol Stream, IL: Tyndale, 2021).

3. Elizabeth Scott, "What Happy People Have in Common," Verywell Mind, updated December 1, 2020, https://www.verywellmind.com/secrets-of-happy-people-3144868.

CHAPTER 5: THE SPONTANEOUS BRAIN TYPE

1. South West News Service, "Acting Spontaneously Might Be the Key to Happiness," *New York Post*, June 11, 2020, https://nypost.com/2020/06/11/is-acting-spontaneously-the-key-to-happiness/.

2. Daniel G. Amen, *Healing ADD from the Inside Out*, rev. ed. (New York: Berkley Books, 2013), chapter 16.

3. Daniel Z. Lieberman and Michael E. Long, *The Molecule of More: How a Single Chemical in Your Brain Drives Love, Sex, and Creativity—and Will Determine the Fate of the Human Race* (Dallas: BenBella Books, 2018), 16.

4. Harry Benson and Rehna Azim, "Celebrity Divorce Rates," Marriage Foundation, January 2016, https://marriagefoundation.org.uk/wp-content/uploads/2016/06/pdf-03.pdf.

5. William H. Church, Ryan E. Adams, and Livia S. Wyss, "Ketogenic Diet Alters Dopaminergic Activity in the Mouse Cortex," *Neuroscience Letters* 571 (June 13, 2014): 1–4, https://www.sciencedirect.com/science/article/abs/pii/S030439401400319X?via%3Dihub.

6. Tiffany Field et al., "Cortisol Decreases and Serotonin and Dopamine Increase following Massage Therapy," *International Journal of Neuroscience* 115, no. 10 (October 2005): 1397–413, https://pubmed.ncbi.nlm.nih.gov/16162447/.

7. Valorie N. Salimpoor et al., "Anatomically Distinct Dopamine Release during Anticipation and Experience of Peak Emotion to Music," *Nature Neuroscience* 14 (January 9, 2011): 257–62, https://www.nature.com/articles/nn.2726.

8. Hsiang-Yi Tsai et al., "Sunshine-Exposure Variation of Human Striatal Dopamine D(2)/D(3) Receptor Availability in Healthy Volunteers," *Progress in Neuro-Psychopharmacology and Biological Psychiatry* 35, no. 1 (January 15, 2011): 107–10, https://pubmed.ncbi.nlm.nih.gov/20875835/.

CHAPTER 6: THE PERSISTENT BRAIN TYPE

1. Ángel Pazos, Alphonse Probst, and J. M. Palacios, "Serotonin Receptors in the Human Brain—IV. Autoradiographic Mapping of Serotonin-2 Receptors," *Neuroscience* 21, no. 1 (April 1987): 123–39, https://www.sciencedirect.com/science/article/abs/pii/0306452287903277?via%3Dihub#!.

2. Simon N. Young, "How to Increase Serotonin in the Human Brain without Drugs," *Journal of Psychiatry and Neuroscience* 32, no. 6 (November 2007): 394–99, https://www.ncbi.nlm.nih.gov/pmc/articles/PMC2077351/#r34-1.

3. Imperial College London, "Rethinking Serotonin Could Lead to a Shift in Psychiatric Care," ScienceDaily, September 4, 2017, https://www.sciencedaily.com/releases/2017/09/170904093724.htm.

4. Rhonda P. Patrick and Bruce N. Ames, "Vitamin D and the Omega-3 Fatty Acids Control Serotonin Synthesis and Action, Part 2: Relevance for ADHD, Bipolar Disorder, Schizophrenia, and Impulsive Behavior," *FASEB Journal* 29, no. 6 (February 24, 2015): 2207–22, https://faseb.onlinelibrary.wiley.com/doi/full/10.1096/fj.14-268342.

5. Tiffany Field et al., "Massage Therapy Effects on Depressed Pregnant Women," *Journal of Psychosomatic Obstetrics and Gynaecology* 25, no. 2 (June 2004): 115–22, https://pubmed.ncbi.nlm.nih.gov/15715034/.

Tiffany Field et al., "Cortisol Decreases and Serotonin and Dopamine Increase following Massage Therapy," *International Journal of Neuroscience* 115, no. 10 (October 2005): 1397–413, https://pubmed .ncbi.nlm.nih.gov/16162447/.

6. Robert N. Golden et al., "The Efficacy of Light Therapy in the Treatment of Mood Disorders: A Review and Meta-Analysis of the Evidence," *American Journal of Psychiatry* 162, no. 4 (April 2005): 656–62, https://ajp.psychiatryonline.org/doi/full/10.1176/appi .ajp.162.4.656.

7. Marije aan het Rot et al., "Bright Light Exposure during Acute Tryptophan Depletion Prevents a Lowering of Mood in Mildly Seasonal Women," *European Neuropsychopharmacology* 18, no. 1 (January 2008): 14–23, https://www.sciencedirect .com/science/article/abs/pii/S0924977X07001137.

8. Elisabeth Perreau-Linck et al., "In vivo Measurements of Brain Trapping of C-labelled Alpha-methyl-L-tryptophan during Acute Changes in Mood States," *Journal of Psychiatry and Neuroscience* 32, no. 6 (November 2007): 430–34, https://www.ncbi.nlm.nih.gov/pmc /articles/PMC2077345/.

CHAPTER 7: THE SENSITIVE BRAIN TYPE

1. Judith Orloff, "How to Thrive as a Sensitive Person, with Dr. Judith Orloff," October 22, 2019, in *Brain Warrior's Way Podcast*, 13:11, https://brainwarriorswaypodcast.com/how-to -thrive-as-a-sensitive-person-with-dr-judith-orloff//.

2. Colin A. Capaldi, Raelyne L. Dopko, and John M. Zelenski, "The Relationship between Nature Connectedness and Happiness: A Meta-analysis," *Frontiers in Psychology* 5 (September 8, 2014): 976, https://www.frontiersin.org/articles/10.3389/fpsyg.2014.00976 /full.

3. Inna Schneiderman, et al., "Oxytocin during the Initial Stages of Romantic Attachment: Relations to Couples' Interactive Reciprocity," *Psychoneuroendocrinology* 37, no. 8 (August 2012): 1277–85, https://www.ncbi.nlm.nih.gov/pmc/articles/PMC3936960/.

Melanie Greenberg, "The Science of Love and Attachment," *Psychology Today*, March 30, 2016, https://www.psychologytoday.com/us/blog/the-mindful-self-express/201603/the -science-love-and-attachment.

Scott Edwards, "Love and the Brain," Harvard Medical School, Spring 2015, https://hms .harvard.edu/news-events/publications-archive/brain/love-brain.

4. Martin Sack et al., "Intranasal Oxytocin Reduces Provoked Symptoms in Female Patients with Posttraumatic Stress Disorder Despite Exerting Sympathomimetic and Positive Chronotropic Effects in a Randomized Controlled Trial," *BMC Medicine* 15, no. 1 (February 2017): 40, https://www.ncbi.nlm.nih.gov/pmc/articles/PMC5314583/.

5. Jessie L. Frijling, "Preventing PTSD with Oxytocin: Effects of Oxytocin Administration on Fear Neurocircuitry and PTSD Symptom Development in Recently Trauma-Exposed Individuals," *European Journal of Psychotraumatology* 8, no. 1 (April 11, 2017): 1302652, https://www.ncbi.nlm.nih.gov/pmc/articles/PMC5400019/.

6. K. Paul Stoller, *Oxytocin: The Hormone of Healing and Hope* (Lagunitas, CA: Dream Treader Press, 2012), 1–3.

7. Lori Singer, "Oxytocin—More than a Love Hormone," Be Her Village, September 24, 2020, https://behervillage.com/articles/oxytocin-more-than-a-love-hormone.

8. Miho Nagasawa et al., "Oxytocin-Gaze Positive Loop and the Coevolution of Human-Dog Bonds," *Science* 348, no. 6232 (April 17, 2015): 333–36, https://science.sciencemag.org /content/348/6232/333.

9. Alan R. Harvey, "Links Between the Neurobiology of Oxytocin and Human Musicality," *Frontiers in Human Neuroscience* 14 (August 26, 2020): 350, https://doi.org/10.3389 /fnhum.2020.00350.

10. Ferris Jabr, "Let's Get Physical: The Psychology of Effective Workout Music," *Scientific American*, March 20, 2013, https://www.scientificamerican.com/article/psychology -workout-music/.

11. Naveen Jayaram et al., "Effect of Yoga Therapy on Plasma Oxytocin and Facial Emotion Recognition Deficits in Patients of Schizophrenia," *Indian Journal of Psychiatry* 55, no. S3 (July 2013): S409–13, https://www.ncbi.nlm.nih.gov/pmc/articles/PMC3768223/.

12. Thomas Christopher, "10 Healthy Ways to Boost Your Happy Hormones," Medium, January 25, 2021, https://medium.com/datadriveninvestor/10-healthy-ways-to-boost -your-happy-hormones-7f6e2535203e.

13. Kerstin Uvnäs-Moberg, Linda Handlin, and Maria Petersson, "Self-Soothing Behaviors with Particular Reference to Oxytocin Release Induced by Non-noxious Sensory Stimulation," *Frontiers in Psychology* 5 (January 12, 2015): 1529, https://www.frontiersin .org/articles/10.3389/fpsyg.2014.01529/full.

14. Takumi Nagasawa, Mitsuaki Ohta, and Hidehiko Uchiyama, "Effects of the Characteristic Temperament of Cats on the Emotions and Hemodynamic Responses of Humans," *PLOS ONE* 15, no. 6 (June 25, 2020): e0235188, https://pubmed.ncbi.nlm.nih.gov/32584860/.

15. Brenda Goodman, "How the 'Love Hormone' Works Its Magic," WebMD, November 25, 2013, https://www.webmd.com/sex-relationships/news/20131125/how-the-love -hormone-works-its-magic.

16. National Institute on Drug Abuse, "Overdose Death Rates," January 29, 2021, https://www.drugabuse.gov/drug-topics/trends-statistics/overdose-death-rates.

17. Kent C. Berridge and Morten L. Kringelbach, "Pleasure Systems in the Brain," *Neuron* 86, no. 3 (May 6, 2015): 646–64.

18. Shiv Basant Kumar et al., "Telomerase Activity and Cellular Aging Might Be Positively Modified by a Yoga-Based Lifestyle Intervention," *Journal of Alternative and Complementary Medicine* 21, no. 6 (June 2015): 370–72, https://www.liebertpub.com/doi /10.1089/acm.2014.0298.

19. P. B. Rokade, "Release of Endomorphin Hormone and Its Effects on Our Body and Moods: A Review" (International Conference on Chemical, Biological and Environment Sciences, Bangkok, December 2011), http://psrcentre.org/images/extraimages/41.%20 1211916.pdf.

20. Rokade, "Release of Endomorphin Hormone."

21. Sandra Manninen et al., "Social Laughter Triggers Endogenous Opioid Release in Humans," *Journal of Neuroscience* 37, no. 25 (June 21, 2017): 6125–31, https://www .jneurosci.org/content/37/25/6125.

22. Ji-Sheng Han, "Acupuncture and Endorphins," *Neuroscience Letters* 361, nos. 1–3 (May 6, 2004): 258–61, https://pubmed.ncbi.nlm.nih.gov/15135942/.

23. David P. Sniezek and Imran J. Siddiqui, "Acupuncture for Treating Anxiety and Depression in Women: A Clinical Systematic Review," *Medical Acupuncture* 25, no. 3 (June 2013): 164–72, https://pubmed.ncbi.nlm.nih.gov/24761171/.

24. Fatma Gülçin Uğurlu et al., "The Effects of Acupuncture versus Sham Acupuncture in the Treatment of Fibromyalgia: A Randomized Controlled Clinical Trial," *Acta Reumatologica Portuguesa* 42, no. 1 (January–March 2017): 32–37, https://pubmed.ncbi.nlm.nih. gov/28371571/.

25. Xuan Yin et al., "Efficacy and Safety of Acupuncture Treatment on Primary Insomnia: A Randomized Controlled Trial," *Sleep Medicine* 37 (September 2017): 193–200, https://pubmed.ncbi.nlm.nih.gov/28899535/.

CHAPTER 8: THE CAUTIOUS BRAIN TYPE

1. Dr. Daniel Amen, "Brittany Furlan Has Her Brain Scanned at Amen Clinics (Part 1)," Facebook, video, 4:28, November 25, 2020, https://www.facebook.com/watch/?v= 414592606488399.

2. Amen Clinics, "Young Entrepreneur Neels Visser Came to Amen Clinics to Get His Brain Scanned Due to Concerns over Keeping His Anxiety in Check," Facebook, video, 7:52, January 27, 2021, https://www.facebook.com/AmenClinic/posts/2073910632740336.

3. Chloe Taylor, "Here's Why People Are Panic Buying and Stockpiling Toilet Paper to Cope

with Coronavirus Fears," CNBC, March 11, 2020, https://www.cnbc.com/2020/03/11/heres-why-people-are-panic-buying-and-stockpiling-toilet-paper.html.

4. "How a Couple Used Their Brains to Escape an Active Shooter at Route 91, with Troy and Shannon Zeeman," *Brain Warrior's Way Podcast*, January 7, 2020, https://brainwarriorswaypodcast.com/how-a-couple-used-their-brains-to-escape-an-active-shooter-at-route-91-with-troy-and-shannon-zeeman/.

5. Crissa L. Guglietti et al., "Meditation-Related Increases in GABAB Modulated Cortical Inhibition," *Brain Stimulation* 6, no. 3 (May 2013): 397–402, https://pubmed.ncbi.nlm.nih.gov/23022436/.

6. Chris C. Streeter et al., "Effects of Yoga versus Walking on Mood, Anxiety, and Brain GABA Levels: A Randomized Controlled MRS Study," *Journal of Alternative and Complementary Medicine* 16, no. 11 (November 2010): 1145–52, https://www.ncbi.nlm.nih.gov/pmc/articles/PMC3111147/.

Chris C. Streeter et al., "Yoga Asana Sessions Increase Brain GABA Levels: A Pilot Study," *Journal of Alternative and Complementary Medicine* 13, no. 4 (May 2007): 419–26, https://pubmed.ncbi.nlm.nih.gov/17532734/.

7. Andrew Steptoe, Jane Wardle, and Michael Marmot, "Positive Affect and Health-Related Neuroendocrine, Cardiovascular, and Inflammatory Processes," *Proceedings of the National Academy of Sciences of the United States of America* 102, no. 18 (May 3, 2005): 6508–12, https://www.ncbi.nlm.nih.gov/pmc/articles/PMC1088362/.

8. Edward J. Sachar, Jeremy C. Cobb, and Ronald E. Shor, "Plasma Cortisol Changes during Hypnotic Trance: Relation to Depth of Hypnosis," *Archives of General Psychiatry* 14, no. 5 (May 1966): 482–90, https://jamanetwork.com/journals/jamapsychiatry/article-abstract/489024.

9. Dawson Church, Garret Yount, and Audrey J. Brooks, "The Effect of Emotional Freedom Techniques on Stress Biochemistry: A Randomized Controlled Trial," *Journal of Nervous and Mental Disease* 200, no. 10 (October 2012): 891–96, https://pubmed.ncbi.nlm.nih.gov/22986277/.

10. Long Zhang et al., "A Review Focused on the Psychological Effectiveness of Tai Chi on Different Populations," *Evidence-Based Complementary and Alternative Medicine* 2012 (2012): 678107, https://www.hindawi.com/journals/ecam/2012/678107/.

11. Tiffany Field et al., "Cortisol Decreases and Serotonin and Dopamine Increase following Massage Therapy," *International Journal of Neuroscience* 115, no. 10 (October 2005): 1397–413, https://pubmed.ncbi.nlm.nih.gov/16162447/.

12. Matthew Thorpe, "11 Natural Ways to Lower Your Cortisol Levels," Healthline, April 17, 2017, https://www.healthline.com/nutrition/ways-to-lower-cortisol.

CHAPTER 9: BRIGHT MINDS ARE HAPPIER

1. Daniel G. Amen, *Memory Rescue* (Carol Stream, IL: Tyndale, 2017).

Daniel G. Amen, *The End of Mental Illness* (Carol Stream, IL: Tyndale, 2020).

2. Stephanie Studenski, et al., "Gait Speed and Survival in Older Adults," *JAMA* 305, no. 1 (January 5, 2011): 50–58, https://www.ncbi.nlm.nih.gov/pmc/articles/PMC3080184/.

3. Gabriele Gratton et al., "Dietary Flavanols Improve Cerebral Cortical Oxygenation and Cognition in Healthy Adults," *Scientific Reports* 10 (November 24, 2020): 19409, https://www.nature.com/articles/s41598-020-76160-9.

4. Paul G. Harch et al., "A Phase I Study of Low-Pressure Hyperbaric Oxygen Therapy for Blast-Induced Post-concussion Syndrome and Post-traumatic Stress Disorder," *Journal of Neurotrauma* 29, no. 1 (January 1, 2012): 168–85, https://pubmed.ncbi.nlm.nih.gov/22026588/.

5. Morteza Azizi et al., "The Role of Cognitive Group Therapy and Happiness Training on Cerebral Blood Flow Using 99mTc-ECD Brain Perfusion SPECT: A Quasi-experimental Study of Depressed Patients," *Nuklearmedizin* 53, no. 5 (2014): 205–10, https://pubmed.ncbi.nlm.nih.gov/24823430/.

6. Angelo Suardi et al., "The Neural Correlates of Happiness: A Review of PET and fMRI Studies Using Autobiographical Recall Methods," *Cognitive, Affective, and Behavioral Neuroscience* 16, no. 3 (June 2016): 383–92, https://pubmed.ncbi.nlm.nih.gov/26912269/.

7. Jun Sugawara, Takashi Tarumi, and Hirofumi Tanaka, "Effect of Mirthful Laughter on Vascular Function," *American Journal of Cardiology* 106, no. 6 (September 15, 2010): 856–9, https://pubmed.ncbi.nlm.nih.gov/20816128/.

8. Cigna, *Loneliness and the Workplace*, 2020, https://www.cigna.com/static/www-cigna-com/docs/about-us/newsroom/studies-and-reports/combatting-loneliness/cigna-2020-loneliness-factsheet.pdf.

9. Wido G. M. Oerlemans, Arnold B. Bakker, and Ruut Veenhoven, "Finding the Key to Happy Aging: A Day Reconstruction of Happiness," *Journals of Gerontology: Series B*, 66B, no. 6 (November 2011): 665–74, https://academic.oup.com/psychsocgerontology/article/66B/6/665/588065.

10. Pedro Marques-Vidal and Virginia Milagre, "Are Oral Health Status and Care Associated with Anxiety and Depression? A Study of Portuguese Health Science Students," *Journal of Public Health Dentistry* 66, no. 1 (Winter 2006): 64–66, https://pubmed.ncbi.nlm.nih.gov/16570753/.

11. Daniel G. Amen et al., "Quantitative Erythrocyte Omega-3 EPA Plus DHA Levels Are Related to Higher Regional Cerebral Blood Flow on Brain SPECT," *Journal of Alzheimer's Disease* 58, no. 4 (2017): 1189–99, https://pubmed.ncbi.nlm.nih.gov/28527220/.

12. Masahiro Matsunaga et al., "Association between Perceived Happiness Levels and Peripheral Circulating Pro-inflammatory Cytokine Levels in Middle-Aged Adults in Japan," *Neuro Endocrinology Letters* 32, no. 4 (2011): 458–63, https://pubmed.ncbi.nlm.nih.gov/21876513/.

13. Nancy L. Sin, Jennifer E. Graham-Engeland, and David M. Almeida, "Daily Positive Events and Inflammation: Findings from the National Study of Daily Experiences," *Brain, Behavior, and Immunity* 43 (January 2015): 130–38, https://www.sciencedirect.com/science/article/abs/pii/S0889159114004073.

14. Meike Bartels, "Genetics of Wellbeing and Its Components Satisfaction with Life, Happiness, and Quality of Life: A Review and Meta-analysis of Heritability Studies," *Behavior Genetics* 45, no. 2 (March 2015): 137–56, https://pubmed.ncbi.nlm.nih.gov/25715755/.

15. Kevin F. Bieniek et al., "Chronic Traumatic Encephalopathy Pathology in a Neurodegenerative Disorders Brain Bank," *Acta Neuropathologica* 130, no. 6 (2015): 877–89, https://www.ncbi.nlm.nih.gov/pmc/articles/PMC4655127/.

16. Daniel G. Amen et al., "Discriminative Properties of Hippocampal Hypoperfusion in Marijuana Users Compared to Healthy Controls: Implications for Marijuana Administration in Alzheimer's Dementia," *Journal of Alzheimer's Disease* 56, no. 1 (2017): 261–73, https://pubmed.ncbi.nlm.nih.gov/27886010/.

17. K. F. Koltyn et al., "Changes in Mood State following Whole-Body Hyperthermia," *International Journal of Hyperthermia* 8, no. 3 (May–June 1992): 305–7, https://pubmed.ncbi.nlm.nih.gov/1607735/.

18. Katriina Kukkonen-Harjula and K. Kauppinen, "How the Sauna Affects the Endocrine System," *Annals of Clinical Research* 20, no. 4 (1988): 262–6, https://pubmed.ncbi.nlm.nih.gov/3218898/.

    Daniela Ježová et al., "Rise in Plasma Beta-endorphin and ACTH in Response to Hyperthermia in Sauna," *Hormone and Metabolic Research* 17, no. 12 (December 1985): 693–94, https://www.thieme-connect.com/products/ejournals/abstract/10.1055/s-2007-1013648.

19. Katriina Kukkonen-Harjula et al., "Haemodynamic and Hormonal Responses to Heat Exposure in a Finnish Sauna Bath," *European Journal of Applied Physiology and Occupational Physiology* 58, no. 5 (1989): 543–50, https://pubmed.ncbi.nlm.nih.gov/2759081/.

20. Giorgio Touburg and Ruut Veenhoven, "Mental Health Care and Average Happiness:

Strong Effect in Developed Nations," *Administration and Policy in Mental Health* 42, no. 4 (July 2015): 394–404, https://pubmed.ncbi.nlm.nih.gov/25091049/.

21. Jerome Sarris et al., "Adjunctive Nutraceuticals for Depression: A Systematic Review and Meta-Analyses," *American Journal of Psychiatry* 173, no. 6 (June 2016): 575–87, https://ajp.psychiatryonline.org/doi/10.1176/appi.ajp.2016.15091228.

22. I first shared Terry's story in *Your Brain Is Always Listening* (Carol Stream, IL: Tyndale, 2021), 111.

23. Yoram Barak, "The Immune System and Happiness," *Autoimmunity Reviews* 5, no. 8 (October 2006): 523–27, https://www.sciencedirect.com/science/article/abs/pii/S1568997206000279.

24. Aiko Tanaka, Nobuko Tokuda, and Kiyoshi Ichihara, "Psychological and Physiological Effects of Laughter Yoga Sessions in Japan: A Pilot Study," *Nursing and Health Sciences* 20, no. 3 (September 2018): 304–12, https://onlinelibrary.wiley.com/doi/abs/10.1111/nhs.12562.

25. Kristen C. Willeumier et al., "Elevated BMI is Associated with Decreased Blood Flow in the Prefrontal Cortex Using SPECT Imaging in Healthy Adults," *Obesity* 19, no. 5 (May 2011): 1095-97, https://pubmed.ncbi.nlm.nih.gov/21311507/.

    Daniel G. Amen et al., "Patterns of Cerebral Blood Flow as a Function of Obesity in Adults," *Journal of Alzheimer's Disease* 77, no. 3 (2020): 1331–37, https://pubmed.ncbi.nlm.nih.gov/32773393/.

    K. Willeumier et al., "Elevated Body Mass in National Football League Players Linked to Cognitive Impairment and Decreased Prefrontal Cortex and Temporal Pole Activity," *Translational Psychiatry* 2, no. 1 (January 17, 2012): e68, https://pubmed.ncbi.nlm.nih.gov/22832730/.

26. Floriana S. Luppino et al., "Overweight, Obesity, and Depression: A Systematic Review and Meta-analysis of Longitudinal Studies," *Archives of General Psychiatry* 67, no. 3 (2010): 220–29, https://pubmed.ncbi.nlm.nih.gov/20194822/.

27. Centers for Disease Control and Prevention, "The Surprising Truth about Prediabetes," last reviewed June 11, 2020, https://www.cdc.gov/diabetes/library/features/truth-about-prediabetes.html.

CHAPTER 10: HAPPY NUTRACEUTICALS

1. Clemens W. Janssen et al., "Whole-Body Hyperthermia for the Treatment of Major Depressive Disorder: A Randomized Clinical Trial," *JAMA Psychiatry* 73, no. 8 (August 1, 2016): 789–95, https://pubmed.ncbi.nlm.nih.gov/27172277/.

2. Daniel G. Amen, *The End of Mental Illness* (Carol Stream, IL: Tyndale, 2020).

3. Jeffrey B. Blumberg et al., "Impact of Frequency of Multi-Vitamin/Multi-Mineral Supplement Intake on Nutritional Adequacy and Nutrient Deficiencies in U.S. Adults," *Nutrients* 9, no. 8, (August 9, 2017): 849, https://pubmed.ncbi.nlm.nih.gov/28792457/.

    Victor L. Fulgoni 3rd et al., "Foods, Fortificants, and Supplements: Where Do Americans Get Their Nutrients?" *Journal of Nutrition* 141, no. 10 (October 2011): 1847–54, https://pubmed.ncbi.nlm.nih.gov/21865568/.

    Maret G. Traber, "Vitamin E Inadequacy in Humans: Causes and Consequences," *Advances in Nutrition* 5, no. 5 (September 2014): 503–14, https://academic.oup.com/advances/article/5/5/503/4565757.

4. Yaron Steinbuch, "90% of Americans Eat Garbage," *New York Post*, November 17, 2017, https://nypost.com/2017/11/17/90-of-americans-eat-like-garbage/.

    Centers for Disease Control and Prevention, "Only 1 in 10 Adults Get Enough Fruits or Vegetables," November 16, 2017, https://www.cdc.gov/media/releases/2017/p1116-fruit-vegetable-consumption.html.

5. Robert H. Fletcher and Kathleen M. Fairfield, "Vitamins for Chronic Disease Prevention in Adults: Clinical Applications," *JAMA* 287, no. 23 (June 19, 2002): 3127–29, https://jamanetwork.com/journals/jama/fullarticle/195039.

6. Mark Hyman, *The UltraMind Solution: Fix Your Broken Brain by Healing Your Body First* (New York: Scribner, 2008), 114.

7. Charles W. Popper, "Single-Micronutrient and Broad-Spectrum Micronutrient Approaches for Treating Mood Disorders in Youth and Adults," *Child and Adolescent Psychiatric Clinics of North America* 23, no. 3 (July 2014): 591–672, https://www .sciencedirect.com/science/article/abs/pii/S1056499314000315?via%3Dihub.

8. Meredith Blampied, "Broad Spectrum Micronutrient Formulas for the Treatment of Symptoms of Depression, Stress, and/or Anxiety: A Systematic Review," *Expert Review of Neurotherapeutics* 20, no. 4 (April 2020): 351–71, https://pubmed.ncbi.nlm.nih. gov/32178540/.

9. Julia J. Rucklidge and Bonnie J. Kaplan, "Broad-Spectrum Micronutrient Formulas for the Treatment of Psychiatric Symptoms: A Systematic Review," *Expert Review of Neurotherapeutics* 13, no. 1 (January 2013): 49–73, https://pubmed.ncbi.nlm.nih.gov /23253391/.

10. Stephen J. Schoenthaler and Ian D. Bier, "The Effect of Vitamin-Mineral Supplementation on Juvenile Delinquency among American Schoolchildren: A Randomized, Double-Blind Placebo-Controlled Trial," *Journal of Alternative and Complementary Medicine* 6, no. 1 (February 2000): 7–17, https://pubmed.ncbi.nlm.nih.gov/10706231/.

11. Julia J. Rucklidge et al., "Vitamin-Mineral Treatment of Attention-Deficit Hyperactivity Disorder in Adults: Double-Blind Randomised Placebo-Controlled Trial," *British Journal of Psychiatry* 204, no. 4 (2014): 306–15, https://www.cambridge.org/core/journals/the -british-journal-of-psychiatry/article/vitaminmineral-treatment-of-attentiondeficit -hyperactivity-disorder-in-adults-doubleblind-randomised-placebocontrolled-trial/6DE CDD36BD673FB31C92C64BAA9BBA14.

12. Julia J. Rucklidge et al., "Shaken but Unstirred? Effects of Micronutrients on Stress and Trauma After an Earthquake: RCT Evidence Comparing Formulas and Doses," *Human Psychopharmacology* 27, no. 5 (September 2012): 440–54, https://onlinelibrary.wiley.com /doi/abs/10.1002/hup.2246.

13. Bonnie J. Kaplan et al., "A Randomised Trial of Nutrient Supplements to Minimise Psychological Stress after a Natural Disaster," *Psychiatry Research* 228, no. 3 (August 30, 2015): 373–79, https://www.sciencedirect.com/science/article/abs/pii /S0165178115003935.

14. Kaplan. "A Randomised Trial of Nutrient Supplements."

15. David O. Kennedy et al., "Effects of High-Dose B Vitamin Complex with Vitamin C and Minerals on Subjective Mood and Performance in Healthy Males," *Psychopharmacology* 211, no. 1 (July 2010): 55–68, https://pubmed.ncbi.nlm.nih.gov/20454891/.

16. Hyman, *UltraMind Solution*, 124.

17. Hyman, *UltraMind Solution*, 129.

18. Charlotte Wessel Skovlund et al., "Association of Hormonal Contraception with Suicide Attempts and Suicide," *American Journal of Psychiatry* 175, no. 4 (April 1, 2018), 336–42, https://pubmed.ncbi.nlm.nih.gov/29145752/.

19. Allen T. G. Lansdowne and Stephen C. Provost, "Vitamin D3 Enhances Mood in Healthy Subjects during Winter," *Psychopharmacology* 135, no. 4 (February 1998): 319–23, https:// link.springer.com/article/10.1007%2Fs002130050517.

20. Harvard T. H. Chan School of Public Health, "Smoking, High Blood Pressure and Being Overweight Top Three Preventable Causes of Death in the U.S.," April 27, 2009, https:// www.hsph.harvard.edu/news/press-releases/smoking-high-blood-pressure-overweight -preventable-causes-death-us/.

21. Erik Messamore et al., "Polyunsaturated Fatty Acids and Recurrent Mood Disorders: Phenomenology, Mechanisms, and Clinical Application," *Progress in Lipid Research* 66 (April 2017): 1–13, https://pubmed.ncbi.nlm.nih.gov/28069365/.

Jerome Sarris, David Mischoulon, and Isaac Schweitzer, "Omega-3 for Bipolar Disorder: Meta-Analyses of Use in Mania and Bipolar Depression," *Journal of Clinical Psychiatry* 73, no. 1 (January 2012): 81–86, https://pubmed.ncbi.nlm.nih.gov/21903025/.

Roel J. T. Mocking et al., "Meta-analysis and Meta-regression of Omega-3 Polyunsaturated Fatty Acid Supplementation for Major Depressive Disorder," *Translational Psychiatry* 6 (March 15, 2016): e756, https://www.nature.com/articles/tp201629.

22. Joseph R. Hibbeln and Rachel V. Gow, "The Potential for Military Diets to Reduce Depression, Suicide, and Impulsive Aggression: A Review of Current Evidence for Omega-3 and Omega-6 Fatty Acids," *Military Medicine* 179, supplement 11 (November 2014): 117–28.

Mingming Huan et al., "Suicide Attempt and n-3 Fatty Acid Levels in Red Blood Cells: A Case Control Study in China," *Biological Psychiatry* 56, no. 7 (October 1, 2004): 490–96, https://pubmed.ncbi.nlm.nih.gov/15450784/.

M. Elizabeth Sublette et al., "Omega-3 Polyunsaturated Essential Fatty Acid Status as a Predictor of Future Suicide Risk," *American Journal of Psychiatry* 163, no. 6 (June 2006): 1100–1102, https://ajp.psychiatryonline.org/doi/full/10.1176/ajp.2006.163.6.1100.

Michael D. Lewis et al., "Suicide Deaths of Active-Duty US Military and Omega-3 Fatty -Acid Status: A Case-Control Comparison," *Journal of Clinical Psychiatry* 72, no. 12 (December 2011): 1585–90, https://pubmed.ncbi.nlm.nih.gov/21903029/.

23. Trevor A. Mori and Lawrence J. Beilin, "Omega-3 Fatty Acids and Inflammation," *Current Atherosclerosis Reports* 6. no. 6 (November 2004): 461–67, https://pubmed.ncbi.nlm.nih.gov/15485592/.

Deddo Moertl et al., "Dose-Dependent Effects of Omega-3-Polyunsaturated Fatty Acids on Systolic Left Ventricular Function, Endothelial Function, and Markers of Inflammation in Chronic Heart Failure of Nonischemic Origin: A Double-Blind, Placebo-Controlled, 3-Arm Study," *American Heart Journal* 161, no. 5 (May 2011): 915.e1–e9, https://pubmed.ncbi.nlm.nih.gov/21570522/.

Jessay Gopuran Devassy et al., "Omega-3 Polyunsaturated Fatty Acids and Oxylipins in Neuroinflammation and Management of Alzheimer Disease," *Advances in Nutrition* 7, no. 5 (September 15, 2016): 905–16.

24. Clemens von Schacky, "The Omega-3 Index as a Risk Factor for Cardiovascular Diseases," *Prostaglandins and Other Lipid Mediators* 96, nos. 1–4 (November 2011): 94–98, https://www.sciencedirect.com/science/article/abs/pii/S1098882311000487.

Seamus Paul Whelton et al., "Meta-analysis of Observational Studies on Fish Intake and Coronary Heart Disease," *American Journal of Cardiology* 93, no. 9 (May 1, 2004): 1119–23, https://www.sciencedirect.com/science/article/abs/pii/S1098882311000487.

25. Catherine M. Milte et al., "Increased Erythrocyte Eicosapentaenoic Acid and Docosahexaenoic Acid Are Associated with Improved Attention and Behavior in Children with ADHD in a Randomized Controlled Three-Way Crossover Trial," *Journal of Attention Disorders* 19, no. 11 (November 2015): 954–64, https://pubmed.ncbi.nlm.nih.gov/24214970/.

Michael H. Bloch and Ahmad Qawasmi, "Omega-3 Fatty Acid Supplementation for the Treatment of Children with Attention-Deficit/Hyperactivity Disorder Symptomatology: Systematic Review and Meta-analysis," *Journal of the American Academy of Child and Adolescent Psychiatry* 50, no. 10 (October 2011): 991–1000, https://pubmed.ncbi.nlm.nih.gov/21961774/.

26. Yu Zhang et al., "Intakes of Fish and Polyunsaturated Fatty Acids and Mild-to-Severe Cognitive Impairment Risks: A Dose-Response Meta-analysis of 21 Cohort Studies," *American Journal of Clinical Nutrition* 103, no. 2 (February 2016): 330–40, https://pubmed.ncbi.nlm.nih.gov/26718417/.

T. A. D'Ascoli et al., "Association between Serum Long-Chain Omega-3 Polyunsaturated Fatty Acids and Cognitive Performance in Elderly Men and Women: The Kuopio Ischaemic Heart Disease Risk Factor Study," *European Journal of Clinical Nutrition* 70, no. 8 (August 2016): 970–75, https://www.nature.com/articles/ejcn201659.

Karoline Lukaschek et al., "Cognitive Impairment Is Associated with a Low Omega-3 Index in the Elderly: Results from the KORA-Age Study," *Dementia and Geriatric Cognitive*

Disorders 42, nos. 3–4 (October 5, 2016): 236–45, https://europepmc.org/article/med/27701160.

27. Charles Couet et al., "Effect of Dietary Fish Oil on Body Fat Mass and Basal Fat Oxidation in Healthy Adults," *International Journal of Obesity and Related Metabolic Disorders* 21, no. 8 (August 1997): 637–43, https://pubmed.ncbi.nlm.nih.gov/15481762/.

Jonathan D. Buckley and Peter R. C. Howe, "Anti-obesity Effects of Long-Chain Omega-3 Polyunsaturated Fatty Acids," *Obesity Reviews* 10, no. 6 (November 2009): 648–59, https://pubmed.ncbi.nlm.nih.gov/19460115/.

28. Maranda Thompson et al., "Omega-3 Fatty Acid Intake by Age, Gender, and Pregnancy Status in the United States: National Health and Nutrition Examination Survey 2003–2014," *Nutrients* 11, no. 1 (2019): 177, https://www.mdpi.com/2072-6643/11/1/177.

Zhiying Zhang et al., "Dietary Intakes of EPA and DHA Omega-3 Fatty Acids among US Childbearing-Age and Pregnant Women: An Analysis of NHANES 2001–2014," *Nutrients* 10, no. 4 (March 28, 2018): 416, https://pubmed.ncbi.nlm.nih.gov/29597261/.

29. Hirohito Tsuboi et al., "Omega-3 Eicosapentaenoic Acid Is Related to Happiness and a Sense of Fulfillment—A Study among Female Nursing Workers," *Nutrients* 12, no. 11 (November 2020): 3462, https://www.ncbi.nlm.nih.gov/pmc/articles/PMC7696953/.

30. Malcolm Peet and Caroline Stokes, "Omega-3 Fatty Acids in the Treatment of Psychiatric Disorders," *Drugs* 65, no. 8 (2005): 1051–59, https://pubmed.ncbi.nlm.nih.gov/15907142/.

David Mischoulon et al., "A Double-Blind, Randomized Controlled Trial of Ethyl-Eicosapentaenoate for Major Depressive Disorder," *Journal of Clinical Psychiatry* 70, no. 12 (December 2009): 1636–44, https://pubmed.ncbi.nlm.nih.gov/19709502/.

Julian G. Martins, "EPA but Not DHA Appears to Be Responsible for the Efficacy of Omega-3 Long Chain Polyunsaturated Fatty Acid Supplementation in Depression: Evidence from a Meta-analysis of Randomized Controlled Trials," *Journal of the American College of Nutrition* 28, no. 5 (October 2009): 525–42, https://pubmed.ncbi.nlm.nih.gov/20439549/.

Jerome Sarris, David Mischoulon, and Isaac Schweitzer, "Omega-3 for Bipolar Disorder: Meta-analyses of Use in Mania and Bipolar Depression," *Journal of Clinical Psychiatry* 73, no. 1 (January 2012): 81–86, https://pubmed.ncbi.nlm.nih.gov/21903025/.

François Lespérance et al., "The Efficacy of Omega-3 Supplementation for Major Depression: A Randomized Controlled Trial," *Journal of Clinical Psychiatry* 72, no. 8 (August 2011): 1054–62, https://pubmed.ncbi.nlm.nih.gov/20584525/.

Mariangela Rondanelli et al., "Long Chain Omega 3 Polyunsaturated Fatty Acids Supplementation in the Treatment of Elderly Depression: Effects on Depressive Symptoms, on Phospholipids Fatty Acids Profile and on Health-Related Quality of Life," *Journal of Nutrition, Health and Aging* 15, no. 1 (January 2011): 37–44, https://pubmed.ncbi.nlm.nih.gov/21267525/.

M. Elizabeth Sublette et al., "Meta-analysis of the Effects of Eicosapentaenoic Acid (EPA) in Clinical Trials in Depression," *Journal of Clinical Psychiatry* 72, no. 12 (December 2011): 1577–84, https://pubmed.ncbi.nlm.nih.gov/21939614/.

31. Michaël Messaoudi et al., "Beneficial Psychological Effects of a Probiotic Formulation (*Lactobacillus helveticus* R0052 and *Bifidobacterium longum* R0175) in Healthy Human Volunteers," *Gut Microbes* 2, no. 4 (July–August 2011): 256–61, https://pubmed.ncbi.nlm.nih.gov/21983070/.

Asma Kazemi et al., "Effect of Probiotic and Prebiotic vs Placebo on Psychological Outcomes in Patients with Major Depressive Disorder: A Randomized Clinical Trial," *Clinical Nutrition* 38, no. 2 (April 2019): 522–28, https://pubmed.ncbi.nlm.nih.gov/29731182/.

32. Nhan Tran et al., "The Gut-Brain Relationship: Investigating the Effect of Multispecies Probiotics on Anxiety in a Randomized Placebo-Controlled Trial of Healthy Young Adults," *Journal of Affective Disorders* 252 (June 1, 2019): 271–77.

33. H. X. Chong et al., "*Lactobacillus plantarum* DR7 Alleviates Stress and Anxiety in Adults:

A Randomised, Double-Blind, Placebo-Controlled Study," *Beneficial Microbes* 10, no. 4 (April 19, 2019): 355–73, https://pubmed.ncbi.nlm.nih.gov/30882244/.

34. Wei-Hsien Liu et al., "Alteration of Behavior and Monoamine Levels Attributable to Lactobacillus plantarum PS128 in Germ-Free Mice," *Behavioural Brain Research* 298, part B (February 1, 2016): 202–09, https://pubmed.ncbi.nlm.nih.gov/26522841/.

35. Renata A. N. Pertile, Xiaoying Cui, and Darryl W. Eyles, "Vitamin D Signaling and the Differentiation of Developing Dopamine Systems," *Neuroscience* 333 (October 1, 2016): 193–203, https://pubmed.ncbi.nlm.nih.gov/27450565/.

36. Sylvie Chalon et al., "Dietary Fish Oil Affects Monoaminergic Neurotransmission and Behavior in Rats," *Journal of Nutrition* 128, no. 12 (December 1998): 2512–19, https://academic.oup.com/jn/article/128/12/2512/4724276.

37. Wei Zhuang et al., "Rosenroot (*Rhodiola*): Potential Applications in Aging-Related Diseases," *Aging and Disease* 10, no. 1 (February 1, 2019): 134–46, https://pubmed.ncbi.nlm.nih.gov/30705774/.

38. Sang Eun Kim et al., "Effect of Ginseng Saponins on Enhanced Dopaminergic Transmission and Locomotor Hyperactivity Induced by Nicotine," *Neuropsychopharmacology* 31, no. 8 (August 2006): 1714–21, https://pubmed.ncbi.nlm.nih.gov/16251992/.

39. Usha Pinakin Dave et al., "An Open-Label Study to Elucidate the Effects of Standardized Bacopa monnieri Extract in the Management of Symptoms of Attention-Deficit Hyperactivity Disorder in Children," *Advances in Mind-Body Medicine* 28, no. 2 (Spring 2014): 10–15, https://pubmed.ncbi.nlm.nih.gov/24682000/.

40. Beenish Mirza, et al., "Neurochemical and Behavioral Effects of Green Tea (Camellia sinensis): A Model Study, Pakistan *Journal of Pharmaceutical Sciences*, 26 no. 3 (May 2013): 511–16, https://pubmed.ncbi.nlm.nih.gov/23625424/.

41. T. Yoshitake, S. Yoshitake, and J. Kehr, "The *Ginkgo biloba* Extract EGb 761® and Its Main Constituent Flavonoids and Ginkgolides Increase Extracellular Dopamine Levels in the Rat Prefrontal Cortex," *British Journal of Pharmacology* 159, no. 3 (February 1, 2010): 659–68, https://pubmed.ncbi.nlm.nih.gov/20105177/.

42. Chandra C. Cardoso et al., "Evidence for the Involvement of the Monoaminergic System in the Antidepressant-like Effect of Magnesium," *Progress in Neuro-Psychopharmacology and Biological Psychiatry* 33, no. 2 (March 17, 2009): 235–42, https://www.sciencedirect.com/science/article/abs/pii/S0278584608003588.

43. Shrinivas K. Kulkarni, Mohit Kumar Bhutani, and Mahendra Bishnoi, "Antidepressant Activity of Curcumin: Involvement of Serotonin and Dopamine System," *Psychopharmacology* 201, no. 3 (December 2008): 435–42, https://pubmed.ncbi.nlm.nih.gov/18766332/.

44. Pradeep J. Nathan et al., "The Neuropharmacology of L-theanine (N-ethyl-L-glutamine): A Possible Neuroprotective and Cognitive Enhancing Agent," *Journal of Herbal Pharmacotherapy* 6, no. 2 (2006): 21–30, https://pubmed.ncbi.nlm.nih.gov/17182482/.

45. Bombi Lee et al., "Berberine Alleviates Symptoms of Anxiety by Enhancing Dopamine Expression in Rats with Post-traumatic Stress Disorder," *Korean Journal of Physiology and Pharmacology* 22, no. 2 (March 2018): 183–92, https://pubmed.ncbi.nlm.nih.gov/29520171/.

46. Wei-Hsien Liu et al., "Alteration of Behavior and Monoamine Levels Attributable to Lactobacillus plantarum PS128 in Germ-Free Mice," *Behavioural Brain Research* 298, part B (February 1, 2016): 202–09, https://pubmed.ncbi.nlm.nih.gov/26522841/.

47. Stuart Brody, "High-Dose Ascorbic Acid Increases Intercourse Frequency and Improves Mood: A Randomized Controlled Clinical Trial," *Biological Psychiatry* 52, no. 4 (August 15, 2002): 371–74, https://www.sciencedirect.com/science/article/abs/pii/S000632230201329X.

48. Kamal Patel, "Lactobacillus Reuteri," *Examine*, last updated January 6, 2021, https://examine.com/supplements/lactobacillus-reuteri/.

49. Lisha J. John and Nisha Shantakumari, "Herbal Medicines Use during Pregnancy: A

Review from the Middle East," *Oman Medical Journal* 30, no. 4 (July 2015): 229–36, https://pubmed.ncbi.nlm.nih.gov/26366255/.

50. Mary L. Forsling and A. J. Williams, "The Effect of Exogenous Melatonin on Stimulated Neurohypophysial Hormone Release in Man," *Clinical Endocrinology* 57, no. 5 (November 2002): 615–20, https://pubmed.ncbi.nlm.nih.gov/12390335/.

51. Tracey Roizman, "Are There Supplements to Take to Increase Endorphins?" LIVESTRONG.com, https://www.livestrong.com/article/500666-supplements-to-take-for-endorphins/.

52. Roizman, "Are There Supplements to Take to Increase Endorphins?"

53. Christel Rousseaux et al., "*Lactobacillus acidophilus* Modulates Intestinal Pain and Induces Opioid and Cannabinoid Receptors," *Nature Medicine* 13, no. 1, (January 2007): 35–37, https://pubmed.ncbi.nlm.nih.gov/17159985/.

54. Shaik Shavali et al., "Melatonin Exerts Its Analgesic Actions Not by Binding to Opioid Receptor Subtypes but by Increasing the Release of Beta-endorphin an Endogenous Opioid," *Brain Research Bulletin* 64, no. 6 (January 30, 2005): 471–79, https://www.sciencedirect.com/science/article/abs/pii/S0361923004002308.

55. Susan C. Ferrence and Gordon Bendersky, "Therapy with Saffron and the Goddess at Thera," *Perspectives in Biology and Medicine* 47, no. 2 (Spring 2004): 199–226, https://pubmed.ncbi.nlm.nih.gov/15259204/.

56. Shahin Akhondzadeh et al., "Comparison of *Crocus sativus* L. and Imipramine in the Treatment of Mild to Moderate Depression: A Pilot Double-Blind Randomized Trial [ISRCTN45683816]," *BMC Complementary and Alternative Medicine* 4 (September 2, 2004): 12, https://www.ncbi.nlm.nih.gov/pmc/articles/PMC517724/.

Shahin Akhondzadeh et al., "A 22-Week, Multicenter, Randomized, Double-Blind Controlled Trial of *Crocus sativus* in the Treatment of Mild-to-Moderate Alzheimer's Disease," *Psychopharmacology* 207, no. 4 (January 2010): 637–43, https://link.springer.com/article/10.1007/s00213-009-1706-1.

Anna V. Dwyer, Dawn L. Whitten, and Jason A. Hawrelak, "Herbal Medicines, Other Than St. John's Wort, in the Treatment of Depression: A Systematic Review," *Alternative Medicine Review* 16, no. 1 (March 2011): 40–49, https://pubmed.ncbi.nlm.nih.gov/21438645/.

Adrian L. Lopresti and Peter D. Drummond, "Saffron (*Crocus sativus*) for Depression: A Systematic Review of Clinical Studies and Examination of Underlying Antidepressant Mechanisms of Action," *Human Psychopharmacology* 29 no. 6 (November 2014): 517–27, https://onlinelibrary.wiley.com/doi/abs/10.1002/hup.2434.

Mohammad Reza Khazdair et al., "The Effects of *Crocus sativus* (Saffron) and Its Constituents on Nervous System: A Review," *Avicenna Journal of Phytomedicine* 5, no. 5 (September–October 2015): 376–91, https://www.ncbi.nlm.nih.gov/pmc/articles/PMC4599112/.

Mohsen Mazidi et al., "A Double-Blind, Randomized and Placebo-Controlled Trial of Saffron (*Crocus sativus* L.) in the Treatment of Anxiety and Depression," *Journal of Complementary and Integrative Medicine* 13, no. 2 (June 1, 2016): 195–99, https://pubmed.ncbi.nlm.nih.gov/27101556/.

Magda Tsolaki et al., "Efficacy and Safety of *Crocus sativus* L. in Patients with Mild Cognitive Impairment: One Year Single-Blind Randomized, with Parallel Groups, Clinical Trial," *Journal of Alzheimer's Disease* 54, no. 1 (August 23, 2016): 129–33, https://content.iospress.com/articles/journal-of-alzheimers-disease/jad160304.

Graham Kell et al., "Affron a Novel Saffron Extract (*Crocus sativus* L.) Improves Mood in Healthy Adults over 4 Weeks in a Double-Blind, Parallel, Randomized, Placebo-Controlled Clinical Trial," *Complementary Therapies in Medicine* 33 (August 2017): 58–64, https://pubmed.ncbi.nlm.nih.gov/28735826/.

Xiangying Yang et al., "Comparative Efficacy and Safety of *Crocus sativus* L. for Treating Mild to Moderate Major Depressive Disorder in Adults: A Meta-analysis of Randomized

Controlled Trials," *Neuropsychiatric Disease and Treatment* 14 (May 21, 2018): 1297–305, https://pubmed.ncbi.nlm.nih.gov/29849461/.

Adrian L. Lopresti et al., "Affron, a Standardised Extract from Saffron (Crocus sativus L.) for the Treatment of Youth Anxiety and Depressive Symptoms: A Randomised, Double-Blind, Placebo-Controlled study," *Journal of Affective Disorders* 232 (May 2018): 349–57, https://pubmed.ncbi.nlm.nih.gov/29510352/.

Mojtaba Khaksarian et al., "The Efficacy of *Crocus sativus* (Saffron) versus Placebo and Fluoxetine in Treating Depression: A Systematic Review and Meta-analysis," *Psychology Research and Behavior Management* 12 (April 23, 2019): 297–305, https://www.ncbi.nlm.nih.gov/pmc/articles/PMC6503633/.

Barbara Tóth et al., "The Efficacy of Saffron in the Treatment of Mild to Moderate Depression: A Meta-Analysis," *Planta Medica* 85, no. 1 (January 2019): 24–31, https://pubmed.ncbi.nlm.nih.gov/30036891/.

Amir Ghaderi et al., "The Effects of Saffron (*Crocus sativus L.*) on Mental Health Parameters and C-reactive Protein: A Meta-analysis of Randomized Clinical Trials," *Complementary Therapies in Medicine* 48 (January 2020): 102250, https://www.sciencedirect.com/science/article/abs/pii/S0965229919313305?via%3Dihub.

Sara Baziar et al., "*Crocus sativus* L. versus Methylphenidate in Treatment of Children with Attention-Deficit/Hyperactivity Disorder: A Randomized, Double-Blind Pilot Study," *Journal of Child and Adolescent Psychopharmacology* 29, no. 3 (April 2019): 205–212, https://www.liebertpub.com/doi/10.1089/cap.2018.0146.

Arezoo Rajabian et al., "A Review of Potential Efficacy of Saffron (*Crocus Sativus* L.) in Cognitive Dysfunction and Seizures," *Preventive Nutrition and Food Science* 24, no. 4 (December 2019): 363–72, https://www.ncbi.nlm.nih.gov/pmc/articles/PMC6941716/.

57. Rebekka Heitmar, James Brown, and Ioannis Kyrou, "Saffron (*Crocus sativus* L.) in Ocular Diseases: A Narrative Review of the Existing Evidence from Clinical Studies," *Nutrients* 11, no. 3 (March 18, 2019): 649, https://pubmed.ncbi.nlm.nih.gov/30889784//.

Stefano Di Marco et al., "Saffron: A Multitask Neuroprotective Agent for Retinal Degenerative Diseases," *Antioxidants* 8, no. 7 (July 17, 2019): 224, https://pubmed.ncbi.nlm.nih.gov/31319529/.

58. Mostafa Asadollahi et al., "Protective Properties of the Aqueous Extract of Saffron (Crocus sativus L.) in Ischemic Stroke, Randomized Clinical Trial," *Journal of Ethnopharmacology* 238 (July 28, 2019): 111833, https://pubmed.ncbi.nlm.nih.gov/30914350/.

59. Seyed Ahmad Hosseini et al., "An Evaluation of the Effect of Saffron Supplementation on the Antibody Titer to Heat-Shock Protein (HSP) 70, hsCRP and Spirometry Test in Patients with Mild and Moderate Persistent Allergic Asthma: A Triple-Blind, Randomized Placebo-Controlled Trial," *Respiratory Medicine* 145 (December 2018): 28–34, https://pubmed.ncbi.nlm.nih.gov/30509713/.

60. Zahra Hamidi et al., "The Effect of Saffron Supplement on Clinical Outcomes and Metabolic Profiles in Patients with Active Rheumatoid Arthritis: A Randomized, Double-Blind, Placebo-Controlled Clinical Trial," *Phytotherapy Research* 34, no. 7 (July 2020), 1650–58, https://onlinelibrary.wiley.com/doi/abs/10.1002/ptr.6633.

61. Marzieh Agha-Hosseini et al., "Crocus sativus L. (Saffron) in the Treatment of Premenstrual Syndrome: A Double-Blind, Randomised and Placebo-Controlled Trial," *BJOG* 115, no. 4 (March 2008): 515–19, https://pubmed.ncbi.nlm.nih.gov/18271889/.

Amirhossein Modabbernia et al., "Effect of Saffron on Fluoxetine-Induced Sexual Impairment in Men: Randomized Double-Blind Placebo-Controlled Trial," *Psychopharmacology* 223, no. 4 (October 2012): 381–88, https://pubmed.ncbi.nlm.nih.gov/22552758/.

Ladan Kashani et al., "Saffron for Treatment of Fluoxetine-Induced Sexual Dysfunction in Women: Randomized Double-Blind Placebo-Controlled Study," *Human Psychopharmacology* 28, no. 1 (January 2013): 54–60, https://pubmed.ncbi.nlm.nih.gov/23280545/.

62. Syed Imran Bukhari, Mahreen Manzoor, and M. K. Dhar, "A Comprehensive Review of the Pharmacological Potential of *Crocus sativus* and Its Bioactive Apocarotenoids," *Biomedicine and Pharmacotherapy* 98 (February 2018): 733–45, https://www.sciencedirect.com/science/article/abs/pii/S075333221735182X.

63. Akhondzadeh et al., "Comparison of *Crocus sativus L.* and Imipramine in the Treatment of Mild to Moderate Depression."

    Dwyer, Whitten, and Hawrelak, "Herbal Medicines, Other Than St. John's Wort, in the Treatment of Depression," 40–49.

    Lopresti and Drummond, "Saffron (*Crocus sativus*) for Depression," 517–27.

    Khazdair et al., "Effects of *Crocus sativus* (Saffron) and Its Constituents on Nervous System," 376–91.

    Mazidi et al., "Double-Blind, Randomized and Placebo-Controlled Trial of Saffron (*Crocus sativus L.*) in the Treatment of Anxiety and Depression," 195–99.

    Kell et al., "Affron a Novel Saffron Extract (*Crocus sativus L.*) Improves Mood in Healthy Adults," 58–64.

    Yang et al., "Comparative Efficacy and Safety of *Crocus sativus* L. for Treating Mild to Moderate Major Depressive Disorder in Adults," 1297–305.

    Lopresti et al., "Affron, a Standardised Extract from Saffron (Crocus sativus L.) for the Treatment of Youth Anxiety and Depressive Symptoms," 349–57.

    Khaksarian et al., "Efficacy of *Crocus sativus* (Saffron) versus Placebo and Fluoxetine in Treating Depression," 297–305.

    Tóth et al., "Efficacy of Saffron in the Treatment of Mild to Moderate Depression," 24–31.

    Ghaderi et al., "Effects of Saffron (*Crocus sativus L.*) on Mental Health Parameters and C-reactive Protein."

64. Khaksarian et al., "Efficacy of *Crocus sativus* (Saffron) versus Placebo and Fluoxetine in Treating Depression," 297–305.

65. Modabbernia et al., "Effect of Saffron on Fluoxetine-Induced Sexual Impairment in Men," 381–88.

    Kashani et al., "Saffron for Treatment of Fluoxetine-Induced Sexual Dysfunction in Women," 54–60.

66. Akhondzadeh et al., "Comparison of *Crocus sativus L.* and Imipramine in the Treatment of Mild to Moderate Depression."

67. Mazidi et al., "Double-Blind, Randomized and Placebo-Controlled Trial of Saffron (*Crocus sativus L.*) in the Treatment of Anxiety and Depression," 195–99.

68. Akhondzadeh et al., "22-Week, Multicenter, Randomized, Double-Blind Controlled Trial of *Crocus sativus* in the Treatment of Mild-to-Moderate Alzheimer's Disease," 637–43.

    Tsolaki et al., "Efficacy and Safety of Crocus sativus L. in Patients with Mild Cognitive Impairment," 129–33.

69. Baziar et al., "*Crocus sativus* L. versus Methylphenidate in Treatment of Children with Attention-Deficit Hyperactivity Disorder," 205–12.

70. Ajaikumar B. Kunnumakkara et al., "Curcumin, the Golden Nutraceutical: Multitargeting for Multiple Chronic Diseases," *British Journal of Pharmacology* 174, no. 11 (June 2017): 1325–48, https://bpspubs.onlinelibrary.wiley.com/doi/full/10.1111/bph.13621.

    Sahdeo Prasad and Bharat B. Aggarwal, "Turmeric, the Golden Spice," in *Herbal Medicine: Biomolecular and Clinical Aspects*, 2nd ed., ed. Iris F. F. Benzie and Sissi Wachtel-Galor (Boca Raton, FL: CRC Press/Taylor and Francis, 2011), chap. 13, https://www.ncbi.nlm.nih.gov/books/NBK92752/.

71. Reza Tabrizi et al., "The Effects of Curcumin-Containing Supplements on Biomarkers of Inflammation and Oxidative Stress: A Systematic Review and Meta-analysis of Randomized Controlled Trials," *Phytotherapy Research* 33, no. 2 (February 2019): 253–62, https://pubmed.ncbi.nlm.nih.gov/30402990/.

72. Vikram S. Gota et al., "Safety and Pharmacokinetics of a Solid Lipid Curcumin Particle

Formulation in Osteosarcoma Patients and Healthy Volunteers," *Journal of Agricultural and Food Chemistry* 58, no. 4 (February 24, 2010): 2095–99, https://pubmed.ncbi.nlm.nih .gov/20092313/.

73. Katherine H. M. Cox, Andrew Pipingas, and Andrew B. Scholey, "Investigation of the Effects of Solid Lipid Curcumin on Cognition and Mood in a Healthy Older Population," *Journal of Psychopharmacology* 29, no. 5 (May 2015): 642–51, https://pubmed.ncbi.nlm .nih.gov/25277322/.

74. Qin Xiang Ng et al., "Clinical Use of Curcumin in Depression: A Meta-Analysis," *Journal of the American Medical Directors Association* 18, no. 6 (June 1, 2017): 503–8, https:// pubmed.ncbi.nlm.nih.gov/28236605/.

75. Matthew A. Petrilli et al., "The Emerging Role for Zinc in Depression and Psychosis," *Frontiers in Pharmacology* 8 (June 30, 2017): 414, https://pubmed.ncbi.nlm.nih.gov /28713269/.

76. Somaye Yosaee et al., "Effects of Zinc, Vitamin D, and Their Co-supplementation on Mood, Serum Cortisol, and Brain-Derived Neurotrophic Factor in Patients with Obesity and Mild to Moderate Depressive Symptoms: A Phase II, 12-Wk, 2x2 Factorial Design, Double-Blind, Randomized, Placebo-Controlled Trial," *Nutrition* 71 (March 2020): 110601, https://pubmed.ncbi.nlm.nih.gov/31837640/.

77. Grzegorz Satała et al., "Allosteric Inhibition of Serotonin 5-HT7 Receptors by Zinc Ions," *Molecular Neurobiology* 55, no. 4 (April 2018): 2897–910, https://link.springer.com /article/10.1007/s12035-017-0536-0.

78. Office of Dietary Supplements, "Zinc: Fact Sheet for Health Professionals" National Institutes of Health, updated March 26, 2021, https://ods.od.nih.gov/factsheets/Zinc -HealthProfessional/.

79. Lazaro Barragán-Rodríguez, Martha Rodríguez-Morán, and Fernando Guerrero-Romero, "Efficacy and Safety of Oral Magnesium Supplementation in the Treatment of Depression in the Elderly with Type 2 Diabetes: A Randomized, Equivalent Trial," *Magnesium Research* 21, no. 4 (December 2008): 218–23, https://pubmed.ncbi.nlm.nih.gov /19271419/.

Emily K. Tarleton et al., "Role of Magnesium Supplementation in the Treatment of Depression: A Randomized Clinical Trial," *PLOS ONE* 12, no. 6 (June 27, 2017): e0180067, https://journals.plos.org/plosone/article?id=10.1371/journal.pone.0180067.

80. Anna-leila Williams et al.,"S-adenosylmethionine (SAMe) as Treatment for Depression: A Systematic Review," *Clinical and Investigative Medicine* 28, no. 3 (June 2005): 132–39, https://pubmed.ncbi.nlm.nih.gov/16021987/.

Jerome Sarris et al., "S-adenosyl Methionine (SAMe) versus Escitalopram and Placebo in Major Depression RCT: Efficacy and Effects of Histamine and Carnitine as Moderators of Response," *Journal of Affective Disorders* 164 (August 2014): 76–81, https://pubmed.ncbi .nlm.nih.gov/24856557/.

George I. Papakostas et al., "S-adenosyl Methionine (SAMe) Augmentation of Serotonin Reuptake Inhibitors for Antidepressant Nonresponders with Major Depressive Disorder: A Double-Blind, Randomized Clinical Trial," *American Journal of Psychiatry* 167, no. 8 (August 2010): 942–48, https://pubmed.ncbi.nlm.nih.gov/20595412/.

R. Andrew Shippy et al., "S-adenosylmethionine (SAM-e) for the Treatment of Depression in People Living with HIV/AIDS," *BMC Psychiatry* 4 (November 11, 2004): 38, https:// bmcpsychiatry.biomedcentral.com/articles/10.1186/1471-244X-4-38#.

K. M. Bell et al., "S-adenosylmethionine Treatment of Depression: A Controlled Clinical Trial," *American Journal of Psychiatry* 145, no. 9 (September 1988): 1110–14, https:// europepmc.org/article/med/3046382.

P. Salmaggi et al., "Double-Blind, Placebo-Controlled Study of S-adenosyl-L-methionine in Depressed Postmenopausal Women," *Psychotherapy and Psychosomatics* 59, no. 1 (1993): 34–40, https://pubmed.ncbi.nlm.nih.gov/8441793/.

K. M. Bell et al., "S-adenosylmethionine Blood Levels in Major Depression: Changes with

Drug Treatment," *Acta Neurologica Scandinavica* 89, no. S154 (May 1994): S15–18, https://onlinelibrary.wiley.com/doi/abs/10.1111/j.1600-0404.1994.tb05404.x.

Roberto Delle Chiaie, Paolo Pancheri, and Pierluigi Scapicchio, "Efficacy and Tolerability of Oral and Intramuscular S-adenosyl-L-methionine 1,4-butanedisulfonate (SAMe) in the Treatment of Major Depression: Comparison with Imipramine in 2 Multicenter Studies," *American Journal of Clinical Nutrition* 76, no. 5 (November 2002): S1172–76, https://pubmed.ncbi.nlm.nih.gov/12418499/.

Anup Sharma et al., "S-adenosylmethionine (SAMe) for Neuropsychiatric Disorders: A Clinician-Oriented Review of Research," *Journal of Clinical Psychiatry* 78, no. 6 (June 2017): e656–67, https://pubmed.ncbi.nlm.nih.gov/28682528/.

81. Vijitha de Silva et al., "Evidence for the Efficacy of Complementary and Alternative Medicines in the Management of Osteoarthritis: A Systematic Review," *Rheumatology* (Oxford) 50, no. 5 (May 2011): 911–20, https://pubmed.ncbi.nlm.nih.gov/21169345/.

82. Klaus Linde, Michael M. Berner, and Levente Kriston, "St John's Wort for Major Depression," *Cochrane Database of Systematic Reviews* 2008, no. 4 (October 8, 2008): CD000448, https://pubmed.ncbi.nlm.nih.gov/18843608/.

Maurizio Fava et al., "A Double-Blind, Randomized Trial of St John's Wort, Fluoxetine, and Placebo in Major Depressive Disorder," *Journal of Clinical Psychopharmacology* 25, no. 5 (October 2005): 441–47, https://pubmed.ncbi.nlm.nih.gov/16160619/.

Siegfried Kasper et al., "Continuation and Long-Term Maintenance Treatment with Hypericum Extract WS 5570 After Recovery from an Acute Episode of Moderate Depression—a Double-Blind, Randomized, Placebo Controlled Long-Term Trial," *European Neuropsychopharmacology* 18, no. 11 (November 2008): 803–13, https://pubmed.ncbi.nlm.nih.gov/18694635/.

Jerome Sarris et al., "Conditional Probability of Response or Nonresponse of Placebo Compared with Antidepressants or St John's Wort in Major Depressive Disorder," *Journal of Clinical Psychopharmacology* 33, no. 6 (December 2013): 827–30, https://pubmed.ncbi.nlm.nih.gov/24091858/.

83. Jerome Serris, et al., "Adjunctive Nutraceuticals for Depression: A Systematic Review and Meta-Analyses," *The American Journal of Psychiatry*, 173, no. 6 (April 26, 2016): 575–87, https://doi.org/10.1176/appi.ajp.15091228.

CHAPTER 11: THE YOU, HAPPIER DIET

1. Morgan Korn, "The Staggering Amounts of Food Eaten on Super Bowl Sunday," ABC News, February 2, 2017, https://abcnews.go.com/US/staggering-amounts-food-eaten-super-bowl-sunday/story?id=45217629.

2. Tom Brady, *The TB12 Method* (New York: Simon & Schuster, 2020), chapters 7 and 8.

Jessica Campbell, "This Is Everything Tom Brady Eats in a Day," *GQ*, January 28, 2021, https://www.gq.com.au/fitness/health-nutrition/this-is-everything-tom-brady-eats-in-a-day/image-gallery/3ba2f38741bc4c1bd68860069b007829?pos=3.

Paul Kita and Temi Adebowale, "Here's What Tom Brady Eats Every Day, and on Game Day," *Men's Health*, January 22, 2021, https://www.menshealth.com/nutrition/a19535249/tom-brady-reveals-insane-diet-in-new-book/.

3. Allyssa Birth, "Comfort Foods, Sickbed Snacks and Celebratory Nosh: What Are Americans' Favorites?" Harris Poll, January 25, 2016, https://theharrispoll.com/theres-really-no-debate-that-food-can-be-a-comfort-whether-stressed-or-depressed-almost-everyone-has-a-favorite-go-to-dish-that-seems-to-help-make-everything-all-better-just-over-half-53/.

4. Felice N. Jacka et al., "Dietary Patterns and Depressive Symptoms over Time: Examining the Relationships with Socioeconomic Position, Health Behaviours and Cardiovascular Risk," *PLOS ONE* 9, no. 1 (January 29, 2014): e87657, https://pubmed.ncbi.nlm.nih.gov/24489946/.

Behnaz Shakersain et al., "Prudent Diet May Attenuate the Adverse Effects of Western

Diet on Cognitive Decline," *Alzheimer's and Dementia* 12, no. 2 (February 2016): 100–109, https://alz-journals.onlinelibrary.wiley.com/doi/full/10.1016/j.jalz.2015.08.002.

Amber L. Howard et al., "ADHD Is Associated with a 'Western' Dietary Pattern in Adolescents," *Journal of Attention Disorders* 15, no. 5 (2011): 403–11, https://journals.sagepub.com/doi/10.1177/1087054710365990.

Giovanni Tarantino, Vincenzo Citro, and Carmine Finelli, "Hype or Reality: Should Patients with Metabolic Syndrome–related NAFLD Be on the Hunter-Gatherer (Paleo) Diet to Decrease Morbidity?" *Journal of Gastrointestinal and Liver Diseases* 24, no. 3 (September 2015): 359–68, https://pubmed.ncbi.nlm.nih.gov/26405708/.

5. Gregory E. Simon et al., "Association between Obesity and Psychiatric Disorders in the US Adult Population," *Archives of General Psychiatry* 63, no. 7 (July 2006): 824–30, https://jamanetwork.com/journals/jamapsychiatry/fullarticle/209790.

Nancy M. Petry et al., "Overweight and Obesity Are Associated with Psychiatric Disorders: Results from the National Epidemiologic Survey on Alcohol and Related Conditions," *Psychosomatic Medicine* 70, no. 3 (April 2008): 288–97, https://pubmed.ncbi.nlm.nih.gov/18378873/.

H. C. Michelle Byrd, Carol Curtin, and Sarah E. Anderson, "Attention-Deficit/Hyperactivity Disorder and Obesity in US Males and Females, Age 8–15 Years: National Health and Nutrition Examination Survey 2001–2004," *Pediatric Obesity* 8, no. 6 (2013): 445–53, https://www.ncbi.nlm.nih.gov/pmc/articles/PMC3638065/.

Michael Hinck, "How Obesity Can Affect Your Teen's Self Esteem," Health Beat, Jamaica Hospital Medical Center, September 26, 2014, https://jamaicahospital.org/newsletter/?p=1337.

6. K. M. Carpenter et al., "Relationships between Obesity and DSM-IV Major Depressive Disorder, Suicide Ideation, and Suicide Attempts: Results from a General Population Study," *American Journal of Public Health* 90, no. 2 (February 2000): 251–57, https://www.ncbi.nlm.nih.gov/pmc/articles/PMC1446144/.

7. Zita Képes et al., "Age, BMI and Diabetes as Independent Predictors of Brain Hypoperfusion," *Nuclear Medicine Review* 24, no. 1 (2021): 11–15, https://pubmed.ncbi.nlm.nih.gov/33576479/.

8. Corby K. Martin et al., "Effect of Calorie Restriction on Mood, Quality of Life, Sleep, and Sexual Function in Healthy Nonobese Adults: The CALERIE 2 Randomized Clinical Trial," *JAMA Internal Medicine* 176, no. 6 (June 1, 2016): 743–52, https://pubmed.ncbi.nlm.nih.gov/27136347/.

9. Stephen Malunga Manchishi et al., "Effect of Caloric Restriction on Depression," *Journal of Cellular and Molecular Medicine* 22, no. 5 (May 2018): 2528–35, https://www.ncbi.nlm.nih.gov/pmc/articles/PMC5908110/.

10. DeAnn Liska et al., "Narrative Review of Hydration and Selected Health Outcomes in the General Population," *Nutrients* 11, no. 1 (January 2019): 70, https://www.ncbi.nlm.nih.gov/pmc/articles/PMC6356561/.

11. Nathalie Pross et al., "Influence of Progressive Fluid Restriction on Mood and Physiological Markers of Dehydration in Women," *British Journal of Nutrition* 109, no. 2 (2013): 313–21, https://www.ncbi.nlm.nih.gov/pmc/articles/PMC3553795/.

12. Nathalie Pross, "Effects of Dehydration on Brain Functioning: A Life-Span Perspective," *Annals of Nutrition and Metabolism* 70, supplement 1 (2017): 30–36, https://www.karger.com/Article/FullText/463060.

13. Daniel G. Amen and Tana Amen, *The Brain Warrior's Way* (New York: New American Library, 2016), 113.

14. Shunquan Wu et al., "Serum Lipid Levels and Suicidality: A Meta-analysis of 65 Epidemiological Studies," *Journal of Psychiatry and Neuroscience* 41, no. 1 (January 2016): 56–69, https://www.ncbi.nlm.nih.gov/pmc/articles/PMC4688029/.

15. Ab Latif Wani, Sajad Ahmad Bhat, and Anjum Ara, "Omega-3 Fatty Acids and the Treatment of Depression: A Review of Scientific Evidence," *Integrative Medicine Research*

4, no. 3 (September 2015): 132–41, https://www.ncbi.nlm.nih.gov/pmc/articles /PMC5481805/.

16. Lenore Arab, Rong Guo, and David Elashoff, "Lower Depression Scores among Walnut Consumers in NHANES," *Nutrients* 11, no. 2 (January 26, 2019): 275, https://pubmed .ncbi.nlm.nih.gov/30691167/.

17. James E. Gangwisch et al., "High Glycemic Index Diet as a Risk Factor for Depression: Analyses from the Women's Health Initiative," *American Journal of Clinical Nutrition* 102, no. 2 (August 2015): 454–63, https://www.ncbi.nlm.nih.gov/pmc/articles/PMC4515860/.

18. Redzo Mujcic and Andrew J. Oswald, "Evolution of Well-Being and Happiness After Increases in Consumption of Fruit and Vegetables," *American Journal of Public Health* 106, no. 8 (August 1, 2016): 1504–10, https://ajph.aphapublications.org/doi/10.2105 /AJPH.2016.303260.

19. Matteo Briguglio et al., "Dietary Neurotransmitters: A Narrative Review on Current Knowledge," *Nutrients* 10, no. 5 (May 13, 2018): 591, https://www.ncbi.nlm.nih.gov/pmc /articles/PMC5986471/.

20. Neuroscience News, "Experiences of PTSD Linked to Nutritional Health," February 3, 2021, https://neurosciencenews.com/ptsd-nutrition-17665/.

21. Mohammad J. Siddiqui et al., "Saffron (*Crocus sativus* L.): As an Antidepressant," *Journal of Pharmacy and BioAllied Sciences* 10, no. 4 (October–December 2018): 173–80, https:// www.ncbi.nlm.nih.gov/pmc/articles/PMC6266642/.

22. Shrikant Mishra and Kalpana Palanivelu, "The Effect of Curcumin (Turmeric) on Alzheimer's Disease: An Overview," *Annals of Indian Academy of Neurology* 11, no. 1 (January–March 2008): 13–19, https://www.ncbi.nlm.nih.gov/pmc/articles/PMC2781139/.

23. Ying Guo et al., "Antidepressant Effects of Rosemary Extracts Associate with Anti -inflammatory Effect and Rebalance of Gut Microbiota," *Frontiers in Pharmacology* 9 (October 2, 2018): 1126, https://www.ncbi.nlm.nih.gov/pmc/articles/PMC6192164/.

24. Farhana Zahir et al., "Low Dose Mercury Toxicity and Human Health," *Environmental Toxicology and Pharmacology* 20, no. 2 (September 2005): 351–60, https://pubmed.ncbi .nlm.nih.gov/21783611/.

25. Arbind Kumar Choudhary and Yeong Yeh Lee, "Neurophysiological Symptoms and Aspartame: What Is the Connection?" *Nutritional Neuroscience* 21, no. 5 (June 2018): 306–16, https://pubmed.ncbi.nlm.nih.gov/28198207/.

26. Samuel O. Igbinedion et al., "Non-celiac Gluten Sensitivity: All Wheat Attack Is Not Celiac," *World Journal of Gastroenterology* 23, no. 40 (2017): 7201–10, https://www.ncbi .nlm.nih.gov/pmc/articles/PMC5677194/.

27. Jessica R. Jackson et al., "Neurologic and Psychiatric Manifestations of Celiac Disease and Gluten Sensitivity," *Psychiatric Quarterly* 83, no. 1 (March 2012): 91–102, https://www .ncbi.nlm.nih.gov/pmc/articles/PMC3641836/.

28. Eleanor Busby et al., "Mood Disorders and Gluten: It's Not All in Your Mind! A Systematic Review with Meta-Analysis," *Nutrients* 10, no. 11 (November 8, 2018): 1708, https:// pubmed.ncbi.nlm.nih.gov/30413036/.

29. Meghan Hockey et al., "Is Dairy Consumption Associated with Depressive Symptoms or Disorders in Adults? A Systematic Review of Observational Studies," *Critical Reviews in Food Science and Nutrition* 60, no. 21 (2020): 3653–68, https://pubmed.ncbi.nlm.nih.gov /31868529/.

30. Pew Charitable Trusts, "Fixing the Oversight of Chemicals Added to Our Food," November 7, 2013, https://www.pewtrusts.org/en/research-and-analysis/reports/2013 /11/07/fixing-the-oversight-of-chemicals-added-to-our-food.

31. Center for Science in the Public Interest, "CSPI Says Food Dyes Pose Rainbow of Risks," June 29, 2010, https://cspinet.org/new/201006291.html.

32. Caroline B. Quines et al., "Monosodium Glutamate, a Food Additive, Induces Depressive -like and Anxiogenic-like Behaviors in Young Rats," *Life Sciences* 107, nos. 1–2 (June

27, 2014): 27–31, https://www.sciencedirect.com/science/article/abs/pii /S0024320514004524.

33. Amen Clinics, "Brain Health Guide to Red Dye #40," June 14, 2016, https://www. amenclinics.com/blog/brain-health-guide-red-dye-40/.

34. N. M. Hussin et al., "Efficacy of Fasting and Calorie Restriction (FCR) on Mood and Depression among Ageing Men," *Journal of Nutrition, Health and Aging* 17, no. 8 (2013): 674–80, https://pubmed.ncbi.nlm.nih.gov/24097021/.

CHAPTER 12: ANCHORING HAPPINESS INTO YOUR NERVOUS SYSTEM

1. A chat room in the early days of the internet allowed users to instantly communicate with each through text-based messages. Here's another interesting tidbit: I couldn't participate in the CNN chat from my office or home. I had to fly to the CNN Center in Atlanta, where I was provided a speedy typist so those in the chat room didn't have to wait too long to read my insights into happiness and good brain function.

2. CNN, "Dr. Daniel Amen: Happiness and Good Brain Function," September 10, 2001, http://www.cnn.com/2001/COMMUNITY/09/09/amen/.

3. Jordan S. Rubin, *The Maker's Diet* (Lake Mary, FL: Siloam, 2004), 56.

4. 2 Corinthians 10:5, ESV

5. "Pollyanna - The Glad Game," September 6, 2012, video, 1:47, from *Pollyanna*, directed by David Swift (Burbank, CA: Walt Disney Productions, 1960), https://www.youtube.com /watch?v=1lhxyf7A1hg.

6. Ruth Graham, "How We All Became Pollyannas (and Why We Should Be Glad about It)," *Atlantic*, February 26, 2013, https://www.theatlantic.com/entertainment/archive/2013/02 /how-we-all-became-pollyannas-and-why-we-should-be-glad-about-it/273323/.

7. Steven C. Hayes, "Psychological Flexibility: How Love Turns Pain into Purpose," TEDx, University of Nevada, February 22, 2016, video, 19:39, https://www.youtube.com/ watch?v=o79_gm05ppg.

8. Steven C. Hayes, "5 Effective Exercises to Help You Stop Believing Your Unwanted Automatic Thoughts," Ideas.Ted.Com, October 22, 2019, https://ideas.ted.com/5-effective -exercises-to-help-you-stop-believing-your-unwanted-automatic-thoughts/.

9. Adam S. Radomsky et al., "Part 1—You Can Run but You Can't Hide: Intrusive Thoughts on Six Continents," *Journal of Obsessive-Compulsive and Related Disorders 3*, no. 3 (July 2014): 269–79, https://www.sciencedirect.com/science/article/abs/pii /S2211364913000675.

10. Shayla Love, "Why You Should Talk to Yourself in the Third Person," *Vice*, December 28, 2020, https://www.vice.com/en/article/k7a3mm/why-you-should-talk-to-yourself-in-the -third-person-inner-monologue.

Igor Grossmann et al., "Training for Wisdom: The Distanced-Self-Reflection Diary Method," *Psychological Science* 32, no. 3 (March 2021): 381–94, https://pubmed.ncbi.nlm .nih.gov/33539229/.

11. Jason S. Moser et al., "Third-Person Self-Talk Facilitates Emotion Regulation without Engaging Cognitive Control: Converging Evidence from ERP and fMRI," *Scientific Reports* 7 (July 3, 2017), https://www.nature.com/articles/s41598-017-04047-3.

12. Critter Control, "Raccoon Sounds," https://www.crittercontrol.com/wildlife/raccoons /raccoon-sounds.

13. Basketball legend "Wilt the Stilt" Chamberlain, at seven feet, one inch, didn't wear rubber bands to snap them every time a bad thought came his way—like when he had to go to the free throw line because he was a notoriously poor free-throw shooter. He started wearing rubber bands around his wrist as a kid in case his socks didn't stay up on their own.

14. Frances A. Yates, *The Art of Memory* (Chicago: University of Chicago Press, 1966), 1–2.

CHAPTER 13: POSITIVITY BIAS TRAINING

1. Justin Bieber: Seasons (YouTube Originals, 2020), episode 9, "Album on the Way," February 17, 2020, video, 9:51, https://www.youtube.com/watch?v=pWcl-BeQqls&t=361s.

   Kerry Breen, "What Is Havening? Experts Weigh In on Justin Bieber's Stress-Relieving Technique," TODAY.com, March 3, 2020, https://www.today.com/health/what-havening-experts-weigh-justin-bieber-s-stress-relieving-technique-t174747.

2. Havening Techniques, "Havening Touch," https://www.havening.org/about-havening/havening-touch.

3. Madhuleena Roy Chowdhury, "19 Best Positive Psychology Interventions + How to Apply Them," PositivePsychology.com, updated May 4, 2021, https://positivepsychology.com/positive-psychology-interventions/.

4. Rob Hirtz, "Martin Seligman's Journey from Learned Helplessness to Learned Happiness," *Pennsylvania Gazette*, January 4, 1999, https://www.upenn.edu/gazette/0199/hirtz.html.

5. Chowdhury, "19 Best Positive Psychology Interventions."

6. Steve Maraboli, *If You Want to Find Happiness, Find Gratitude* (self-pub., 2020).

7. Martin E.P. Seligman, *Flourish* (New York: Free Press, 2011), chapter 2.

8. Timothy D. Windsor, Kaarin J. Anstey, and Bryan Rodgers, "Volunteering and Psychological Well-Being among Young-Old Adults: How Much Is Too Much?" *Gerontologist* 48, no. 1 (February 2008): 59–70, https://pubmed.ncbi.nlm.nih.gov/18381833/.

9. Bryant M. Stone and Acacia C. Parks, "Cultivating Subjective Well-Being through Positive Psychological Interventions," in *Handbook of Well-Being*, ed. Ed Diener, Shigehiro Oishi, and Louis Tay (Salt Lake City: DEF Publishers, 2018), https://www.nobascholar.com/chapters/59/download.pdf.

10. Matthew A. Killingsworth and Daniel T. Gilbert, "A Wandering Mind Is an Unhappy Mind," *Science* 330, no. 6006 (November 12, 2010): 932, https://pubmed.ncbi.nlm.nih.gov/21071660/.

11. Daniel G. Amen, *Your Brain Is Always Listening* (Carol Stream, IL: Tyndale, 2021), 63–64.

12. Courtney E. Ackerman, "How to Live in the Present Moment: 35 Exercises and Tools (+ Quotes)," PositivePsychology.com, updated January 30, 2021, https://positivepsychology.com/present-moment/.

13. Ackerman, "How to Live in the Present Moment."

14. University College London, "Repetitive Negative Thinking Linked to Dementia Risk," ScienceDaily, June 7, 2020, https://www.sciencedaily.com/releases/2020/06/200607195008.htm.

15. Byron Katie with Stephen Mitchell, *Loving What Is: Four Questions That Can Change Your Life* (New York: Harmony Books, 2002).

16. Jennifer Aaker and Naomi Bagdonas, *Humor, Seriously: Why Humor Is a Secret Weapon in Business and Life* (New York: Currency, 2021), 22.

17. Janelle Ringer, "Laughter: A Fool-Proof Prescription," Loma Linda University Health, April 1, 2019, https://news.llu.edu/research/laughter-fool-proof-prescription.

18. Elisabeth Sifton, *The Serenity Prayer: Faith and Politics in Times of Peace and War* (New York: Norton, 2003).

CHAPTER 14: HAPPY CONNECTIONS

1. Arthur L. Brody et al., "Regional Brain Metabolic Changes in Patients with Major Depression Treated with Either Paroxetine or Interpersonal Therapy: Preliminary Findings," *Archives of General Psychiatry* 58, no. 7 (July 2001): 631–40, https://pubmed.ncbi.nlm.nih.gov/11448368/.

2. Pim Cuijpers et al., "Interpersonal Psychotherapy for Mental Health Problems: A Comprehensive Meta-Analysis," *American Journal of Psychiatry* 173, no.7 (April 1, 2016): 680–87, https://ajp.psychiatryonline.org/doi/10.1176/appi.ajp.2015.15091141.

3. Daniel G. Amen, *Feel Better Fast and Make It Last* (Carol Stream, IL: Tyndale, 2018), chap. 6.

4. Dennis Prager, "Why Be Happy?" PragerU, July 20, 2014, video, 5:05, https://www
.youtube.com/watch?v=_Zxnw0l499g.

5. Gottman Institute, "Research," https://www.gottman.com/about/research/.

6. Gary R. Birchler, Robert L. Weiss, and John P. Vincent, "Multimethod Analysis of Social
Reinforcement Exchange between Maritally Distressed and Nondistressed Spouse and
Stranger Dyads," *Journal of Personality and Social Psychology* 31, no. 2 (1975): 349–60,
https://psycnet.apa.org/record/1975-11572-001.

J. M. Gottman and R. W. Levenson, (1992). "Marital Processes Predictive of Later
Dissolution: Behavior, Physiology, and Health," *Journal of Personality and Social
Psychology* 63, no. 2 (1992): 221–233, https://doi.org/10.1037/0022-3514.63.2.221.

7. Marshall Lev Dermer, "Towards Understanding the Meaning of Affectionate Verbal
Behavior; Towards Creating Romantic Loving," *Behavior Analyst Today* 7, no. 4 (2006):
452–80, https://doi.apa.org/fulltext/2010-10811-002.html.

8. John M. Gottman and Robert W. Levenson, "Marital Processes Predictive of Later
Dissolution: Behavior, Physiology, and Health," *Journal of Personality and Social
Psychology* 63, no. 2 (1992): 221–33, https://psycnet.apa.org/record/1992-42807-001.

9. Marcial Losada and Emily Heaphy, "The Role of Positivity and Connectivity in the
Performance of Business Teams: A Nonlinear Dynamics Model," *American Behavioral
Scientist* 47, no. 6 (February 1, 2004): 740–65, https://journals.sagepub.com/doi/10
.1177/0002764203260208.

10. Loren Toussaint et al., "Effects of Lifetime Stress Exposure on Mental and Physical
Health in Young Adulthood: How Stress Degrades and Forgiveness Protects Health,"
Journal of Health Psychology 21, no. 6 (June 2016): 1004–14, https://pubmed.ncbi.nlm.nih
.gov/25139892/.

11. John Maltby, Liza Day, and Louise Barber, "Forgiveness and Happiness. The Differing
Contexts of Forgiveness Using the Distinction between Hedonic and Eudaimonic
Happiness," *Journal of Happiness Studies* 6, no. 1 (March 2005): 1–13, https://link
.springer.com/article/10.1007/s10902-004-0924-9.

12. Kirsten Weir, "Forgiveness Can Improve Mental and Physical Health," *Monitor on
Psychology* 48, no. 1 (January 2017): 30, http://www.apa.org/monitor/2017/01/ce-corner
.aspx.

13. I wrote about the REACH method in *Your Brain Is Always Listening* (Carol Stream, IL:
Tyndale, 2021), 53–54.

Everett Worthington, "Research," http://www.evworthington-forgiveness.com/research.

14. Amen, *Your Brain Is Always Listening*.

CHAPTER 15: HAPPINESS AROUND THE WORLD

1. Jason Richards, "It's an Annoying Song (After All)," *Atlantic*, March 13, 2012, https://www
.theatlantic.com/entertainment/archive/2012/03/its-an-annoying-song-after-all/254429/.

2. Steven Taylor et. al., "Musical Obsessions: A Comprehensive Review of Neglected
Clinical Phenomena," *Journal of Anxiety Disorders* 28, no. 6 (August 2014): 580–89, https://
pubmed.ncbi.nlm.nih.gov/24997394/.

3. Sally Robertson, "Earworms—Why Do Songs Get Stuck in Your Head?" News Medical,
February 26, 2019, https://www.news-medical.net/health/Earworms-Why-do-Songs-Get
-Stuck-in-Your-Head.aspx.

4. Anne Margriet Euser, Menno Oosterhoff, and Ingrid van Balkom, "Stuck Song Syndrome:
Musical Obsessions—When to Look for OCD," *British Journal of General Practice* 66,
no. 643 (February 2016): 90, https://pubmed.ncbi.nlm.nih.gov/26823252/.

5. Dewayne Bevil, "John Stamos Turns to Disney Tune for Comfort," *Orlando Sentinel*, March
17, 2020, https://www.orlandosentinel.com/coronavirus/os-ne-coronavirus-disney-john
-stamos-small-world-20200317-gfkgs4i3rjefhfiw7ytoyubflu-story.html.

6. Harry Walker and Iza Kavedžija, "Values of Happiness," in "Happiness: Horizons of

Purpose," special issue, *HAU: Journal of Ethnographic Theory* 5, no. 3 (Winter 2015): 1–23, https://www.journals.uchicago.edu/doi/pdfplus/10.14318/hau5.3.002.

7. Denmark.dk, "Why Are Danish People So Happy?" https://denmark.dk/people-and -culture/happiness.

8. Anna Altman, "The Year of Hygge, the Danish Obsession with Getting Cozy," *New Yorker*, December 18, 2016, https://www.newyorker.com/culture/culture-desk/the-year-of -hygge-the-danish-obsession-with-getting-cozy.

9. Altman, "The Year of Hygge."

10. UN Environment Programme, "#Friday Fact: The Netherlands Is Home to More Bicycles Than People!" March 23, 2018, https://www.unep.org/news-and-stories/story/fridayfact -netherlands-home-more-bicycles-people.

11. Stuff Dutch People Like, "No. 2 Gezelligheid," https://stuffdutchpeoplelike.com/2015/09 /23/gezelligheid-gezellig/.

12. The Germans capitalize *Gemütlichkeit*, but Americans are more relaxed about that.

13. When the Disney movie *The Jungle Book* came out in 1967, the title of the memorable song, "Bare Necessities," was translated into German as "Probier's mal mit Gemütlichkeit," which literally means, "Try It with Coziness."

14. Rob Jordan, "Stanford Researchers Find Mental Health Prescription: Nature," Stanford News, June 30, 2015, https://news.stanford.edu/2015/06/30/hiking-mental-health -063015/.

15. Jordan, "Stanford Researchers Find Mental Health Prescription."

16. United Nations Department of Economic and Social Affairs, "68% of the World Population Projected to Live in Urban Areas by 2050, Says UN," May 16, 2018, https://www.un.org /development/desa/en/news/population/2018-revision-of-world-urbanization-prospects .html.

17. Jen Rose Smith, "What Is 'Friluftsliv'? How an Idea of Outdoor Living Could Help Us This Winter," *National Geographic*, September 11, 2020, https://www.nationalgeographic.com /travel/article/how-norways-friluftsliv-could-help-us-through-a-coronavirus-winter.

18. Prevagen.com, "More Mess Means More Stress: How Clutter Affects Your Brain," https:// www.prevagen.com/brain-health-tips/how-clutter-affects-your-brain/.

19. Peter's Yard, "Lagom: The Swedish Art of Eating Harmoniously," https://www.petersyard .com/journal/lagom-the-swedish-art-of-eating-harmoniously/.

20. Orla Thomas, "Cultural Encounters in Istanbul," BBC, September 9, 2010, http://www.bbc .com/travel/story/20100909-cultural-encounters.

21. Ized Uanikhehi, "How Ancient Knowledge Inspires African Tech to Flourish," CNN, March 26, 2018, https://www.cnn.com/2018/03/26/africa/ubuntu---the-african-concept-of -community-.

22. Uanikhehi, "How Ancient Knowledge Inspires."

23. JackyYenga.com, "The Spirit of Ubuntu," March 6, 2015, http://www.jackyyenga.com/the -spirit-of-ubuntu/.

24. The Philippines is the only Christian nation in Asia, with more than 86 percent of the population calling themselves Roman Catholics. See Jack Miller, "Religion in the Philippines," Asia Society, Center for Global Education, https://asiasociety.org/education /religion-philippines.

25. Tianna Haas, "Filipino Christians Provide Relief Goods during Pandemic," SIM, April 9, 2020, https://www.sim.org/w/filipino-christians-provide-relief-goods-during-pandemic.

26. Christy Anne Jones, "Shinrin-Yoku: The Japanese Art of Forest Bathing," Savvy Tokyo, July 9, 2020, https://savvytokyo.com/shinrin-yoku-the-japanese-art-of-forest-bathing/.

27. If you feel you need a cell phone for safety reasons or have to be available, then turn off the ringer.

28. The saddest state in the US is West Virginia, followed by Arkansas and Oklahoma. See

Adam McCann, "Happiest States in America," WalletHub, September 22, 2020, https://wallethub.com/edu/happiest-states/6959.

29. Tribe Talk, "How Practicing Ho'oponopono Can Nourish Your Soul," Hawaiian Healing, September 5, 2019, https://www.hawaiianhealing.com/blogs/news/how-practicing-hooponopono-can-nourish-your-soul.

30. James Hamblin, "This Is Your Brain on Fish," *Atlantic*, August 7, 2014, https://www.theatlantic.com/health/archive/2014/08/this-is-your-brain-on-fish/375638/.

31. Scott Neuman, "Bhutan's New Prime Minister Says Happiness Isn't Everything," NPR, August 3, 2013, https://www.npr.org/sections/parallels/2013/08/03/208299418/bhutans-new-prime-minister-says-happiness-isnt-everything.

32. UN News, United Nations, "Happiness Should Have Greater Role in Development Policy—UN Member States," July 19, 2011, https://news.un.org/en/story/2011/07/382052.

33. John F. Helliwell, Richard Layard, and Jeffrey D. Sachs, eds., *World Happiness Report 2019* (New York: Sustainable Development Solutions Network), 88.

Laura Begley Bloom, "Ranked: 10 Happiest and 10 Saddest Countries in the World," *Forbes*, March 25, 2019, https://www.forbes.com/sites/laurabegleybloom/2019/03/25/ranked-10-happiest-and-10-saddest-countries-in-the-world/?sh=8c3656063745.

CHAPTER 16: CLARITY

1. I've written about the One Page Miracle in many of my books, starting with *Change Your Brain, Change Your Life* (New York: Times Books, 1998), chap. 8.

2. Walter Isaacson, *American Sketches: Great Leaders, Creative Thinkers, and Heroes of a Hurricane* (New York: Simon and Schuster, 2010), 136.

3. Hans Küng, "Freud and the Problem of God," *Wilson Quarterly* 3, no. 4 (Autumn 1979): 162–71, https://www.jstor.org/stable/40255732?seq=1.

4. Jeanne McCauley et al., "Spiritual Beliefs and Barriers among Managed Care Practitioners" *Journal of Religion and Health* 44, no. 2 (Summer 2005): 137–46, https://pubmed.ncbi.nlm.nih.gov/16021729/.

Harold G. Koenig, "Religion, Spirituality, and Health: The Research and Clinical Implications," *ISRN Psychiatry* 2012 (2012): 278730, https://www.ncbi.nlm.nih.gov/pmc/articles/PMC3671693/.

5. Shanshan Li et al., "Religious Service Attendance and Lower Depression among Women—a Prospective Cohort Study," *Annals of Behavioral Medicine* 50, no. 6 (December 2016): 876–84, https://academic.oup.com/abm/article/50/6/876/4562664.

Full Gospel Businessmen's Training, "47 Health Benefits of Prayer," https://fgbt.org/Health-Tips/47-health-benefits-of-prayer.html.

6. Patricia A. Boyle et al., "Effect of a Purpose in Life on Risk of Incident Alzheimer Disease and Mild Cognitive Impairment in Community-Dwelling Older Persons," *Archives of General Psychiatry* 67, no. 3 (March 2010): 304–10, https://www.ncbi.nlm.nih.gov/pmc/articles/PMC2897172/.

7. Aliya Alimujiang et al., "Association between Life Purpose and Mortality among US Adults Older Than 50 Years," *JAMA Network Open* 2, no. 5 (May 3, 2019): e194270, https://pubmed.ncbi.nlm.nih.gov/31125099/.

8. Andrew Steptoe, Angus Deaton, and Arthur A. Stone, "Subjective Wellbeing, Health, and Ageing," *Lancet* 385, no. 9968 (February 14, 2015): 640–48, https://pubmed.ncbi.nlm.nih.gov/25468152/.

9. Anthony L. Burrow and Nicolette Rainone, "How Many *Likes* Did I Get? Purpose Moderates Links between Positive Social Media Feedback and Self-Esteem," *Journal of Experimental Social Psychology* 69 (March 2017): 232–36, https://www.sciencedirect.com/science/article/abs/pii/S0022103116303377.

10. Elisabeth Kübler-Ross, *Death: The Final Stage of Growth* (New York: Simon & Schuster, 1986), 164. See also Elisabeth Kübler-Ross, *On Death and Dying: What the Dying Have to*

Teach Doctors, Nurses, Clergy and Their Own Families, 50th anniversary ed. (New York: Scribner, 2014).

11. Chinese proverb, Goodreads, https://www.goodreads.com/quotes/7956059-if-you-want-happiness-for-an-hour-take-a.

12. Laura Clery, "Getting Honest in Therapy," March 18, 2021, Facebook, video, 11:38, https://www.facebook.com/laura.clery/videos/5242240365847022.

CONCLUSION: THE DAILY JOURNEY OF HAPPINESS

1. Christopher Bergland, "Morning Exercise May Improve Decision-Making during the Day," *Athlete's Way* (blog), *Psychology Today*, April 30, 2019, https://www.psychologytoday.com/us/blog/the-athletes-way/201904/morning-exercise-may-improve-decision-making-during-the-day.

2. Lin Yang et al., "Trends in Sedentary Behavior among the US Population, 2001–2016," *JAMA* 321, no. 16 (April 23, 2019): 1587–97, https://jamanetwork.com/journals/jama/article-abstract/2731178.

3. Daniel G. Amen and Tana Amen, *The Brain Warrior's Way* (New York: New American Library, 2016), 177–79.

Index

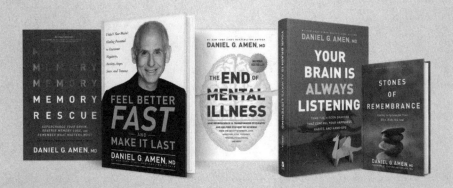